P9-DXT-470

MASTERMIND

MASTERMIND

THE MANY FACES OF THE 9/11 ARCHITECT, KHALID SHAIKH MOHAMMED

RICHARD MINITER

SENTINEL

SENTINEL
Published by the Penguin Group
Penguin Group (USA) Inc., 375 Hudson Street,
New York, New York 10014, U.S.A.
Penguin Group (Canada), 90 Eglinton Avenue East, Suite 700,
Toronto, Ontario, Canada M4P 2Y3
(a division of Pearson Penguin Canada Inc.)
Penguin Books Ltd, 80 Strand, London WC2R 0RL, England
Penguin Ireland, 25 St. Stephen's Green, Dublin 2, Ireland
(a division of Penguin Books Ltd)
Penguin Books Australia Ltd, 250 Camberwell Road, Camberwell,
Victoria 3124, Australia
(a division of Pearson Australia Group Pty Ltd)
Penguin Books India Pvt Ltd, 11 Community Centre, Panchsheel Park,
New Delhi—110 017, India
Penguin Group (NZ), 67 Apollo Drive, Rosedale, Auckland 0632,
New Zealand (a division of Pearson New Zealand Ltd)
Penguin Books (South Africa) (Pty) Ltd, 24 Sturdee Avenue,
Rosebank, Johannesburg 2196, South Africa

Penguin Books Ltd, Registered Offices:
80 Strand, London WC2R 0RL, England

First published in 2011 by Sentinel,
a member of Penguin Group (USA) Inc.

10 9 8 7 6 5 4 3 2 1

Photograph credits
Insert page 1 (top): AP Photo/File
1 (bottom): AP Photo/www.muslm.net
2 (top): AP Photo/B. K. Bangash
2 (bottom): AP Photo/Janet Hamlin/Pool
3 (top): Jeffrey Markowitz/Sygma/Corbis
3 (bottom), 7 (bottom), 8 (bottom): Federal Bureau of Investigation
4 (top and bottom), 7 (top): Thomson Reuters
5 (top): Getty Images News
5 (middle and bottom): Courtesy of the author
6 (top and middle): Time & Life Images/Robert Nickelsberg/Getty Images
6 (bottom): AFP/Jay Directo/Getty Images
8 (top): Rewards for Justice Program, United States Department of State

Library of Congress Cataloging-in-Publication Data

Miniter, Richard.
Mastermind : the many faces of the 9/11 architect, Khalid Shailk Mohammed / Richard Miniter.
p. cm.
Includes bibliographical references and index.
ISBN 978-1-59523-072-0
1. Mohammed, Khalid Shaikh, 1965- 2. Terrorists. 3. September 11 Terrorist Attacks, 2001. I. Title.
HV6430.M64M56 2011
363.325092—dc22
[B]
2010047777

Printed in the United States of America
Set in Simoncini Garamond
Designed by Pauline Neuwirth

To Lisa Merriam, a true friend

Contents

Introduction

From a cage in Guantánamo Bay, Khalid Shaikh Mohammed is on the verge of satisfying his life's biggest ambitions: to be a world-famous performer and to die a martyr. The man that prosecutors and the press call "the 9/11 mastermind" couldn't be happier. He plainly relishes the CIA's description of him as "one of history's most famous terrorists."[1]

That America, the enemy he swore to destroy, is giving him a global stage and a way to a jihadi death is either an irony or a gift from Allah.

The first time he had a stage in America, Khalid was a student doing college comedy skits in North Carolina for *The Friday Tonight Show*, with an informal Muslim group that met near his college campus.[2] His performances were biting and, former classmates say, very funny. One former student called him "the king of comedy."[3] Another told me "he loves the attention."[4] By all accounts he is going to enjoy every moment of a public trial. It may be his last chance to perform before a large audience.

KSM, as he is universally known in intelligence circles, has put himself at the center of every major Al Qaeda plot for the past fifteen years, leading U.S. intelligence officials to call him "the Forrest Gump of al Qaeda."[5] Indeed, KSM was involved with so many major terror plots that some knowledgeable observers, like noted Pakistani journalist Rahimullah Yusufzai, wonder if he is exaggerating his role.[6] In fact, the opposite may be true. Intelligence analysts say the "9/11 mastermind" is still being tied to *more* plots, including ones that will be made public for the first time in this book.

He admitted to planning the 1993 bombing of the World Trade Center (killing six), the bombing of two nightclubs in Bali (killing 202), Richard Reid's "shoe bomber" plot (which would have killed hundreds aboard a Miami-bound flight), the September 11 attacks (killing nearly three thousand), and plots to bomb London's Heathrow Airport (one of the world's busiest), the Big Ben clock tower, and the Empire State Building (where more than a thousand people work). He also confessed to schemes to kill office workers in skyscrapers in Los Angeles, Seattle, and Chicago.[7] He even planned to bomb the Panama Canal, which would have devastated world shipping and strangled the U.S. economy. KSM was an endless fountain of plans to bomb, murder, and maim.

Nor did KSM ever cease trying to hit targets inside the United States. After the September 11 attacks, he twice tried to infiltrate the American mainland with Al Qaeda–trained terrorists. But both were captured before reaching their destinations, thanks to interrogations and phone taps.[8]

When not engaged in large-scale killings, KSM focused on individual murders. He plotted to assassinate President Bill Clinton and twice tried to kill Pope John Paul II. Several prime ministers of Pakistan narrowly escaped his bombs.

KSM is proud of his central role in the kidnapping and murder of *Wall Street Journal* reporter Daniel Pearl, who innocently wanted to get "both sides" of the Al Qaeda story. KSM boasted: "I decapitated with my blessed right hand the head of the American Jew, Daniel

Pearl, in the city of Karachi, Pakistan. For those who would like to confirm, there are pictures of me on the Internet holding his head."[9] His tone of voice revealed more than his words; he was boasting while playing to an audience of jihadis worldwide.

KSM likes to present himself as a strictly observant Muslim, but he picks and chooses which Islamic laws to follow. In college in North Carolina, he would go to Burger King and order hamburgers without the meat, telling his classmates that he couldn't be sure that the beef met Islamic standards of purity.[10] While in U.S. custody, he has grown a long traditional beard and is often seen in flowing robes, handling prayer beads. Yet in the Philippines, he plotted terror attacks over tropical cocktails beneath brass poles of swinging teenage strippers, against a backdrop of pounding rock music. Murder, instrumental music, public nudity, and alcohol consumption are all forbidden by Islamic law.

At times in college and afterward he refused to be photographed because images of living things were "un-Islamic." Later he spent weeks getting a video of himself onto Al Jazeera (see chapter 11) and hours posing for a Red Cross photographer in prison (see photo section).

In the most famous photograph taken at his capture, KSM seems like a bear of a man. That photo shows a bulky man with a carpet of chest hair and intense, dark eyes. In fact, he is more of a chimp than a bear. He is five feet four inches tall[11] and speaks with an accent that one American official at Guantánamo Bay likened to that of Apu, the Indian owner of the Kwik-E-Mart on *The Simpsons.*[12]

He isn't an impressive speaker in Arabic, either. One Al Jazeera reporter who interviewed him described KSM's Arabic as "crude and colloquial,"[13] and another, who watched his testimony at Guantánamo, said he was like "a Pakistani Jackie Mason."[14]

The diminutive terrorist displays a Napoleonic urge to dominate other people, a trait that some interrogators and guards find humorous.

KSM poses as a romantic, but only when the mood suits him. He adores the grand gesture—writing love poems to the wife of his CIA interrogator or, during a break in planning the pope's assassination, buzzing with a rented helicopter the dental clinic where a Catholic Filipina girlfriend worked. KSM (and his nephew Ramzi Yousef) smiled down at her, while slowly unfurling a banner reading I LOVE YOU.[15]

Still, his romanticism had limits. A laptop seized by Philippine police features audio recordings of him mocking the whores he had rented. He was also an avid consumer of porn. "The vast majority of the captured hard drives of terrorists," said former CIA case officer Marc Sageman, "is taken up with porn. Don't think of these guys as strict Muslims. They are essentially seventeen-year-olds."[16] Again, hardly the mark of a devout Muslim.

KSM's life is built on a highly disciplined secrecy, but he is, at heart, a publicity hound. During the many terror operations he supervised, he instructed cell leaders never to phone or e-mail him—he would contact *them*, using prepaid cell phones or coin-operated pay phones, which are harder to track. He wanted to be mysterious, even to his coconspirators. Many of his comrades in terror never knew his real name. He used more than two dozen aliases.[17] "He behaves like an intelligence officer," said Colonel Rodolfo Mendoza, who ran the intelligence section of the Philippines National Police while KSM was there. "He appears and disappears. He is very, very clever."[18]

Yet he wanted the world to know his name. In one of the early versions of the 9/11 plot, in November 1998, he wanted to personally land one of the hijacked planes, release the women and children, and hold a press conference. An incredulous Osama bin Laden vetoed this idea.[19]

He presents himself as an earnest idealist motivated by the torments of the globe's Muslims, but in fact he simply went into the family business. His father was a preacher of radical Islam at the dinner table and in the mosque. His three older brothers (Zahid, Abed, and Aref) plunged into the secret world of armed Islam, blazing the way for bookish young Khalid. When he did become an active terrorist, he was soon joined by his nephew Ramzi Yousef (the leader of the cell that bombed the World Trade Center in 1993), two other nephews, and a brother-in-law. KSM's relatives, well connected in Pakistani terrorist circles, helped him meet the men who had founded Al Qaeda.

KSM's extended family is intricately intermarried and interconnected with extremism. Another nephew,[20] whose mother is one of KSM's two sisters, is Ammar al-Baluchi, who helped KSM coordinate the 9/11 attacks and the Richard Reid shoe bomb plot. Ammar's sister is KSM cousins Ramzi Yousef's wife.[21] Ramzi Yousef's father (and KSM's brother), Mohammed Abdul Karim, is one of the leaders of Sipah-e-Sahaba Pakistan, a terror group based in Pakistan that targets Shia Muslims and others. Two of KSM's nephews (brothers of Ramzi Yousef), Abdul Muneim and Abdul Karim, are also linked to terror attacks.[22] KSM's sister-in-law Aafia Siddiqui, an MIT-trained neuroscientist, was later charged with the attempted murder of a U.S. soldier and was linked to a plot to bomb gas stations in Baltimore. She was allegedly casing targets for KSM when she attracted the FBI's attention.

KSM's clan is dedicated to terrorism the way some families are devoted to winemaking or movie production. "The family specializes in killing," one of the KSM clan's former civilian-defense attorneys, Scott Fenstermaker, told me. "And they are really good at it."[23]

America and its allies have become really good at disrupting KSM family plots and capturing most of the clan. KSM and his nephew Ammar al-Baluchi are currently in U.S. custody and may well be sentenced to death. His brothers Abed and Aref died in Afghanistan. Ramzi Yousef is in the supermax federal prison in Colorado, where he is scheduled for outdoor exercise at the same time as the Unabomber.[24] (We can only wonder about their conversations.) Many of KSM's other relatives are either in custody or actively being hunted by the world's intelligence services.

The KSM family's hatred of America and its allies is based not on ignorance but on personal knowledge. KSM and many of his extended family were educated in America or have traveled widely in the West. As we will see in chapter 2, KSM even had some run-ins with the police in North Carolina. He later bragged to his CIA interrogator that he'd been radicalized in the United States. A CIA report concludes that KSM's time in North Carolina "almost certainly helped propel him on his path to become a terrorist."[25]

But, as we shall see, the real story is far more complicated. While he was radicalized before he arrived in America, the Americans he met only confirmed his ideological prejudices. He mostly met Americans in adverse circumstances, after he had injured them in a car accident or, because of his limited English, failed to do his part in college lab work. Unsurprisingly, he didn't find these Americans to be very friendly. He explained their behavior as "racist" or "anti-Arab," while refusing to acknowledge his own role in the encounters. Nor did he seek out Americans to befriend. He kept to himself and his clique while blaming the world for his exclusion—speeding him on his way to terrorism. According to a CIA report once marked TOP SECRET, "his contacts with Americans, while minimal, confirmed his view that the United States was a debauched and racist country."[26] America's failure to follow Muslim (Sharia) laws and its support for Israel and various Arab autocrats (including the Saudis) were his main complaints. KSM is akin to Brutus in George Bernard Shaw's play *Julius Caesar* who insists that the laws of his tribe are the laws of nature.[27]

The laws of his tribe—the jihadi network he has served for more than half his life—are also dictating the script of his last act, his courtroom performances. He is playing a role. Al Qaeda manuals found in Afghanistan instruct "the brothers" that if they are captured by American or Western European forces, they are to vocally and repeatedly demand a public trial for propaganda and martyrdom purposes. He is dutifully, even joyfully, following orders.

In the course of researching and writing this book, I have often been asked "Why?" The families of September 11 victims were concerned that I was going to lionize KSM. Turning down an interview with me in Paris, Daniel Pearl's widow pointedly asked, "What in your right mind makes you think I would want to do this?"[28] Some members of the intelligence community thought I was going to portray him as "superhuman," while critics of the Bush administration feared I was going to render him as an evil genius who single-handedly justifies the war on terror. KSM is a kind of Rorschach blot whom others fear you will see differently than they do.

For this reason, I feel compelled to address why I wrote this book. It is an attempt to answer three important and interrelated questions:

- Since the 1970s, the Western world has been plagued by hijackings, assassinations, kidnappings, bombings, and mass murders of civilians. What unites all these atrocities is an ideology that goes by many names, including "radical Islam." (Perhaps the best name for a global terrorist movement, borrowing from intelligence reports on the Indian subcontinent, is "jihadi," someone who uses mass murder to terrify civilians into submission to bring about their dark, coercive utopia.) Most of the perpetrators (known as jihadis) are well educated and hail from intact, middle-class families. Why do they do it? Why do promising young Muslims, many of whom are educated in North America or Western Europe, become remorseless killers of people who wish them no harm? To shrink that question down to manageable size: What made Khalid Shaikh Mohammed into an eager planner of mass murder?

- Al Qaeda is an organization of people devoted to killing other humans. It is distinct from an army, which in democracies exists to defend civilians. Al Qaeda seeks to kill noncombatants (in passenger planes, train terminals, office buildings, or at beachside resorts). Its members routinely kill prisoners, often after they have tortured or dismembered them. No Western army routinely does these things—indeed, their officers and enlisted soldiers are punished for far smaller transgressions of the laws of war. As different as Al Qaeda is, we must understand its inner workings if we are to combat it. What does KSM's dogged rise inside that terror network tell us about the internal workings of Al Qaeda?

- Interrogating captured Al Qaeda figures has become incredibly controversial on both sides of the Atlantic. Critics call it "torture." Others object to holding terrorists without a trial, on constitutional and human-rights grounds. What does KSM's interrogation and treatment tell us? If we look into the internal deliberations and CIA memos concerning KSM, what do we learn about the trade-off between "humane treatment" (however defined) and gleaning information that saves innocent lives?

These questions are important because how terrorists are made, how Al Qaeda works on the inside, and the true nature of CIA interrogations—the three key issues in this book—are the three key issues driving U.S. foreign policy and how Western nations deal with terrorism. The answers to these questions determine how we confront terrorism now and how we eventually end it.

In the course of my investigation, I interviewed current and former intelligence officers, investigators, and analysts in the United States, Europe, and the Arab world. I sought out eyewitnesses and others who knew him firsthand. I interviewed intelligence and military officials involved in hunting the mastermind.

I also pored over government documents and court records in Europe and North America as well as every cataloged newspaper, magazine, and broadcast transcript available in English and many others available in translation. I examined captured and other records at the National Archives, in Washington, D.C. I traveled to the campuses of Chowan University and North Carolina Agricultural and Technical State University, the two places where KSM studied in America. In the college libraries, I examined the student newspapers and yearbooks of KSM's years in North Carolina and tracked down his former professors and classmates.

I did these things in hopes of taking the reader inside Al Qaeda's inner circle and into the mind of the man who planned and supervised the deadliest terror attack in world history. My aim here is not to create sympathy but to establish a frank and sober understanding of the 9/11 mastermind. Ultimately, we have to understand what shapes and drives men like KSM or terrorism will go on forever.

Richard Miniter
Arlington, Virginia

BOOK I

ORIGINS

BOOK I

1

The Outsider

The plot to kill nearly three thousand people on a sunny morning in New York began fifty years earlier on an equally sunny morning off the coast of Kuwait, on a small, rusty freighter poorly equipped for passengers.

On board was a tall, wiry man with a black beard and a foreign turban. As he walked along the dock leading to the newly prosperous oil emirate, he began to make a series of commonplace choices that would set in motion a chain of events that would create one of the world's most successful terrorist clans and trigger the deadliest attacks in American history on September 11, 2001.

The city was Fahaheel. It had once been a fishing village where local men dived bare-chested for pearls. By 1950, most of the men were digging for a richer buried treasure: oil. An industrial skyline of derricks, pipes, and steel scaffolds overwhelmed the village, a visual metaphor for Fahaheel's new and larger ambitions. At night, the sputtering torches of gas flares made it hard to see the stars.

The bearded man was Mohammed Ali Dustin al-Balushi,[1] and he had come from the highlands of Iran's Baluchistan region to find work. He would later be known simply as Shaikh Mohammed.

Very little is known and even less is certain about Shaikh Mohammed's life. What we know has to be stitched together from the interrogations of his son Khalid Shaikh Mohammed and other members of his family, together with the recollections of neighbors and government officials. Official documents are largely nonexistent, as Kuwait did not issue birth and death certificates in the 1950s. Immigration documents from the period are also sparse. There is precisely one Arab-language newspaper account in which a member of Mohammed's family discusses the family's formative years.[2]

Walking amid the boom of metal on metal in the towering steel skeleton of the oil industry, Shaikh Mohammed found rows of neat, prosperous brick houses. These were for British engineers and other Western professionals employed by the oil companies.[3] For poor and poorly educated immigrants, housing and work were found far from the British-built town center. In the hot inland, in the southern reaches of Fahaheel in a neighborhood known as Badawiya, a shantytown of concrete block huts with corrugated metal roofs sprang up. It was home to a bewildering array of people from the economic and geographic margins of the Muslim world: Afghans, Baluch (like him), Palestinians, Pakistanis, Indians, and others from Pacific islands. Fleeing war and poverty, they had come to the burning desert of Kuwait for a better life.

Traveling on Pakistani passports, he and his ethnic Baluchi wife, Halema,[4] arrived with four children. Five more would be born in Kuwait, including Khalid Shaikh Mohammed.[5]

Slowly, like other immigrants, Shaikh Mohammed built a life. Slaving as a laborer, he saved enough to become a merchant who sold food and sundries to oil workers. On Fridays, he would preach in the mosque.

By the time his youngest son arrived, in April 1965,[6] Shaikh Mohammed had carved out a measure of status and security. The "honorific 'Shaikh' was added to his name in recognition of his knowledge" of the Koran and his teaching abilities.[7] By then the family was living in nearby Al Ahmadi, an immigrant town near Fahaheel, less than a thirty-minute bus ride from Kuwait City. Shaikh Mohammed had become a preacher at an Al Ahmadi mosque, and his family lived in a small home attached to the mosque.[8]

They named their youngest boy Khalid Shaikh Mohammed. He was known to the family as simply "Khalid Shaikh."

But the family's bright future soon darkened. Shaikh Mohammed got into a dispute with a powerful Kuwaiti merchant family and appears to have lost his Kuwaiti citizenship and his place at the mosque. Others dispute this account, contending that he was never a citizen and his mosque job was temporary. What is undisputed is that the Mohammed family was officially "*bidoon*"—legal residents of Kuwait but without the rights of citizenship. While roughly half of Kuwait's population is ineligible for citizenship, it was an embittering second-class status. As a result, as young Khalid was undoubtedly later told, his father's fight with a Kuwaiti sheikh was not evenly matched.

Then, in 1969, before Khalid started school, his father died.[9] The government of Kuwait has no record of the cause of his death or even the date. In those days, vital statistics on immigrants were not tracked by the Kuwaiti government.

Shaikh Mohammed Ali Dustin al-Balushi, who had brought his heritage and his ideas from the distant mountains, was gone before he could bring his family back to respectability. If he had lived, Khalid's painful early years may have been different.

As a widow with no hope of government aid, Halema was left on her own to raise nine children in an unforgiving land. Halema survived by eking out a living washing female corpses for burial, traditionally a very low-status occupation.[10]

Khalid Shaikh earned good grades in nearby government-sponsored Fahaheel Secondary School, a three-story brown-brick structure almost a city block long. He played on the streets with his best friend, Abdul Basit Mahmoud Abdul Karim, the son of KSM's older sister, Hameda. Wiry, with jet-black hair, Abdul had one lazy eye that made it hard for him to read for a prolonged period. Though they were officially uncle and nephew, they were only three years apart and, by all accounts, inseparable. Abdul Basit would later become known to the world as Ramzi Yousef, the man behind the 1993 bombing of the World Trade Center.[11] (I will refer to him as Ramzi Yousef throughout, for clarity's sake.)

Family ties aside, KSM and Ramzi Yousef had a lot in common. Both had Baluchi fathers and grew up in strict Islamic homes.[12] Both were poor and, initially, had no connections to call on. They had only the advantages of outsiders: their wits, their confidence, and their willingness to take risks.

The role of Ramzi Yousef's father, Mohammed Abdul Karim, as a shaper of Khalid's thinking is hard to ignore and harder to quantify. He worked as a low-level engineer for Kuwait Airways. "According to those who knew him in Baluchistan he is not particularly religious or politically sophisticated. He is said to have only two passions—Baluchi nationalism and an abiding hatred of Islam's minority Shiite sect," writes Mary Anne Weaver, who traveled to Fahaheel before the September 11 attacks and found residents who had known Ramzi's father. "In the early nineteen-eighties, [Ramzi's father] was introduced to the puritanical Wahhabi school of Sunni Islam and to a fundamentalist group closely associated with it, known as the Salafis. Wahhabism is the dominant form of Islam in Saudi Arabia. According to the doctrine of the Salafis, Shiites are infidels. The most extreme members of the group believe that Shiites should not simply be shunned or converted; they should be killed."[13] These anti-Shiite convictions would later be converted into bombings.

A familiarity with the tenets of the Saudi school of Ibn Wahhab and the Salafis (Osama bin Laden is one) would later be a major advantage to an intelligent, ambitious boy who wanted to join the global jihad. Many Sunni terror groups share a Salafi viewpoint and, in the 1980s and 1990s, financing from Saudi sheikhs.

Together, Khalid and Ramzi took risks. One day, a teenage Khalid and Ramzi decided to rip down the Kuwaiti flag from their own Fahaheel Secondary School, a symbolic act of defiance. In those stricter days, they risked expulsion and the future their education could give them. But they did it anyway.[14] The flag and the school were symbols of the authority that they yearned to defy. (Like rebellion, terrorism begins as romantic defiance, with human costs only as an exclamation point. Later, the exclamation points become the point.) Apparently it was Khalid's idea, and he had Ramzi scramble up the pole.[15] It was part of a pattern that would repeat in ever larger challenges to authority.

KSM's hold over his nephew Ramzi Yousef was total and complete. If anything, the relationship had intensified over the years. Al Jazeera reporter Yosri Fouda, who met KSM in 2002, describes the mastermind's relationship with Ramzi Yousef: "All along, Khalid was developing his ideas, knowing that his young nephew would be willing to take almost any risk to carry out his relative's requests."[16]

Why would KSM risk his future on a school prank? What were the ideas and events shaping him in the 1970s? These seemingly simple questions are hard to answer.

CIA and other interrogators rarely, if ever, asked KSM and other "high-value detainees" about their pasts, as Governor Thomas Kean, chairman of the 9/11 Commission, lamented.[17] Instead, interrogators were more interested in future attacks and organizational capabilities. Very little about KSM's childhood development was collected, and virtually nothing has been released to the public. In addition, KSM, when he was free, said very little about his formative years. His contemporaries were similarly circumspect. What we have is a bare set of facts and inferences that can be cautiously drawn from them.

With those limits in mind, three forces doubtlessly had a powerful shaping effect on KSM: his Baluch identity and ties to the Palestinian cause, his membership in the Muslim Brotherhood, and the events of 1979 that transfixed and transformed the Arab world. In that year, Ayatollah Khomeini seized power in Iran, the hostages were taken at the Grand Mosque in Mecca, and the Soviets invaded Afghanistan. To get an idea of KSM's intellectual development, we will examine each in turn.

Baluchistan

Following Friday night prayers, his relatives and older brothers would usually dine around a low table. Talk would often shift to world events. Young Khalid listened as his in-laws and older brothers talked of their lives and their native land of Baluchistan, which sprawls over three modern-day countries: Iran, Pakistan, and Afghanistan. Ramzi's father, Mohammed, was obsessed with the Baluchi cause and would move to the Pakistani portion of Baluchistan in 1986.[18]

Baluchistan is also the name of one of Pakistan's four provinces; it is the largest (44 percent of the total landmass) and least populated (less than 5 percent of the population of 132 million). And it is the poorest.[19] Home to more than seventy tribes, many of which are mutually antagonistic,[20] the province's three main tribes—the Marris, the Bugtis, and the Mengals—have a long history of violence against Pakistan's central government, especially its natural gas pipelines.[21]

For much of the 1970s, during Khalid's childhood years, Baluchistan's armed revolt against Pakistan's central government made news across the Muslim world. The revolt was debated for years afterward, like a kaleidoscope that never got new stones but was constantly turned into fascinating new combinations.

Khalid's homeland of Baluchistan never really wanted to be part of Pakistan. Instead, many Baluch longed for a reunification of their traditional lands, which had been divided by Britain's nineteenth-century imperial officials. Yet British maps did not change Baluchi hearts. Many tribal leaders wanted independence from Britain, India, and, later, the new nation of Pakistan. The British government promised Mir Ahmed Yar Khan, Baluchistan's principal ruler in the 1940s, that his people would be able to choose between total independence or union with India or Pakistan. In 1947, during Pakistan's messy birth, the Khan declared Baluchistan's independence. The Khan believed that restoring independence was part of his princely agreements with the British Empire over the past century and that it was broadly in line with the will of his people. Pakistan's central government saw it differently, threatening to send its army against the Khan. Realizing the full might of the Pakistani army, and after a long period of deliberation, the Khan surrendered. Baluchistan's independence had lasted a bittersweet 225 days.[22]

Nevertheless, guerrilla and terrorist attacks against Pakistani soldiers and installations continued for years. Sometimes the battles were large, involving hundreds of armed men on both sides. The Baluch fought pitched battles in 1958, 1964, and 1965.[23] Ambushes and shootings have continued in a steady trickle ever since. In turn, Pakistan was a brutal foe, repeatedly breaking promises of amnesty and executing tribesmen who had surrendered.[24]

In the 1970s, as in so many places in the wider world, the situation in Baluchistan worsened. In 1973, under a new constitution, Zulfikar Ali Bhutto came in as prime minister of Pakistan. Noting that Baluchistan had not elected a single member of his party to the national parliament he was also suspicious of its new nationalist-Marxist local leader, Nawab Khair Bakhsh Marri, elected to run the provincial government in 1970. Bhutto also opposed Baluchistan's calls for more autonomy in the federal system and its bid for a more equitable distribution of the natural gas revenues generated from its lands. He dismissed Baluchistan's provincial government (as allowed in the national constitution) and sent in the army.

Bhutto soon won over foreign allies. Fearful of the Baluch living in the southeastern corner of his country, the Shah of Iran joined Bhutto's war. He dispatched American-made Huey-Cobra gunships, manned by Iranian pilots and gunners, to attack Baluchi strongholds in Pakistan.[25]

Though both the national government and the Baluchi rebels were Muslim, Pakistan's identity was avowedly Islamic. The Baluch, at the time, were not known for their religiosity. Yet the war soon became a kind of jihad for both sides.

Pakistan's central government considered Islam inseparable from its politics and its identity. The country was founded expressly as a Muslim state, is officially known as the Islamic Republic of Pakistan, and its capital city is Islamabad. Both its 1962 and 1973 constitutions instituted an official government body, the Council of Islamic Ideology, to "ensure all laws were in keeping with the tenets of Islam."[26]

But Islam alone turned out to be a poor glue for holding the new nation together. Tribal and regional identities proved stronger than religious ties. Muslim-majority East Pakistan split off from West Pakistan in 1971, forming Bangladesh. In 1973, fearing that the Baluch wanted to reduce the size of Pakistan even further, the prime minister sent the army to occupy the restive province. Claims of a shared religion did little to mollify the Baluch.

By 1977, the Baluch were defeated and had resigned themselves to Pakistani rule—for now.

Throughout his life, KSM's actions and statements showed a great hatred of the Pakistani state. He made several attempts to kill Pakistan's prime ministers. And he clung firmly to his Baluchi identity—even using it [al-Baluchi] in many of his aliases. No matter how Islamic Pakistan might be, it could never make up for its treatment of Baluchistan in KSM's eyes.

KSM's Baluchi identity was hardly trendy. In 1970s Kuwait, few of Khalid's neighbors were awed by the Baluchi mystique. Instead, the Baluch were seen as a cheap, disposable people who came from afar to mop hotel floors, tighten bolts on oil pipelines, haul rubble from construction sites, and, as Khalid's father did, sell or preach to the other hardworking immigrants. The storied history of the Baluch contrasted with their present, humble reality as a defeated and dispersed people.

Money was not the only, or even the main, divider. Cultural and racial differences made the Baluch a distinct and distrusted minority. While Islam is officially universalist and egalitarian, in practice in Kuwait at the time, the Baluch were often made to feel inferior. As always, the discrimination was sharply felt by the minorities who spent most of their time around the cultural majority—boys like Khalid. Kuwaiti officials who've spoken to me—on a not-for-attribution basis given the political sensitivity of the topic—often say the feeling of discrimination existed more in the minds of the newcomers than in the mouths of the Arabs. Still, no one disputed that the feelings of cultural superiority and inferiority were real.

Khalid strongly identified with the Baluch and endured the discrimination that came from being one of them. In this way do identities harden and sharpen, becoming weapons.

The Muslim Brotherhood

Khalid Shaikh's older brothers Zahid and Abed joined the student wing of the Muslim Brotherhood sometime in the mid-1970s. KSM and his nephew Ramzi soon followed.

To boys in Khalid's position, the Brotherhood appealingly taught that all Muslims were equal, no matter their wealth or ethnicity. He could join as an equal and delight in a culture counter to the one he experienced daily in Kuwait. Often meeting under tents in the desert or in the larger homes of more prosperous members, Khalid heard lectures and debates and even got the chance to perform in skits and plays meant to dramatize political messages.

The Brotherhood gave Khalid two important building blocks: an integrated philosophy of life, politics, and religion, and a connection to a network of jihadis who challenged governments around the world. Suddenly the world made sense to him, and his membership gave him a kind of status.[27]

Understanding the Muslim Brotherhood's origins and philosophy gives some insights into KSM's intellectual development, albeit indirectly. It was his first ideological education, outside of his home.

The Muslim Brotherhood (known in Arabic as Al-Ikhwan Al-Muslimin) was founded in Egypt by Hassan al-Banna. Al-Banna, born in 1906, was schooled in Islam by a strict father, a respected Muslim scholar who ran a watch-repair shop near Alexandria, Egypt. Both father and son were devoted readers of *al-Manar*, a magazine edited by a Syrian named Rashid Rida[28] that was obsessively concerned "with the decline of Islamic civilization relative to the West."[29]

Instead of blaming a backward clergy, as many Muslim scholars did at the time, Rida, and later al-Banna, blamed the Arab world's impure understanding and practice of Islam. Going back to the original seventh-century version of Islam, al-Banna believed, would bring Muslims success just as it had in that earlier era.

Al-Banna's ideal was Islam's "golden age" that lasted from A.D. 622 to 660, when the Prophet Mohammed and the four "rightly guided" caliphs (rulers) ran a united Muslim empire. That his utopia lasted only thirty-eight years and that two of the four "rightly guided caliphs" were assassinated did not bother al-Banna at all.[30] "The subsequent fourteen centuries are considered less important, even objectionable," writes Gilles Kepel, one of France's most influential scholars of contemporary Islam. Kepel contrasts al-Banna's ideal of Mecca, which vanished fourteen centuries ago, with the Western ideal of Pericles' Athens, which disappeared more than twenty centuries ago. While many supporters of democracy cite ancient Athens as an archetype, Kepel writes, no one wants to "copy all of the features of Athenian society," such as slavery, ostracism, or fewer rights for women. Al-Banna, by contrast, wanted to bring back seventh-century Mecca in every detail, except perhaps technology.[31] Rather than learning from the past, he wanted to re-create it. Can a historical-cultural moment be reassembled and maintained, when the incentives and ideas acting on individuals, societies, and states have fundamentally changed? Al-Banna never seemed to address that question.

Hassan al-Banna's main political message was that Islam is a "total solution." Al-Banna's intellectual successor, Yusuf al-Qaradawi, summed up al-Banna's view vividly: "Islam is a comprehensive school of thought, a creed, an ideology, and cannot be completely satisfied but by [completely] controlling society and directing all aspects of life, from how to enter the toilet to the construction of the state."[32]

Al-Banna believed that going back to the time and teachings of the Prophet Mohammed was the only way to take on the Christian West. After all, he reasoned, in the time of the Prophet, all Muslims were unified under a single law and leader, when Arab armies rode triumphantly from the shores of the Atlantic Ocean to the foothills of the Himalayas, conquering all in their path.

Al-Banna's first goal was to turn Egypt into an Islamic state, to be ruled by Islamic law. Over time, he believed, the rest of the Muslim world would fall. "It is the nature of Islam to dominate, not to be dominated, to impose its laws on all nations, and to extend its power to the entire planet," he wrote.[33]

While al-Banna's ideal was ancient, his methods were modern.

When he arrived in Cairo in 1923 to be trained as a schoolteacher, he was surprised by what he described as "the wave of atheism and licentiousness."[34] With a charismatic presence and a commanding voice, al-Banna recruited fellow students to preach traditionalist Islam not only in the mosques but in the sidewalk cafés.[35]

Al-Banna, after graduation, was hired as a schoolteacher in Ismailia, a hamlet in the British-run Suez Canal Zone. He continued to agitate and organize, eventually forming the Brotherhood in 1928.[36] The Brotherhood leaders openly admired Hitler and Mussolini, partly for their shared antipathy to the British Empire (which ran Egypt at the time) and partly for their hostility to Jews and individual rights.[37] For siding with the Axis powers of the Nazis and the Fascists during World War II, al-Banna was briefly jailed by the British.

The Brotherhood's appeal was similar to that of early Western labor unions—it was most powerfully felt among the self-educated strivers. Like early unions, it grew rapidly.

In 1946, al-Banna set up the "Special Apparatus," a secret division for terrorist attacks. The Special Apparatus bombings accelerated across Egypt as British troop numbers declined from 1946 to 1948. Movie theaters and hotel bars were favorite targets, because they were frequented by Westerners and Westernized Egyptians and because movies and alcohol were forbidden by their version of Islam.

Government officials soon became targets. When an Egyptian judge handed down long jail terms to several Brotherhood members convicted of murdering and maiming innocents, another Special Apparatus unit killed the judge.[38]

In their investigation, the Egyptian police found the Special Apparatus's arms caches and written evidence of plots to kill other officials. The police informed the prime minister, who banned the Brotherhood. In months, the prime minister was killed.

The police intensified their crackdown, ultimately gunning down al-Banna himself in 1949. He was left to slowly bleed to death.[39] He was forty-three and almost immediately was hailed as a martyr.

In the wake of Britain's departure, Egypt was plunged into turmoil as communists, nationalists, and Islamists vied to seize power from the king and his prime minister.

Then a new player emerged: a clique of army officers led by Colonel Gamal Abdel Nasser. In July 1952, they captured the palace and the country. For the first time in sixty centuries, Egypt was not ruled by a monarch.

Incredibly, the military chose to ally itself with the Brotherhood, which was reliably anticommunist and anti-British. The Brotherhood brought the military junta a vital asset: a grassroots network. By 1948, one in every eighteen Egyptians was a member of the Brotherhood—more than one million men.[40] Its vast reach included its own hospitals, schools, factories, and support programs for widows, orphans, and the poor.[41] The Brotherhood had grown rapidly by recruiting future professionals (engineers, doctors, lawyers) and paraprofessionals (teachers, police, military) in universities and technical schools. As these young men graduated, they joined and ultimately dominated the professional unions. (Doctors, lawyers, and virtually every other profession in Egypt is unionized.) Many of the most educated, modernized Egyptians now wanted to upend the modern world and return to an ancient Islamic ideal.

Naturally, the honeymoon didn't last. The Brotherhood was disappointed when the military had no interest in imposing strict Islamic law and the military found the Brotherhood hard to work with.

By the early 1950s, Brotherhood leaders began to complain of Colonel Nasser's "pharaoh-like tendencies." Those were fighting words. When a Brotherhood operative tried to kill Nasser in October 1954, the strongman retaliated. Thousands of Brotherhood members were arrested and tortured.[42]

One of the arrested was Sayyid Qutb, who used his prison cell to become the Brotherhood's intellectual leader. His books, all written in Egyptian jails, advanced the ideology of al-Banna with a new twist: armed jihad was permitted, even required, against rulers who were insufficiently Muslim. (The concept of holy war against Muslim rulers was an innovation and, some Islamic scholars say, a questionable one.) Nevertheless, Qutb's books became an underground sensation; during a 1965 crackdown in Egypt, they were found in "virtually every house the police searched."[43] KSM almost certainly read Qutb's books, especially *Milestones* and *In the Shade of the Koran.*

Thanks to Qutb, jihad became a defining element of Islamist movements across the Arab world.

Qutb was hanged for treason in 1966, but his ideas and books lived on. Indeed, his books continued to kill. After Nasser died, in 1970, Anwar el-Sadat took control of Egypt. Eleven years later, he was killed because of peace efforts with Israel as well as his arrests of Brotherhood members. His killers said publicly they were inspired by Qutb's books. In time, Qutb's writings became one of the primary intellectual sources for Al Qaeda.

KSM would later be connected to two of the key figures in the Sadat plot. One of the plotters against Sadat was Dr. Ayman al-Zawahiri, currently Al Qaeda's number two. KSM would meet him repeatedly in Pakistan. Also linked to the plot to kill Sadat was Sheikh Omar Abdel Rahman, later known in the American press as "the Blind Sheikh." Abdel Rahman would come to play a critical role in KSM's first attack on the World Trade Center.

The antagonism between the Egyptian government and the Brotherhood, though it waxes and wanes, persists to this day.

Meanwhile, the Brotherhood established chapters in every Arab country, as well as Europe and the United States. While the chapters operate separately, in response to local politics, their goals and philosophy remain the same. Middle East scholar Barry Rubin calls it "by far the most successful Islamist group in the world."[44]

The Brotherhood created Hamas, which today rules the Gaza Strip, and has inspired armed rebellions in Syria, Sudan, and elsewhere. It is the intellectual breeding ground of every major Islamist terror group, including Al Qaeda, even though the Brotherhood officially opposes terrorism.

For KSM in his teenage years, the Brotherhood supplied two important and intoxicating ideas: that the Wahhabi (or Salafi) version of Islam could be combined with a utopian version of seventh-century Arabia to form a real challenge to the West's dominance of the world, and that armed jihad was the best way to bring that utopia into being.

The Brotherhood gave him more than ideas. It taught him how to use guns in its desert training sessions[45] and provided him with a web of connections that could be tapped to finance terror attacks.

Palestinians

The bottom of any society is where the speed of the mixture moves the fastest. On the streets and in the classrooms of Fahaheel, Khalid met many Palestinians, who made up roughly 40 percent of the boomtown's population in the 1960s and 1970s.[46] The two groups that had the largest impact on the thinking of immigrants in Fahaheel at the time were "the Palestinian Marxists and the Islamists"[47] of the Muslim Brotherhood. "The Palestinians, in fact, predominated in the lower middle class and in the professional ranks of teachers and engineers. These included most of the teachers at the Kuwaiti schools attended by" KSM.[48]

KSM so closely identified with the Palestinian cause that, his college friends say, he would spend hours justifying their attacks on Israeli soldiers and civilians and, sometimes, claim a Palestinian heritage.

It is easy to see why KSM would believe he has much in common with the Palestinians he met. While the Palestinians were Arabs, they, too, were strangers in Kuwait, often living without papers and sometimes without jobs. Both peoples were Muslims whose ancestral lands are now ruled by distant, bureaucratic governments that they are powerless to displace and largely unwilling to share power with. Both peoples have lost lopsidedly when they have gone to war with what they each called the "occupying power." Armed rebellions by the Baluch were brutally crushed by the Pakistani government in 1973, just as the Israelis rapidly defeated the Arab armies sent on behalf of the Palestinians that same year.

Both peoples imagine a glorious past, a legacy that they say has been robbed from them. Glorious pasts are depressing places to spend time in and they defy physics by glowing brighter as they move further away in time.

In general, both peoples adapted to the modern world very quickly as individuals and very poorly as groups. On their own, they became doctors, merchants, engineers, and scientists, building better futures for their families. But too often their organizations look backward with longing and use violence to try to turn the present into a utopian mirage of the past.

But there the similarities end. Palestinians played a pivotal role in the development of Sunni Arab terror organizations, while the Baluch were largely foot soldiers.

Clearly the Palestinian cause was a powerful inspiration for Khalid and his nephew Ramzi Yousef. Khalid speaks Arabic with a distinctive Palestinian accent. (A longtime friend denies this, saying Khalid's Arabic has a Kuwaiti accent. He himself is a Palestinian from Kuwait.) Al Qaeda rarely, if ever, cited the Palestinian cause as justification for terror attacks—until KSM moved into a senior role. His nephew Ramzi shares his accent and strong identification with the Palestinian cause. He later told Raghida Dergham, of Jordan's *Al Hayat* newspaper, that "my grandmother is Palestinian."[49] In reality, his grandmother was a Baluch from Iran. Yet there is no reason to doubt the sincerity of KSM's devotion to the Palestinian cause or to believe he is simply playing to a Western audience obsessed with

Israel. He advocated their cause for years before carrying out any terror attacks.

Khalid's three principal influences—Baluch nationalism, Palestinian radicalism, and the Muslim Brotherhood—each have long histories of terrorist attacks under the banner of Islam. To this fuel, the world would add the fire of revolutionary events.

The Events of 1979

In a single thunderbolt of a year, a series of nearly unbelievable events transformed the Muslim world and, most likely, the thinking of young Khalid. He was fourteen, and the year was 1979.

Iran

The Shah of Iran, Mohammed Reza Pahlavi, fled his kingdom on January 17, 1979. Briefly, the Middle East's first spontaneously formed democracy emerged in Tehran. The new government's prime minister, Shapour Bakhtiar, quickly attracted two powerful enemies, the then-communist-oriented Mujahideen-e Khalq (known as the MEK) and the radical followers of Ayatollah Ruhollah Mousavi Khomeini. Democracy never had a chance. Within months, Khomeini would have total mastery over Iran.

While distinct, Khomeini's thought was similar to that of the Muslim Brotherhood, especially in its choice of enemies. Like the Brotherhood, he saw "pure" Islam as the answer and "secular" Middle Eastern leaders, including the Shah, as the enemy.

Khomeini was opposed to the animating idea of democracy—that voters can change the law through peaceful elections—because he believed that the law is an unchangeable transmission from Allah, as represented in the Koran and the sayings of the Prophet. The law can be modified only through the interpretation of religious scholars, like Khomeini himself. And the room for interpretation is very small.

Khomeini's life and ideas matter because they had an enormous impact on the thinking of radical Arab Sunni groups, including the yet-to-be-created organization known as Al Qaeda. American intelligence analysts and academics have long asserted that the vehement hatred between some Sunnis and some Shia prevents the transmission of ideas and techniques from the Islamic Republic of Iran to Sunni terror groups. In practice, as we shall see, the barrier between Persian and Shia and Arab and Sunni proved to be quite permeable in the 1970s and 1980s. In his book *Knights Under the Prophet's Banner*, Al Qaeda's number two, Dr. Ayman al-Zawahiri, repeatedly cites Iranian Shia sources to establish various doctrinal points or to provide a real-world example of those points.

In addition to believing that the Koran and the Prophet's words should govern every aspect of human affairs, no matter how personal, Khomeini advocated a dictatorship of the clerics. Scholars of Marx will see a familiar concept in Khomeini's thought—handing absolute power to small, pure groups (a vanguard) to act on behalf of the majority, which is mired in false consciousness. While Khomeini never publicly acknowledged his intellectual debt to atheistic communism, the regime he created had striking parallels. Little dissent was tolerated. News and entertainment were aggressively censored. Individual rights, the idea that government is barred from invading certain freedoms, were dispensed with as unwanted Western imports. Tellingly, Khomeini had a scholar's impatience with ordinary people's quotidian concerns.

Khomeini's ideas were intoxicating. For the first time, a state run according to Islamic principles seemed possible, an electric idea that surged across the Muslim world. He was succeeding where the Muslim Brotherhood had so far failed. A new intellectual movement was emerging, in different forms, across the Muslim world—one that would soon threaten the communist East and the democratic West.

Khomeini's impact was soon felt by American diplomats in neighboring Afghanistan. In 1979, the U.S. ambassador to Afghanistan was Adolph Dubs,[50] but he was generally known by his World War II–era nickname, "Spike," because, he said, "no good American should go by the name Adolph."[51] After his tour as chargé d'affaires in the Moscow embassy, he was sent to Kabul in July 1978.[52] The trim fifty-eight-year-old was an expert on Soviet affairs, and Afghanistan was the newest satellite to join the Soviet orbit. At the time, the Soviets ruled Afghanistan through their proxy, the Afghan Communist Party.

In February 1979, Dubs was captured at gunpoint by four Shia Muslim terrorists and held in room L121 of the Kabul Hotel.[53]

His captors demanded the release of three Shia clerics that they believed the Soviet-backed Afghan government was holding incommunicado. The Afghan government denied it had jailed the religious leaders and refused to negotiate, despite the pleading of U.S. embassy officials.

Instead, Soviet advisers and Afghan paramilitaries ringed the hotel. "When we left that morning for our sightseeing tour," an American businessman said, "we had passed 10 soldiers with submachine guns and plainclothes men with drawn revolvers in the corridor."[54]

From the hotel hallway, Afghan police shot their way through the wooden door. One bullet found a water pipe, but others found the captive and the kidnappers. The pipe spewed water onto the floor, sluicing away the blood.[55] The four kidnappers were dead, and so was the American ambassador.

In Washington, President Carter was reported to be "very angry"[56] about the Soviet Union's failure to consult with U.S. officials before storming the kidnappers.

Only an unnamed *Washington Post* editorial writer noticed the "coincidence that, within hours yesterday, a respected American diplomat, Adolph Dubs, was killed in Afghanistan, and the American Embassy with 100 people was temporarily captured in Iran."[57] Even that prescient writer failed to grasp that both events were most likely engineered by Ayatollah Khomeini, writing, "The problem there lay in the difficulty that Ayatollah Khomeini is having in disciplining and disarming the thousands of Iranian revolutionaries who helped him achieve power."[58]

In fact, both the kidnapping of Ambassador Dubs in Kabul and the temporary takeover of the U.S. embassy in Tehran were feints by the wily Ayatollah. He wanted to see what America would do. When all the democratic superpower did was lodge diplomatic protests and urge the roughly seven thousand Americans, largely oil contractors, to leave Iran, the Ayatollah knew America was a paper tiger. The *Washington Post*'s sympathy for the Ayatollah's difficulty in governing his Islamic republic was a wry bonus.

This would prove to be a dangerous lesson to teach the Ayatollah.

On March 31, 1979, Khomeini had staged a referendum (the very electoral device he opposed for decades) and formally seized power. A second referendum, in November 1979, made Khomeini "Supreme Guide" of Iran. (The same title is used by the head of the Muslim Brotherhood.) By November 4, Khomeini had driven out the lawful parliament, and his partisans controlled many of Iran's key government ministries.

A student group allied with Khomeini stormed the U.S. embassy in Tehran in October 1979. Unlike the embassy takeover in March 1979, this invasion was not temporary. Ultimately, fifty-two diplomats were held hostage for 444 days, while a helpless President Carter futilely tried to negotiate.

The hostage crisis helped cement Khomeini's hold on power, even as it cost President Carter his presidency. A month into the hostage crisis, official Tehran radio reports claimed that 95.6 percent of Iranians had voted to make Khomeini dictator "for life." The results were not surprising, because the ballot was not secret. Muslim clerics watched the balloting, noting who deposited a green "yes" ballot and who dared a red "no" ballot.[59] The first radical Islamic terror state, Iran, was born.[60]

While KSM was the kind of Sunni who hated Shia Muslims—he and his nephew would later plot to bomb a Shia holy site—Iran's experience still provided certain encouraging lessons for him. It showed him that the Muslim Brotherhood's idea of an Islamic state was possible, and it suggested that the United States would not dare move against it. But what about the Arab dictators and the Soviet Union? The next few months would answer that question, too.

The Grand Mosque Takeover

While American diplomats were held at pistol point in Tehran, another set of Islamic radicals was preparing another daring takeover. On November 20, 1979, some five hundred armed men seized Al-Masjid al-Haram, the so-called Grand Mosque in Mecca, Saudi Arabia, the holiest site in Islam.

By the Islamic calendar, it was New Year's Day of the year 1400.[61] Some fifty thousand worshippers had gathered for the final day of the pilgrimage that their Muslim faith urges.[62]

Hundreds of them were taken hostage, and the group's leader, Juhayman al-Oteibi, a onetime Saudi National Guard corporal turned preacher, said that the Mahdi had returned. The Mahdi is a messianic figure that Islam teaches will appear at the end of time. Al-Oteibi said that all Muslims worldwide were commanded to obey the so-called Mahdi, Mohammed Abdullah al-Qahtani, who turned out to be al-Oteibi's brother-in-law. (The two ringleaders had met in prison, and al-Qahtani later married al-Oteibi's sister.) Like Khomeini, the group hoped to create an Islamic dictatorship.

A siege began, making the Saudis look increasingly powerless with each passing day. The Saudis were unable to take back the mosque, which was honeycombed with bombs and pious civilians begging for their lives—while the Arab world watched in absorbing horror.

A series of Saudi police and commando assaults failed, including a suicidal helicopter assault on the main courtyard of the mosque. The commandos were shot dead as they slid down ropes from helicopters.

After two weeks of fruitless assaults and hundreds killed, the Saudi king put Prince Turki al-Faisal in charge. Prince Turki phoned Count Claude Alexandre de Marenches, the French spy chief, who agreed to send a three-man French commando team. Non-Muslims are forbidden by custom and Saudi law from entering Mecca, so the team quickly converted to Islam in a Saudi Arabian airport and arrived in Mecca for reconnaissance. They pumped pressurized nonlethal gas into the underground prayer rooms that had become the rebel bunker. It didn't work. Next, Saudi troops carved holes into the floor of the mosque and threw grenades into the subterranean lair, killing hostages and hostage takers alike. As some of the rebels fled, Saudi sharpshooters gunned them down. The "Mahdi" was found among the dead.[63]

After two more weeks of gun battles, the rebels surrendered.

Some sixty-three radicals were taken alive. They were secretly tried and publicly beheaded on January 9, 1980. Never before in Saudi history had so many been beheaded on a single day.[64]

To a young radical steeped in the ideology of the Muslim Brotherhood, the events in Tehran and Mecca seemed to confirm the rightness of those beliefs. See how America trembled? See how it took the Saudis weeks to regain control of the Grand Mosque? With just a hard shove, the old order could be brought down. Despite its conclusion, the takeover of Mecca's Grand Mosque had actually encouraged jihadis.

But what about the Soviets?

The Soviet Invasion of Afghanistan

Soviet tanks rumbled through the snow-slicked streets of Kabul on December 25. The Soviets, frustrated by the difficulties of dealing with their puppet government in Afghanistan, had decided to rule the country directly.

In Moscow, the invasion seemed unlikely to shift the gears of history. The Soviets had sent tanks into Budapest in 1956 and into Prague in 1968, and the result had been greater Soviet control. Why should an impoverished backwater, with no strategic value to anyone but the Soviets themselves, pose a real problem?

As it happened, the war in Afghanistan would fundamentally weaken the Soviet Union and present Muslim extremists with their first opportunity for a modern jihad. The Soviets failed to anticipate that Islamist groups, which were largely unsuccessful against their own governments, would see the liberation of Muslim Afghanistan as a major opportunity to establish a Sunni Islamic state to rival the new Shia Islamic state in Iran.

Soon the Soviets were bogged down in a guerrilla war that they could not win. The Russian bear no longer seemed so fearsome. It would bleed for ten long years and ultimately have to retreat to central Asia.

The events of 1979 taught KSM that the three largest threats to establishing an Islamic state—Arab dictators, American presidents, and Soviet premiers—were toothless. He and many other jihadis were encouraged and energized.

The Afghan jihad, which began in 1980 and accelerated throughout the decade, soon became a kind of Woodstock for indoctrinated Muslim youth. Every radical—from Morocco to Indonesia—wanted to get there to validate his credentials.

KSM was no different. By 1981, when he was sixteen, he was training at Muslim Brotherhood–run military-style camps in the Kuwaiti desert, according to the 9/11 Commission Report.[65] He was training to fight, and even to die, in Afghanistan in the great anti-Soviet jihad.

While his jihad training continued, Khalid finished his formal schooling in Kuwait, graduating from the all-boys Fahaheel Secondary School in 1983.[66] He wanted to follow his older brothers to Afghanistan.

But that was not to be.

Apparently, his family decided that Khalid should be the one to go to college. If every family member was committed to jihad, all would remain poor. If KSM got an engineering degree from an American college, he could support them all. It seemed like a good bet. "Khalid was very genius; in everything he is smart," said Sheikh Ahmed Dabbous, his high school principal. "From the beginning of his studies it's science. He wanted to go to America for this reason. He wanted to become a doctor [Ph.D.] there."[67]

Far from science, his American education would accelerate him in a very different direction.

2

Campus Radical

The two-lane road to Chowan University climbs over a swamp and winds lazily past corn and cotton fields, square brick houses and double-wides, past plaques commemorating Confederate generals and the birthplace of Richard Jordan Gatling, the inventor of the first mass-produced machine gun.

The campus is in Murfreesboro, North Carolina, a rural enclave some one hundred miles southwest of Norfolk, Virginia. In 1983, the town (pop. 2,045[1]) had no bars and no diversions except a lone pizza shop. It closed at 9 P.M.[2]

Chowan's then dean of admissions, Clayton Lewis, went to pick KSM up at Norfolk International Airport. A genial, NPR-listening liberal, he was proud to bring foreign students to campus. Lewis told me he doesn't remember the short, thick-bearded student, and it's very likely they didn't talk at all. KSM's English wasn't good enough for conversation anyway.

Looking out the car's passenger window, KSM saw an alien planet. Kuwait's familiar pale, dry skies were gone; here the sky was dark blue and heavy with humidity. And the trees! In Kuwait, they mainly appeared in wealthy neighborhoods, behind high walls. Here the trees ran riot in a continuous green canopy that lined the road and sometimes leaped across it.

The window also showed a moving picture of how America's rural middle class lived. Extra cars were parked under trees. There were birdbaths and chairs on the lawn for watching the sunset and homemade signs offering pet grooming or fresh produce. These were enterprising and open people who didn't live out their lives behind thick walls but displayed them along the main thoroughfare. In the Arab world, windows are smaller, and little of family life happens in public view. Not so in America.

America would be good to KSM. In return, he would use his college years to make alliances he would need in future terror attacks and plot his first assassination on American soil, which will be discussed here for the first time.

America would require a myriad of minor adjustments. Everything seemed backward here. In Murfreesboro, people disappeared after sunset, while in Kuwait people appeared only after the cooler darkness fell.

Chowan College,[3] as it was known then, is a three-hundred-acre mostly wooded campus a few blocks off Murfreesboro's main street. At the heart of the campus stands an immense, white-columned pre–Civil War mansion. Spreading out like arms on both sides of the antebellum manse is a chain of charmless 1960s-era boxes, where the upperclassmen live. Thus, the campus is a meeting of the Old and New South.

Founded in April 1848 by a collection of Virginia and North Carolina Baptist families, Chowan takes its name from the language of the Algonquin Chowanoc tribe. In Algonquin, *chowan* means "people of the South," and is still pronounced by graduates in the Algonquin manner: *"chow-wahn."* Originally, the name referred to the southernmost Algonquin tribe, then it came to informally stand for the non-Indian people of the southern United States. By the 1980s, when

KSM arrived, the name seemed to stand for the "global South," the ambitious Third World.

Faced with declining enrollment and shrinking income, Clayton Lewis decided to aggressively recruit Arab students from across the Middle East. When he became dean of students at Chowan in 1968, he'd told the college president, "I didn't want a student body of all Baptists."[4] He drove to Washington, D.C., to meet with officials at foreign embassies to pitch the small college. When the first foreign students arrived, they were greeted like celebrities and asked to speak at Rotary Clubs and public schools. That feeling had worn off when KSM arrived in 1984.

KSM chose Chowan, an explicitly Christian school, because, unlike many American colleges, it had comparatively weak entrance requirements.[5] It didn't even require an SAT exam.[6]

And it had lax English-language standards. While strong in math and science he was very weak in English. His plan seemed to be to use Chowan as a landing pad to improve his language skills before transferring to a better school offering a four-year degree in engineering.[7]

KSM also found Chowan attractive because of North Carolina's politically active Muslim community, numbering as many as fourteen thousand across the state.[8] It was perhaps the most active in the country at the time.

A classmate of KSM's (a source), met me in a Greensboro coffeehouse. A large, likable, intelligent man, he is now an imam at five mosques in the Greensboro area. The source lays out more than a dozen different Arabic-language newsletters from 1984. The Kuwait-born Palestinian fans his hand across the newsletters, saying Greensboro was a "star city" of Arab activism. Murfreesboro, Raleigh, and Greensboro formed an active triangle of Muslim Brotherhood and Salafi activity. Front groups, social activities—a complete counterculture in Arabic.[9] (Later, Abdul Hakim Murad, a childhood friend of KSM's, would take flying lessons at Coastal Aviation, in New Bern, North Carolina. He would be part of KSM's plot to detonate eleven airliners in midair in 1994. And the 9/11 hijackers would be told about the North Carolina school as well.[10] So much history seemed to follow in the groove cut by KSM's casual decisions.)

Meanwhile, Chowan chose him largely because he said he had the ability to pay. Sitting in a favorite rocking chair, Lewis isn't willing to say that money was the main motivation for admitting KSM and other Arab students, but, he allows, "I'm sure their money was helpful."[11]

KSM kept his side of the bargain. Chowan officials showed me KSM's college application—which has never been made public before—indicating that he paid $2,245 on August 8, 1983. The payment arrived with his application,[12] Chowan records show. "Khalid's bill was paid in full on the date of his matriculation," Joshua E. Barker, Chowan's director of university relations, tells me, "with no indication of who paid it."[13] That is, Chowan doesn't know where he got the money.

KSM later told other students that his "family" had given him the money.[14] This may have been true, in a way. His family had decided that he was the son it was going to invest in. But where did the family get the money? They were apparently too poor to afford a phone in Kuwait.

Most likely, the Kuwaiti branch of the Muslim Brotherhood had advanced part of the money. The organization has a large charitable division to promote the education of its members. The Brotherhood was KSM's second family, and his brother Zahid had connections among its leaders.

Mysteriously, unlike most Middle Eastern students, KSM came to Chowan on an F-1 visa, indicating that he had a "private sponsor,"[15] unlike ordinary student visas. There is no indication of who that private sponsor might have been. Chowan's paper records have long since been purged, and computerization didn't begin until 1985. Curiously, the 9/11 Commission did not probe the matter.

Given that KSM paid his tuition in August 1983 and didn't arrive until January 1984, Lewis speculates that he had "passport problems." This is unlikely, since KSM received his passport more than six months before applying to Chowan. How he got the passport is an interesting question. He had no birth certificate, driver's license, or national identity card. He received his first official document of any kind on December 6, 1982, a passport (numbered 488555) from the Pakistani embassy in Kuwait City.[16] Into its blank pages was soon posted a valid visa for travel to the United States.

So KSM's "private sponsor," his tuition money, and his delay in Kuwait remain a mystery.

More than money and language set KSM apart. While the student body was diverse in the 1980s—almost evenly balanced between black and white Americans—KSM was different in almost every way. At five feet four inches and perhaps 135 pounds, KSM was physically smaller than most of the other male students. His long black hair and full beard were unusual in North Carolina in the 1980s.[17] And strangely, he made no attempt to befriend his American-born classmates.

KSM left little impression on the then-junior college. He was on campus for a single semester, in the spring of 1984, and did not stay long enough to appear in the yearbook.[18] Indeed, "there do not seem to be any photos of Khalid while he was here," Barker tells me.[19] A search of library and student archives confirms this. KSM was a ghost.

KSM may have been alienated by Chowan's robust Christian identity. The college required all students—Muslim, Christian, and Jewish, believers or nonbelievers—to attend chapel services and take classes on the Christian Bible, every Friday at 10 A.M. Professors were charged with taking attendance and reporting missing students to the college chaplain, who could take disciplinary action.

It was KSM's first experience hearing about Christian beliefs. KSM, a Muslim prayer leader's son and Muslim Brotherhood member, sat with the other Muslim students and endured the experience.[20]

Chowan administrators caution that the Christian experience was academic and ecumenical and that the school was liberal and accommodating toward Muslims. And the college provided a room in Marks Hall for Muslims to pray in. Then-dean Clayton Lewis says he had "no complaints about chapel" requirements.[21]

The factual nature of the theological discussion was probably debatable to KSM. The Koran mentions many of the Hebrew prophets (by the same or similar names) and discusses Jesus extensively. But the Koran's account of the prophets and Jesus differs substantially from the version presented in Hebrew and Christian holy books, which agree on the Hebrew prophets. To the son of a respected teacher of the Koran, the lectures on the Bible must have seemed sectarian and wrong. But, by all accounts, KSM did not bother to debate the matter in class. He either didn't have the English or didn't have the interest to present his views for debate.

Twenty-nine of KSM's fifty-three fellow Chowan science freshman students were Middle Easterners.[22] Virtually all were practicing Muslims, who quickly formed a distinct subculture. Even in the Carolina heat, they would never wear shorts. A source explains: "Shorts are *haram*," forbidden.

Shorts, for the strict Muslims, would make an unwelcome political and religious statement. Counterterrorism expert Daveed Gartenstein-Ross, who spent a year inside an extremist (Salafi) organization as an observant Muslim, explains that strict forms of Islam have many complicated rules about clothing, even for men. Pants must cover the knee and most of the calf, but may not cover the ankle, he explains.[23] Therefore, most American shorts would be *haram* by a certain interpretation of Islam.

Generally, the Muslim students were self-segregated, devoting their time to study, prayer, and shared meals. Occasionally they would play soccer when other students drank, danced, and flirted, three activities the strict Muslims abhorred. "They seemed to be praying all the time," says John Franklin Timberlake, a 1984 Chowan graduate who's now a police officer in Murfreesboro. "Just chanting, like. We never understood a word of it. Sometimes we'd come home late on a weekend night, maybe after we'd had a few beers, and they'd still be praying."[24]

Chowan required that KSM live in a dorm alongside American

students. The Chowan spokesman is not even sure what dormitory he stayed in. "Supposedly Khalid stayed in Parker Hall, but I have nothing to verify that."[25] He cautions that he doesn't know the room number, "or even if any school records show that KSM lived there at all, only hearsay."[26]

Parker Hall is a 1970s-era brick tower with rusting air conditioners beneath every window. The eight-story tower is the tallest in Hertford County; when it went up, the county fire department had to buy a truck with a longer ladder.[27] From the dorm windows one can see a baseball diamond backed by a fringe of scrub trees, a football practice field, and a murky pond the campus map refers to magnificently as Lake Vann. It is at the margins of the campus.

The only Chowan professor who remembers KSM is Garth Faile, who has been teaching chemistry at the college for nearly forty years. (In 2009 he was named teacher of the year.) A traditionalist who still teaches in a coat and tie, Faile was almost halfway through his career when KSM arrived in 1983.

He knew KSM as "Khalid Mohammed" and taught him General Chemistry 102-103 in a white cinder-block room on the third floor of Camp Hall.

He remembers the young KSM thanks to his meticulous notebooks, which go back to 1971, his first year at Chowan. They are small graph-paper-ruled notebooks with black-tape bindings. He pulls one from the shelf behind his desk. Consulting his notebook from 1984, Faile finds that KSM earned one of the highest grade-point averages in freshman chemistry and a perfect score on his final laboratory exam. He was bright, not brilliant. A "B student," Faile told me. He believes that KSM had a good science and math background in Kuwait and was skating through his class. "He was learning English more than he was learning chemistry."[28]

Certainly the demanding curriculum did not allow a lot of time for class discussion of contemporary political issues. Just equations, formulas, elements, and molecules.

One thing concerns Faile. Part of the course curriculum had a section on the uses of nitrates and nitroglycerin, later a key ingredient in his bomb designs. "I didn't teach him to make bombs," Faile said, "but I taught him chemistry."

As his first and only semester at Chowan was ending, KSM applied to transfer to North Carolina Agricultural and Technical State University. He knew how the system worked, and worked it adroitly. A&T's 1984 standards for transfer students did not require an English exam. If he had applied as a freshman or an international student, he would have had to show, in the words of the 1984 college handbook, "considerable facility in the use of the English language."[29] Once again, as when he chose Chowan College for its weak requirements, he had found a loophole.

KSM's first summer in America revealed a different side of the quiet student: a dangerous driver with a daredevil streak. KSM treated traffic laws as "optional," explained his friend Sammy Zitawi.[30]

When I asked the source about a car accident, he asked: "Which car accident?" There were many.

In the summer of 1984, KSM crashed into a car with two women inside. His subsequent actions are telling, a story that can be told in full for the first time here.

On August 8, 1984, KSM was speeding along when he recklessly collided with Deloris Christian Davis, who was driving her 1978 Pontiac, Guilford County records show. Both Davis and her younger sister, Letha Christian, were seriously injured. (Interestingly, KSM's passenger was Abdul Karim Mahmood Abdul Karim, the brother of Ramzi Yousef, the future World Trade Center bomber. Abdul Karim had departed from Kuwait with KSM and had studied for a year at an Oklahoma college. He transferred to North Carolina A&T, partly to join KSM. He would go on to have an Al Qaeda career of his own, in Pakistan.)

KSM was convicted of "failure to reduce his speed" on August 30, 1984, according to Guilford County police records.

The women were so injured and angry that they sued KSM for damages in a civil-court proceeding. KSM ignored a May 14, 1985, summons to appear in court. KSM must have dodged the sheriff's deputies who came to hand him the summons personally. At length, the plaintiffs were forced to serve KSM "by publication," buying an advertisement in the local newspaper. KSM ignored that, too.

Despite his initial disregard for American law and legal procedures, KSM eventually visited attorney Stephen J. Teague, who was representing Davis and Christian. He came with a posse, including an Arab student he called his "translator," and announced that he would be his own defense attorney. KSM clearly seemed to be enjoying the possibility of a public role. He lectured the North Carolina lawyer about Middle East politics for almost an hour.

Teague was surprised by his boldness, and even more surprised when KSM never bothered to show up at trial. The judge handed down a ruling, a default judgment, compelling KSM to pay $10,697.12 in damages, plus $1,500 in attorney's fees. The judgment included $705 worth of damage to the car and medical bills for Deloris Christian Davis ($5,538.05) and Letha Christian ($4,450.07). Though the record is silent on their exact injuries, the amounts of the medical bills—substantial for 1985—and the fact that they pressed the matter in court for more than a year suggest that their injuries were severe.

When KSM failed to pay, his driver's license was suspended.

He didn't learn from the experience. At another police stop, in January 1986, KSM was found to be driving with an invalid license. He was convicted and briefly jailed.[31] (News accounts that say he was jailed for not paying his bills are untrue.)

Even jail time didn't force a change in KSM's driving habits. Burke County records show that KSM also received a speeding ticket on October 20, 1985. He was going sixty-nine miles per hour in a fifty-five-mile-per-hour zone. He received citation number 611669.[32]

He was reckless, even with the lives of others, and arrogantly refused to pay either civil or criminal fines or even to appear in court in response to a summons. Unfortunately, he learned that he could safely mock American justice. This, too, would be a lesson that would stick with him.

In the fall of 1984, he started classes at North Carolina Agricultural and Technical State University.[33] The land-grant university had been chartered by the North Carolina legislature in 1891 to educate "the colored race," and retained its identity as a historically black university. Administrators are proud that the university trains the nation's largest number of African American engineers and second-largest number of African American accountants to this day. Its alumni include the Reverend Jesse Jackson Sr.; Ronald E. McNair, an astronaut who died in the 1986 *Challenger* space shuttle explosion; and the "Greensboro Four," who famously fought to desegregate a lunch counter in that city.

For KSM, Greensboro might as well have still been segregated. Again, he made little effort to live or eat alongside non-Muslim students. While college records show KSM's address as Post Office Box 20886, it appears he lived in apartment 333-B on Montrose Drive, near West Market Street in Greensboro,[34] roughly five miles off campus. The Muslim students turned one of the apartments into a makeshift mosque.[35] He was seen on campus only to go to a classroom or the library.

KSM stood out among Muslim students, although not among his professors. "Khalid, he was so, so smart. He came to college with virtually no English. But he entered directly in advanced classes," Mohammed al-Bulooshi, a Kuwaiti of Baluch origin who attended college with him, told the *Financial Times*.[36]

Native English-speaking students had less exalted views of the young KSM. "The English of most of the guys was absolutely terrible. I was paired up with [Khalid Shaikh] in a senior design class. I would always get paired with one of these guys. There was much frustration. Talentwise, I questioned how they could have gotten that far," said Quentin Clay.[37]

His professors have a less vivid memory of him. David Klett, a mechanical engineering professor at NC A&T, was KSM's student adviser.[38] "He just didn't leave an impression, which means he was probably a very quiet, low-key guy," Klett said. "He didn't do anything that stuck out in my mind and causes me to remember him."[39]

As at Chowan, a group of Muslim North Carolina A&T students emerged to keep the others in line with severe teachings. "We called them the 'mullahs,'" recalled Waleed M. Qimlass, a 1985 A&T graduate. "Basically, the [foreign-born Muslim] students at Greensboro were divided into the mullahs and the non-mullahs."[40]

Naturally, KSM was one of the mullahs.[41] "They [the devout Muslims at A&T] wouldn't listen to music, they wouldn't play music," says Zitawi. "He wouldn't take a picture back then because they thought it was against religion."[42]

These positions—against music and photography—are not required by traditional Islam, which generally bars only instrumental music and is silent on photography. Indeed, the Sufi tradition in Islam is known for its a cappella songs during its services. A source, a Salafi classmate who is now a leader of five mosques in the Greensboro area, does listen to non-instrumental Islamic praise songs. And most Muslims in the Middle East listen to Arabic-language pop music and watch television, including Al Jazeera. But Salafi Islam forbids music, television, movies, and all images of living things. (Indeed, bin Laden, who was a fan of horse racing, would put his fingers in his ears when the race's opening horn sounded at the Khartoum racetrack.)[43] KSM's views on photography and music demonstrate a schooling in extremist doctrines.

KSM, though quiet in class and among American-born students, was a boisterous attention seeker when he was among Arab students. Every Friday and Saturday night, he and other Muslim students would share a halal dinner, a little taste of home. (Halal is to Islam what kosher is to Judaism.) "We used to go to the farmers, buy a lamb or a goat, and butcher it with a knife," Zitawi said.[44]

The Friday night dinners would attract upward of twenty-five Muslim students.[45] Afterward, they would pray as a group. The evening ended with comedy routines or homemade plays. "The men called it *The Friday Tonight Show*."[46]

Again, KSM is best remembered by the Muslim students he exclusively socialized with. KSM's lab partner Sammy Zitawi was a Palestinian who also grew up in Kuwait. "This guy was funny, he could make you laugh," Zitawi said. "He could make fun out of everything."[47]

KSM's nickname was "Blushi," playing on his Baluch origin and the work of then-famous comic John Belushi.[48]

Other Muslim classmates share Zitawi's view. "Whenever the Muslim Student Society had a gathering, he'd keep people laughing—imitating Arab leaders, that kind of thing," a source says.[49]

He remembers KSM's ability to draw a crowd and generate a partylike atmosphere. "His apartment used to be the place where everyone liked to hang out."[50] The apartment was more than what he called "a nonstop comedy zone." It was also a center for hard-line politics and where "everyone" went to pray.[51]

"Basically, what you saw was a microsociety of our home," said Mahmood Zubaid, a Kuwaiti architectural engineer. Even the Arab Muslim students were divided by nationality. "We hung around only with Kuwaitis. The community we were in, out of the two hundred or three hundred [Arab Muslims], was actually only about twenty people."[52]

The "mullahs" at North Carolina A&T were very effective at recruiting newly arrived Arab students, sometimes even meeting them at the airport. "Your first day in Greensboro, you didn't know anybody, maybe your English is not so good, and they met you at the airport and helped you get started," Zubaid said.[53]

The indoctrination didn't necessarily please Kuwaiti parents, especially the ones who weren't that religious at home. "We had a lot of our students coming back from the U.S. radicalized. I'm not talking about religious guys going to the U.S. and coming back as fundamentalists. I'm talking about cool guys," he said.[54] The guys who drank and went to discos would come home as bearded hard-liners.

"Why would they flip religiously? It happens there," another Kuwaiti student told a reporter.[55] "When we are there we are very vulnerable. That's why we get into groups—to protect each other. The religious guys work on them. Why is it so easy? The key thing, I think, is the political views more than the religious."[56]

Why were they becoming radicalized on American campuses? North Carolina A&T, like most other universities, did little to make foreign students feel at home with the larger student body. There was no serious effort to integrate them and no organized activity that would break up their cliques and lead to bonds with new people. As a result, a handful of students could guide, even rule over, most of the students of their nationality. Over time, many became radicalized because they were not presented with any alternatives and knew that bucking the hard-liners would leave them friendless and alone. There are numerous examples of civilian schools in America and Western Europe hosting students who became terrorists. Curiously, there seem to be no examples of students from public or private military schools who became radicalized on campus. One reason may be that military schools make a more robust effort to unify the student body, creating a shared identity between foreign students and their American classmates. We will never know how KSM and his fellow foreign students would have changed if the civilian colleges were less laissez-faire about student life.

KSM was not radicalized, but a radicalizer of others. His summer vacations in Pakistan (and perhaps Afghanistan) energized this process. KSM's three brothers—Aref, Zahid, and Abed—had moved to Peshawar, Pakistan, to a border town that fed the Afghan resistance with arms and ideology. Indeed, most of his extended family decamped from Kuwait for the war zone while he was in college. On at least one summer vacation, KSM joined them.[57]

Pakistan, roiling with billions of dollars in American and Saudi aid for anti-Soviet fighters in Afghanistan, was the seething center of jihadi ideology at the time. If anything, this visit intensified KSM's ambitions toward a terrorist career.

Sheikh Ahmed Dabbous, KSM's high school teacher, talked to him during his pivotal college years. *Los Angeles Times* reporter Terry McDermott tracked Dabbous down, and Dabbous recalled a telling conversation with KSM while he was visiting Kuwait in his college years:

> "When he goes there [the United States] he sees most Americans don't like Arabs and Islam," said Sheikh Ahmed Dabbous, his high school teacher: "Why?" I ask him.

> "Because of Israel," he says. "Most Americans hate Arabs because of this."
>
> "He's a very normal boy before. Kind, generous, always the smiling kind. After he came back, he's a different man. He's very sad. He doesn't speak. He just sits there.
>
> "I talked to him to change his mind, to tell him this is just a few Americans. He refused to speak to me about it again. He was set. This was when he was on vacation from school. When KSM said this I told him we must meet again. He said, 'No, my ideas are very strong. Don't talk with me again about this matter.' "[58]

As a result of his foreign trips[59] and his self-segregation on both of his American campuses, KSM's English did not improve, and neither did his view of Americans. As for his idea that most Americans hate Arabs because of Israel, it seems like a pose. He simply didn't have any relationships with American students close enough to have in-depth political conversations.

Indeed, it appears that KSM spent part of his college years plotting his first assassination on American soil, the killing of Meir Kahane in 1990.

When Meir Kahane, a rabbi who founded the Jewish Defense League and later became a member of Israel's Knesset, came to speak on North Carolina A&T's campus, KSM became enraged.

Kahane's views could not have been more noxious to KSM. Kahane advocated the forcible "transfer" of more than one million Palestinians living inside Israel to Arab lands. (KSM favors exactly the opposite policy, the forcible exit of all Jews from the Holy Land.) "I say that if any Arab raises a hand against a Jew, no more hand," Kahane said in 1986. "If any Arab raises his head against a Jew, no more head."[60]

Kahane was a great comfort to the many working-class Jews who were forced to leave Arab lands between 1948 and 1973—often with no compensation for their seized property and nothing more than the clothes on their backs. By contrast, more than one million Muslims live peacefully in Israel, protected by its laws and voting in its elections. As for the Palestinians who fled their homes in 1948, Kahane pointed out, they were not deported by any government but left fearing that Israelis would do to them what they would do to the Jews if the power positions were reversed. To this day, millions of Palestinians live in refugee camps supported by the United Nations and Western governments, while there is no provision (except by Israel) for the throngs of Jews displaced from Arab lands.

Still, to many Israelis and Americans, Kahane sounded less like a humanitarian than a provocateur. Kahane's views on Israel could be sufficiently captured by this line: "No guilt, no apologies, and the hell with the rest of the world." It is not hard to see why KSM would want Kahane dead.

KSM later admitted to his CIA interrogators that he planned to murder Kahane. That remark was put into the CIA's top-secret interrogation memos, which were later reviewed by Dieter Snell and other members of the 9/11 Commission staff. The 9/11 Commission Report, which noted KSM's desire to kill Kahane in a single line, immediately dismissed KSM's claim as "uncorroborated," adding that it "may be mere bravado."[61] Perhaps. But the simple fact is that the U.S. government does not know whether KSM was involved, even indirectly, in Kahane's assassination. In fact, there are good reasons to believe KSM was telling the truth about his murderous intent toward Kahane.

Virtually all of the players in the 1990 Kahane assassination would reappear in the 1993 World Trade Center bombing, which KSM funded and his nephew orchestrated. This cannot be a coincidence, yet to this day it has largely been ignored by investigators.

As Kahane stepped from the podium at New York's Marriott East Side Hotel, a man approached him, smiling.[62] The smiling stranger pulled out a chrome-plated .357 Magnum handgun and shot Kahane in the chest and in the head. Kahane was pronounced dead within the hour.

The smiling assassin, El Sayyid Nosair, ran for the exit. He was chased by Irving Franklin, a seventy-three-year-old man. Nosair stopped, turned, and shot at Franklin, grazing his leg.

On the street, Nosair urgently looked for his getaway car, a taxi driven by Mahmud Abouhalima.[63] Later, Abouhalima would be the driver for the 1993 World Trade Center bombers. He was also a part-time driver for the "Blind Sheikh," Omar Abdel Rahman, a longtime associate of Osama bin Laden, who was later convicted of a wide-ranging plot to blow up New York City landmarks. KSM met Abdel Rahman during one of his visits to Pakistan in the early 1990s.

But Nosair got into the wrong taxi.

Inside a strange cab, Nosair ordered the driver to speed through a red light. The cabbie refused. Nosair shoved open the taxi door and burst onto Lexington Avenue. On the sidewalk, he ran into Carlos Acosta, an armed detective for the U.S. Postal Service. Nosair shot him in the arm, and Acosta returned fire, hitting Nosair in the neck. Nosair was taken to the same hospital as Kahane.

Investigators later examined an amateur video made during Kahane's speech and identified a man in the crowd as Mohammed Salameh.[64] Most likely, Salameh was there to witness Nosair's "heroic deed." Salameh, one of Nosair's cousins, was later part of the 1993 World Trade Center bombing, supervised by KSM's nephew and sidekick Ramzi Yousef.

Nosair; his getaway driver, Abouhalima; and his accomplice in the crowd, Salameh, were each questioned by police. But the investigators never realized the significant connections among them (they lived in the same apartment buildings, worshipped at the same mosque, and each had ties to terrorists).

Nosair's history should have raised more questions by investigators. Nosair, who had worked for New York City's water department until he was let go in 1990, partly for trying to convert his coworkers to Islam, had bombed a Greenwich Village gay bar, Uncle Charlie's, in April 1990, but wasn't linked to that crime until 1995.[65] Nosair said he objected to homosexuality because it violated Islamic tenets. Four days before killing Kahane, Nosair was spotted meeting with the Blind Sheikh. "They were deep in conversation."[66] Radical Islam would have been a legitimate angle of investigation in the Kahane assassination, but New York Police Department Chief of Detectives

Joseph Borelli ordered investigators to "abandon any broad conspiracy theory."[67] Abouhalima and Salameh were never charged.

Instead, the NYPD detectives treated the Kahane murder as the act of a random crackpot. So, the more than forty boxes of evidence that police collected from Nosair's Cliffside, New Jersey, apartment were not translated for his trial and were never presented in court.

Nosair maintained that he was "framed by a guy with a yarmulke."

Denied key evidence, the jury was so confused, it acquitted him of the murder but convicted him of illegal possession of the gun that killed Kahane. Who shot the assassin's gun that Nosair possessed, the jury never explained. The terrorism angle was not really considered at the time.

Nor did the FBI treat it as a terrorism case. "I was in charge of bureau operations at the time," Buck Revell said, "and I never received any information that the assassin of Meir Kahane was connected with any sort of organization that might have a terrorist agenda."[68]

One problem was analytic. The FBI and New York Police Department's intelligence units were used to looking for terrorists who were disciplined and operated inside rigid, hierarchical organizations. The Kahane murder was essentially free-form, put together by a group of relatives and friends who attended the same mosque. It was a new pattern, one they weren't yet accustomed to spotting. And no one asked why Nosair had decided to target Kahane. That trail, if pursed, might have led to the Blind Sheikh and eventually perhaps to KSM.

Another problem: most of the seized evidence wasn't carefully scrutinized until years later. Part of the reason was bureaucratic infighting. The FBI seized twenty-four of the forty boxes of evidence from the New York Police Department. Two days later, Manhattan District Attorney Robert Morgenthau's office got the evidence from the FBI. The officials spent so much time fighting over who had control of the evidence taken from Nosair's apartment that no one actually looked inside the boxes.[69]

What was in them? Investigators found manuals for making bombs, newspaper articles about assassinations, and piles of Arabic-language documents. Among the papers was a bomb-making formula "almost identical to the one used at the World Trade Center."[70] In the evidence collected in Nosair's apartment were pages from U.S. Army manuals—some marked TOP SECRET—translated into Arabic. The manuals seem to have been stolen from U.S. Special Forces.

How did Nosair, a former city worker with no military background, come to have Arabic translations of secret U.S. Army manuals? Years later, FBI agents and New York City police officers would learn that Khalid Ibrahim, who had run a fund-raising operation for Osama bin Laden's various groups since 1989,[71] introduced Nosair to Ali Mohammed, an instructor for the U.S. Special Forces at Fort Bragg in New Jersey.

Mohammed, a former Egyptian army officer, did more than give Nosair manuals; he gave him training. Mohammed often hosted Nosair as well as two future World Trade Center bombers (Ibrahim Elgabrowny and Mahmud Abouhalima) at firing ranges in New Jersey and Connecticut. The future bombers returned the favor. One of the demands made after the 1993 World Trade Center bombing was the release of Nosair from prison.

Ali Mohammed, meanwhile, met frequently with bin Laden in Sudan and later Afghanistan.

The Blind Sheikh was tied to both Nosair and the World Trade Center bombers—and he seems to have been influential in choosing the twin towers as an appropriate target. He had written several fatwas authorizing Muslims to "rob banks and kill Jews,"[72] like Kahane. His sermons were even more direct. He called for attacks on America and other Western countries, telling his followers to "destroy their economy, burn their companies, eliminate their interests, sink their ships, shoot down their planes, kill them on the sea, air, or land."[73]

Indeed, many of the World Trade Center bombers met one another through the blind cleric's Al-Salam mosque, a dark, dirty series of rooms located over the Sultan Travel Agency, at 2484 Kennedy Boulevard in Jersey City.[74] The Blind Sheikh had been tried and acquitted three times in Egypt for the assassination of Anwar el-Sadat, Egypt's president who made peace with Israel; he was also a spiritual adviser to Egyptian Islamic Jihad, the terrorist group that killed Sadat and merged with Al Qaeda in 1998.

Finally, it appears that it was the Blind Sheikh who first gave KSM the idea for attacking the World Trade Center. His 1992 fatwa, which quickly became legendary in jihadi circles, warned Muslims not to attack the United Nations building (it would turn too much of the world's opinion against the Islamic cause), recommending the World Trade Center as a better target.

The Blind Sheikh's fatwas did not attract much interest among American intelligence officials, but they were closely studied by one analyst working for the Mossad, Israel's intelligence agency. I spoke with this analyst on the condition of anonymity. He explained that the Blind Sheikh's fatwa recommending the World Trade Center as a target had had a huge impact in jihadi circles in the early 1990s. Attacking the World Trade Center immediately became "a fixed idea inside Al Qaeda" and related groups, he told me. "That fatwa gave KSM the idea for the World Trade Center," he said.[75]

Is it possible that KSM passed along the idea of targeting Kahane to the Blind Sheikh, who in turn told Nosair and Abouhalima? There is an old saying in intelligence circles: there are no coincidences.

With the Kahane plot set in motion, KSM could return to his studies. He graduated with a degree in mechanical engineering on December 18, 1986,[76] having earned his degree in less than three years.[77]

Upon graduation, KSM quickly left the country for Pakistan, where his brothers and Ramzi Yousef's father waited for him in Quetta, a town near the Durand Line, which divides Pakistan from Afghanistan. (Other relatives of KSM's had moved to Iran.)

KSM learned more than a little broken English and a lot of engineering in America. He learned from his arrest and other traffic run-ins with the authorities that America's police are governed by laws and procedures that give the accused an array of rights. This is something the clever game player could exploit. He learned that there was a well-integrated Muslim community that could be helpful to operatives, as long as it did not know that it would be aiding terror attacks. (This would be useful intelligence for the San Diego cell in the 9/11 attack's early stages.) He learned from the Blind Sheikh that the World Trade Center was a religiously acceptable (and even desirable) target.

Unfortunately, none of these lessons would go to waste.

3

Searching for War

Above the smoke and dust of Pakistan's Jalozai refugee camp loomed a mud-walled fortress, ringed with razor wire and machine-gun emplacements. From its high walls you could look down the Khyber Pass and see the peaks of Afghanistan, where war had displaced almost two million people since 1979.

A small car wormed and bounced its way up to the main gate, a mud-brick arch guarded by young men with new beards and old Kalashnikovs.

A sign in English and Arabic read, THE UNIVERSITY OF DAWA AND JIHAD (see photo section). *Dawa* means "call," and suggests a religious duty, while *jihad* means "holy war." This strange, fortified campus, built with Saudi money, was fueled by Saudi ideology and manned by Muslims from across the Arab world.

The driver rolled down his window as a guard leaned in. Zahid Shaikh Mohammed explained that his brother, the wiry kid in the passenger seat, was there to meet the emir.

The gate opened and the car rolled into the sandy compound. It was a motley collection of buildings. A rare luxury winked in the sun: new air conditioners were stuck into the faces of the decrepit structures. In one courtyard, young men shouted during a synchronized martial drill.

At a main building, KSM and his brother Zahid explained again that they were there to see Sheikh Sayyaf.

Zahid had spent the past few years getting to know everyone of consequence in Pakistan. Zahid was running operations for the Committee for Islamic Appeal, a Kuwait-based charity that aided Arabs fighting in Afghanistan. The committee was one of the largest charities active in the region and had considerable clout.[1] Sheikh Sayyaf was one of his most important contacts.

Abdul Rasul Sayyaf, an Afghan warlord who spoke perfect Arabic, ran the University of Dawa and Jihad and headed the Hizbul-Ittihad El-Islami (Islamic Union Party), which briefly unified the various Arab factions fighting the Soviets. Among the university's donors were Osama bin Laden and a host of Saudi and Persian Gulf–state Arab sheikhs.

Zahid introduced KSM to a vigorous man with intense, coal-black eyes and a beard that hung from his jaw to the center of his chest, falling in thick black ringlets. The beard was as famous as the man, a raffish signature known throughout the jihadi world. From out of that beard would come words that would change KSM's life.

Increasingly, KSM's future seemed to lie in Pakistan. Most of his family had moved there while he was studying in the United States. His brothers, uncles, and cousins were scattered across Pakistan and were involved in various capacities in the war against the Soviets. Some made bombs, some carried messages. Along the border with Afghanistan, the only work was "war work."[2]

KSM had arrived in Pakistan when the anti-Soviet jihad was at its peak. The Saudi government was spending roughly $1 billion per year to transport, equip, and train fighters from across the Arab-speaking world. Arab governments had obliged the Saudi effort by emptying their jails of Islamist radicals, who were released on the sole condition that they depart immediately for Afghanistan. In short, the Arab world was exporting its problem people and making a problem for the Soviet invaders of Afghanistan at the same time. Once in neighboring Pakistan, these radicals were met by the followers of Sheikh Sayyaf, Osama bin Laden, or others and given food, housing, military training, and ideological indoctrination. Those who lived through the Afghan jihad ended up with valuable combat experience and a network of like-minded contacts that stretched from Indonesia to Algeria. Far from exhausting the jihadi threat to Arab states through the fight against the Soviets, ultimately the Afghan jihad created a much more able foe, one that was more confident, more professional, and more global in its reach.

Meanwhile, American contributions—another $1 billion—flowed to seven different Afghan factions (but not to Osama bin Laden or other Arab jihadis). Two CIA station chiefs responsible for managing the Afghan war in the 1980s, Bill Peikney and Milton Bearden, told me that no U.S. funds went to bin Laden or other Arab groups.[3] Marc Sageman, a CIA case officer working under Bearden in Islamabad, agrees, adding that he didn't even meet any Arabs.[4] The CIA was focused on funding the Afghans.

The flood of funds meant that Pakistan's borderlands were awash with arms and men eager to use them. For KSM, it was a tremendous opportunity.

Sheikh Sayyaf greeted him with tea in handleless glass cups.

Abdul Rasul Sayyaf allowed himself no luxuries (except, incredibly, a nightly game of tennis on a dry-mud court). He had established a network of perhaps a dozen military-style training camps in Afghanistan and Pakistan's North-West Frontier Province. The rite of initiation into the jihad was attending one of Sheikh Sayyaf's camps.

But first, KSM had to win the approval of the sheikh himself. KSM's education, deep ideological understanding, and extensive family connections to the jihadi network quickly met with Sayyaf's approval.

Sheikh Sayyaf sent KSM to the Sada camp, in eastern Afghanistan.[5] Its name means "echo," and it was formed to handle the overflow from Khaldan camp, the first large-scale terror training facility in Afghanistan. The camp was overseen by Abu Burhan al-Iraqi, a burly, bearded man who had briefly worked for Saddam Hussein's government. (Abu Musab al-Zarqawi, the head of Iraq's Al Qaeda wing until his death in June 2006, attended the same camp.)[6]

Sheikh Sayyaf's camps were populated mainly by Muslims from Indonesia, Malaysia, the Philippines, and other parts of Southeast Asia. This was no accident. Recruits tended to cluster where their countrymen had studied. This was not out of blind national or regional loyalty but a function of the fact that recruiting tends to flow along family trees and other social networks. The Asians generally spoke English, not Arabic, so the clustering effect of recruitment also made it easier for Sayyaf to appoint instructors that they could understand. The harsh conditions—the cold nights (a shock to tropical recruits) and the cold, grain-based meals (another shock), combined with the rigorous regime of exercise and prayer—forged close bonds among the men.

One man in particular would have an enormous impact on KSM's fate. His name was Abdurajak Janjalani. After returning to the Philippines, he would establish the Abu Sayyaf terror group (named after their Afghan patriarch) and invite Ramzi Yousef to train his men in bomb making. At the Sada camp, KSM also met a man we now know as Hambali, a leading Indonesian terror leader. These relationships would later draw both KSM and Ramzi Yousef to Indonesia and the Philippines, the sites of some of their boldest plans.

After a three-month stint at the training camps in Afghanistan, KSM was summoned by Abdullah Azzam, the mentor of Osama bin Laden. Azzam was a Palestinian-Jordanian who had been educated at Egypt's famous Al-Azhar University and later taught in Jeddah, Saudi Arabia. He was a fiery speaker who traveled across the Middle East, Europe, and America, raising money and men for jihad. His passion and his eloquence could move men to quit their studies, leave their jobs, and travel far from their wives—just to have a chance to die for the cause of Islam. His speaking power was similar to that of John Wesley and other eighteenth-century evangelicals who could bring solid skeptics to tears in twenty minutes and order them to action in sixty minutes. Azzam was like Wesley in another way: devoutly religious people couldn't understand his appeal. KSM's classmate told me he found Azzam boring.

KSM could hardly have been luckier. Perhaps his brother's networking had paid off again. Azzam was the mentor of Osama bin Laden. The jihadi movement was small enough at the time that an ambitious and capable lad could meet everyone of importance.

Azzam put KSM to work at Mercy International, one of Azzam's many front groups. Working in the media office, KSM came in contact with a number of wealthy Gulf Arabs, men who would later prove useful to him in financing various bomb plots.

KSM and Ramzi Yousef almost certainly saw each other at Sheikh Sayyaf's remote university or in his sprawling network of camps.

Ramzi Yousef, who had completed his education in electrical engineering at the West Glamorgan Institute of Higher Education, in Swansea, Wales, took basic training in firearms and bomb making at Sayyaf's infamous Khaldan camp. Omar Nasiri, while working undercover for French intelligence, also trained at the Khaldan camp and described it as "an oasis among the black hills," with a few crude buildings wedged into a steep gorge. A cold river flowing through the camp made the immediate surroundings lush in a scorched desert.[7] It had a mosque, a barracks with hard dirt floors, and another ramshackle structure where meals were taken and instructions given.

Ramzi Yousef found time to marry a Baluch girl, Latifa Abdul Aziz, paying her father a dowry of ten thousand Pakistani rupees (roughly $400).[8] By 1990 he was a respected instructor in Sayyaf's camps, teaching young terrorists how to make nitroglycerin and other explosives. He was known as "the Chemist."[9] His engineering degree had proved useful after all. But it is clear how Ramzi Yousef saw himself in the business card he had printed up. It featured his name in bold print, below which was his job title: INTERNATIONAL TERRORIST.[10]

For a time, KSM was a teacher, instructing students in engineering at Sayyaf's university.[11]

He also found time to get married to a Pakistani woman who had lived in the Jalozai refugee camp, on the flatlands below Sayyaf's hill-top university. KSM's brother Zahid later married her sister.[12] (KSM's wife and children are now believed to be living in Iran.)

With a new wife, KSM had to make some decisions about where his life was going.

By 1992 the jihad was winding down in Afghanistan. The USSR had retreated in 1989 and dissolved in 1990, and the United States ended its involvement at the same time. The Northern Alliance—which was distinctly unfriendly to bin Laden and the other "Arab Afghans"—had seized power in Kabul. (The Taliban would not be created, by Pakistani intelligence, for another two years.)

The major Arab Afghan figures had decamped to other nations. Osama bin Laden had gone home to Saudi Arabia in 1990, and when his meetings with known terrorists aroused the attention of the oil kingdom's intelligence service, he moved to Sudan in 1992.[13] The Filipino followers of Sheikh Sayyaf returned to the southern isles of the Philippines, where they formed an eponymous terror group. Dr. Ayman al-Zawahiri (who later became Al Qaeda's number two, following the merger of his Egyptian Islamic Jihad into bin Laden's organization) moved to North Africa and later several of the former Soviet republics of central Asia.

Finally, the money for jihad flowing in from Persian Gulf states slowed to a trickle.

The Afghan jihad had ended before KSM or his nephew Ramzi Yousef had a chance to distinguish themselves as leading figures in the global jihad. They would have to find another way.

Bosnia was the obvious choice. Since the role of radical Islam in the Bosnian conflict is not well known, I will outline some of it here.

Conquered by the Ottoman Turks in 1463, the Bosnian elite had converted to Islam and ruled the Christian population for nearly five hundred years.

In those days, Christians had no legal rights. Very few could even own land. If a Muslim robbed or murdered a Christian, the Christian had no legal recourse. By law, no nonbeliever could testify against a Muslim. Only Christians and Jews were required to pay the *jizya,* a confiscatory tax that kept non-Muslims poor. Worse still was the annual "blood tax," in which Christian boys were forcibly taken from their families to be made into soldiers or eunuch slaves. Girls were often taken for harems or the slave trade. These and other humiliating legal measures formed a deep and lasting resentment among Christians and a countervailing fear of reform and equality by Muslim Bosnians.

In 1870, the Turks were compelled to turn Bosnia over to the Austro-Hungarian Empire. The hopes of Christians and the fears of Muslims were soon dashed. In the name of civil peace, few reforms were made, and the Muslim landowning class was largely left in charge. While Christians could now build churches, own land, and seek higher education, the legal system—headed by Muslim judges—was still biased against them.

Austro-Hungarian universities introduced Christians to the ideas of nationalism and self-determination, planting an idea that would become deadly in the 1990s. The end of World War I (which had begun with a shot fired by a Serbian nationalist) brought independence to Yugoslavia (including Bosnia). The much-feared retribution against Muslims never came, but economic and legal reforms at last made citizens equal under the law.

World War II ended the hopes of a democratic Balkans. The Muslim Youth, an offshoot of Egypt's Muslim Brotherhood, had brought radical Islamist ideas to Bosnia's Muslim intellectuals. When the Nazis invaded, these Muslim radicals joined the side of Adolf Hitler. While the SS unit of Muslim Bosnians failed to be an effective fighting force, the plainclothes Muslim militias soon became notorious for their pogroms against Christian farmers suspected of siding with the anti-Nazi partisans. These atrocities were soon merged into the Bosnian Christian historical narrative, deepening the divisions between Christians and Muslims.

Marshal Josip Broz Tito swept to power in 1945, at the close of World War II, with his own brand of nationalistic communism. As an avowedly atheistic force, Tito-style communism attempted to heal the social divisions by banishing all traces of religion from Balkan life in the early Cold War years.

But the seed of jihadism in Bosnia was too hardy to die. In 1948, the communist regime put a number of Muslim Youth members on trial for plotting to overthrow the government, in hopes of replacing it with an Islamic state. Their political goals were entirely copied from the works of the Muslim Brotherhood of Egypt, including Qutb. Its leaders convicted and imprisoned, the Muslim Youth in Bosnia went underground. Its secret meetings would continue for decades.

Meanwhile, Tito's Yugoslavia managed to stay out of the orbits of the Soviet and Chinese communist empires and began courting the "nonaligned" nations of the Third World. By the 1960s, the Yugoslav Communist Party officials believed that Muslim party members would be ideal to help Yugoslavia's efforts to connect to the Arab world. Beginning in 1964, Yugoslavia allowed sectarian Muslim groups to meet and to publish. By the 1970s, the Muslim Youth, still led by the same set of old men from the 1940s, reemerged. It again tried to overthrow the government, provoking another trial for seditious conspiracy. Again, the Muslim Youth went underground.

In 1990, Yugoslavia, racked with international debts and social payments it could no longer afford, collapsed. The Muslim Youth was waiting in the wings; its hour upon the stage had finally come.

A new political party for Muslims, the Party of Democratic Action, was born. Despite attempts by Croatian Christians to join, the party was exclusively for Muslims and openly supported the dictatorships of Iran and Iraq. It set its sights on seizing power in an independent Bosnian Muslim state and maneuvered for civil war. At each step, it was covertly aided by the Islamic Republic of Iran.

Torn apart by civil war (or jihad), Bosnia was an ideal place for a budding terrorist to go. KSM made his way there in 1992 and served with the El Mujahid ("the holy warriors") Detachment of the Bosnian Muslim government.[14] The Muslim government reportedly gave him a Bosnian passport.[15] Again, he made valuable contacts.

Former National Security Agency analyst John Schindler, an expert on the Balkans, notes that KSM's time in Bosnia seems to have been "more formative of his development in Al Qaeda than his time in Afghanistan."[16] Schindler adds: "The neglected truth is that in the 1990s, Bosnia played an identical role in the global jihad to that of Afghanistan in the 1980s, serving as a convenient place to wage war against the infidel while providing sanctuary and training for the next generation of militants."[17]

Among the contacts KSM made in Bosnia were Khalid al-Mihdhar and Nawaf al-Hazmi, two Saudi nationals who would later achieve infamy as hijackers of American Airlines Flight 77 on September 11, 2001.[18] These two "muscle" hijackers helped corral the passengers on the plane that was purposely smashed into the Pentagon. As we shall see, these two hijackers were an endless source of trouble for KSM in the run-up to the 9/11 massacre. But all of that drama still lay ahead.

Dejected, KSM returned from Bosnia in 1994 with no great victory to claim.

After a brief stay with his extended family in Pakistan, he worked his network of Gulf Arabs. He had contacted them for funding prior operations of Azzam and Sayyaf; now he needed something for himself. Abdullah bin Khalid al-Thani, a member of Qatar's ruling family and then minister of religious affairs, agreed to give KSM a no-show job at the Ministry of Electricity and Water and a government-sponsored apartment. Until 1996, this Qatar apartment and salary would be his safe haven and his lifeline as he traveled the world.

KSM drifted back to Pakistan, where he reconnected with nephew Ramzi Yousef. KSM had an idea. It involved a first-class trip to New York and a walk down memory lane.

Like many terrorist recruits, Ramzi Yousef maintained good contacts with the alumni of Khaldan camp in Afghanistan.

At Khaldan, Ramzi Yousef had met Ahmed Mohammed Ajaj, who had worked as a pizza delivery man in Texas[19] before joining the jihad. Ajaj was not a U.S. citizen and had overstayed his U.S. visa before heading to Saudi Arabia and Pakistan. Still, he was eager to be useful, and Ramzi Yousef had a cruel use for him.

Ramzi Yousef bought two first-class tickets to New York. The second ticket was for Ajaj, whose luck was about to run out.[20] Within hours, he would be swept up in what was then the largest terrorist plot in American history.

BOOK II

A TERRORIST CAREER

BOOK II

4

Tradebom

In the first-class section of a jumbo jet roaring toward New York, Ramzi Yousef innocently asked Ajaj if he could store some of his belongings in Ajaj's luggage. They were brothers from the camps, and, Yousef explained, his small carry-on was bursting.

Ajaj readily agreed, sealing his fate.

Ramzi Yousef handed Ajaj his notebooks, which U.S. Customs inspectors later realized were manuals for making bombs. It had page after page of handwritten bomb recipes, like a cookbook. If Ajaj got into the United States with bomb manuals, they would be helpful to Ramzi Yousef. If not, then the manuals would make Ajaj a target, not Yousef.

At the John F. Kennedy International Airport immigration checkpoint, the two purposely got into separate lines. When Ajaj approached an inspector, he was immediately suspicious of Ajaj's Swedish passport. The photograph seemed too thick. She ran her fingernail along the edge, peeling off the photo of Ajaj. Underneath was a picture of another man.

Yousef watched calmly as Ajaj was arrested. Ajaj would spend the next six months in an American prison awaiting trial and deportation, and would later be rearrested, charged, and convicted for his transitory role in a plot to kill 250,000 Americans. But Ajaj's arrest had provided Ramzi Yousef with a valuable distraction.

Yousef presented himself as Azan Muhammad, a victim of Iraqi dictator Saddam Hussein. He had a valid Iraqi passport in that name, but no visa allowing entry into the United States.[1] Claiming he'd been persecuted by Iraqi soldiers during the invasion of Kuwait, he asked for political asylum.[2] Immigration inspector Martha Morales did not want to admit Ramzi Yousef, but she was overruled by her supervisors.[3]

He was questioned, processed, and released. Within twelve hours he was freely walking the streets of New York. Under the law, political-asylum applicants must be held in a detention center until their request is granted or they are deported. But the detention facility was already at its legal maximum occupancy, so he was asked to report back in November for a hearing.[4] That suited him. He would have at least two months before anyone in the U.S. government would be looking for him.

Ramzi Yousef had a simple plan: find the Blind Sheikh, Omar Abdel Rahman, and the accomplices of El Sayyid Nosair, the imprisoned killer of Meir Kahane, and put a team together.

Ramzi Yousef went to a storefront mosque at 552 Atlantic Avenue, in Brooklyn Heights, which locals called "the jihad office."[5] It was officially known as Alkifah Refugee Center[6] and had been set up by Abdullah Azzam, KSM's employer in Pakistan. Azzam had links to the Muslim Brotherhood, the Muslim World League, the still-embryonic Al Qaeda, and Saudi intelligence. He had come to Jersey City in 1988 and, in a speech to several hundred Muslims at Al-Salam mosque (where the Blind Sheikh also preached), said, "Blood and martyrdom are the only way to create a Muslim society. . . . However, humanity won't allow us to achieve this objective because all humanity is the enemy of every Muslim."[7] (Interestingly, Azzam had been accompanied on that U.S. trip by Kahane's assassin, El Sayyid

Nosair.) Azzam later sent Mustafa Shalabi to establish a permanent jihadi base, for fundraising and recruitment, in the United States in the 1980s. Above the Alkifah Refugee Center was a mosque. The Blind Sheikh preached at that mosque and the more radical Al-Salam, in Jersey City.

Yousef soon found his team through the mosque and the "jihad office."

His "wheelman" would be Mohammed Salameh, who had played a role in the Kahane assassination. An illegal immigrant with eyesight so poor that he had failed his New Jersey driver's license exam four times,[8] Salameh was an odd choice. He had already spectacularly failed to remain unnoticed or effective in the Kahane murder. Yet, as with Ajaj, Ramzi Yousef had a use for Salameh. His trusting nature only made that use easier. Salameh even let Yousef share his small Jersey City apartment.

Another accomplice would be Mahmud Abouhalima, who like Salameh had played a role in the Kahane assassination. He had abjectly failed in his duties as the driver of the getaway car.

Others would be added along the way, including Abdul Rahman Yasin, an epileptic Muslim on welfare who lived with his mother a floor above Salameh. While Yasin's mother cooked them Arabic food, Ramzi Yousef persuaded Yasin to join their terror operation.[9]

Yousef introduced himself to all of these terror-team members by his alias, Rashid al-Iraqi (meaning Rashid the Iraqi). A key component of the "tradecraft" that KSM taught his nephew was to trust no one with your real name.

KSM, through his phone calls to Yousef, would be the moneyman and, most likely, the operational commander. In December, Ramzi Yousef made numerous conference calls to various phone numbers in the Baluchistan province of Pakistan, where KSM was at the time. Yousef was diligent. He even made calls to KSM from his hospital bed after Salameh had gotten the two of them into a traffic accident. (Interestingly, Yousef's bomb-making manual was left in the back of Salameh's car, which was impounded by New Jersey police, who dutifully handed the manuals back to Yousef.) Yousef also tried to hide his electronic fingerprints through "three-way calling," then a new phone feature.[10] As agreed, KSM was never mentioned by name or alias to the other members of the terror cell. KSM would be a ghost.

The only trace of KSM would be a single wire transfer. Transaction records show that on November 3, 1992, $660 was sent from a "Khaled Shaykh," in Doha, Qatar (where KSM was living without an alias), to Mohammed Salameh, Nosair's accomplice in the Kahane assassination.[11] It was an unusual slipup. While presumably one of many wire transfers believed to have occurred between KSM and Ramzi Yousef, this was the only one found by Justice Department investigators.

The next few months are a blur of false starts and careful purchases of industrial chemicals. When his accomplices were unable to buy the needed chemicals, Ramzi Yousef stepped in, coolly telling suppliers he was an "Israeli."[12] This convenient lie seemed to ease concerns, and with his more confident, businesslike demeanor, Ramzi Yousef won the trust of the suppliers.

By January 1993, the men were mixing chemicals in a run-down Jersey City apartment. The noxious vapors collected on the walls, leaving telltale blue stains.[13] Next, they moved their makeshift laboratory to Space Station storage locker number 4344.[14] From the front door of the Space Station they could see the twin towers of the World Trade Center, gleaming in the moonlight across the Hudson River. But there was no time to gape. They had a bomb to build.

Just before dawn on February 26, 1993, they packed a bright yellow Ford Econoline van with fifteen hundred pounds of ammonium nitrate, three long, heavy tanks of hydrogen gas, four containers of nitroglycerin, and four twenty-foot fuses.[15] The explosive contraption cost less than four hundred dollars.[16]

The rented van was followed by a midnight-blue Honda sedan. This was their getaway car.

By noon, the van was heading down the ramp beneath the World Trade Center's north tower. They stopped at a predetermined spot in the vast parking garage. Ramzi Yousef calmly lit the four fuses on the fifteen-hundred-pound bomb. He ran to the getaway car—in exactly twelve minutes the bomb would explode.

The Honda raced up the ramp, but their escape was blocked by a truck. Abouhalima leaned on the horn. The truck didn't move. *What's the hurry?* Its driver kept looking for an opening in traffic. Five painful minutes ticked by.[17]

The fuses kept burning, at one and a half inches per second.

Abouhalima honked again. Were they going to be among the tens of thousands they hoped to murder? The truck, at last, shifted gears and inched into traffic. Finally free, the bombers drove away into the snowy afternoon.

Minutes later, at 12:17 P.M., the Ryder rental truck exploded.

The blast threw cars against concrete pillars, smashed down through three concrete floors, and rained down cinder blocks onto the north tower's heat pumps on level B5.[18] It caused destruction in seven levels, six of them underground.

A crater opened in the basement of the World Trade Center, almost two hundred feet wide and sixty feet deep. The blast sliced open electrical cables, which became snakes hissing sparks and starting fires, while smashed pipes discharged sewage and filthy air-conditioner fluid. In the apocalyptic darkness, fires feasted on the carrion of smashed cars. The fire devoured the available oxygen, creating howling wind. Total damage and lost revenue would exceed $550 million.

Within minutes, the New York City Fire Department arrived. Trucks and crews kept coming all afternoon. Eventually, the fire department deployed some 750 vehicles and 40 percent of its on-duty personnel—the largest contingent ever, until September 11, 2001.

FBI assistant director James Fox established a command post in a nearby federal building. They would have to find out what happened and who did it. Had an electric transformer blown? Was it a bomb?

Within hours, Fox was visited by David Williams, the FBI's senior bomb expert. He had conducted extensive tests on the soil in the crater. It was a bomb, he said.

Fox asked how he could be so sure.

"I have examined ten thousand bombings," Williams said.

"That's good enough for me," said Fox.[19]

The FBI investigation was soon officially code-named "Tradebom."

The World Trade Center bomb would turn out to be "the largest improvised explosive device the Bureau had ever encountered."[20]

But who did it and why? All of the early guesses—a bank heist gone bad, a Serbian terrorist attack—proved wrong. Instead, the initial evidence didn't make any sense.

The date of the bombing wasn't the anniversary of any significant world event. While various groups had contacted the police or the press to take credit—including Ramzi Yousef, who claimed to represent the "Fifth Battalion" of an imaginary terrorist army—none seemed capable of an attack of this size. The bomb design didn't fit the pattern of any established terrorist group.

Then the FBI got lucky. At the bottom of the bomb crater, investigators found a differential housing, a part that connects the two rear axles of a van. The metal housing was from the van that carried the bomb. And, incredibly, it had an intact vehicle identification number stamped on it, allowing the FBI to trace it to a Ryder leasing outfit in New Jersey.

Then the Bureau got another lucky break. An FBI special agent phoned the rental agency. The manager said the vehicle had been rented by an Arab guy, who had reported it stolen. The manager explained that the man had called repeatedly to get back his four-hundred-dollar deposit. When he called again, the manager switched over to the line with the FBI agent on it.

"It's the Arab guy I told you about," he explained.

"Invite him over," suggested the FBI special agent.[21] The agents raced over as the counter clerk asked the "Arab guy" to come in.

The "Arab guy" was arrested on the spot.

He turned out to be Mohammed Salameh, the wheelman for the bombers. He desperately needed the money to pay for his escape. The airline ticket that Ramzi Yousef had given him was for an infant's plane fare. Without the money to upgrade the ticket, he would be trapped in the United States. That was what Ramzi Yousef wanted. His capture would be another helpful distraction.

Salameh's phone records and storage unit keys (which he foolishly kept in his pocket) connected the rest of the dots. In days, the FBI had the bomb-making laboratory and leads on other members of the cell.

Ramzi Yousef was disciplined. Within eight hours of the blast, he was onboard a Pakistani Airlines flight to Islamabad. First class, of course. He didn't stick around to gloat and soak up the media coverage—or get arrested.

His accomplices were less disciplined and soon caught. That might have been their main role all along. Indeed, they may have been chosen precisely because they'd done a poor job with the Kahane killing. Because most of the cell members were amateurs and easily rounded up, federal investigators did not spend a lot of time wondering whether the bombing was funded by a foreign power.

Where did KSM get the funds for the 1993 World Trade Center attack? An analysis by RAND, the respected think tank that works closely with the CIA and the Defense Department, points out that amateur terrorists, by themselves, do not rule out the possibility of sponsorship by a foreign government or a foreign terrorist organization:

> This use of amateur terrorists as dupes or cut-outs to mask the involvement of a foreign patron or government could potentially benefit terrorist state sponsors by enabling them to more effectively conceal their involvement and thus avoid potential military retaliation or diplomatic and economic sanctions. The prospective state sponsors' connection could be further obscured by the fact that much of the amateur terrorists' equipment, resources, and even funding could be entirely self-generating.[22]

If it turned out that KSM had received money from the government of Iraq or Iran, then the World Trade Center bombing ceases to be a criminal matter. It becomes an act of war. So far, the only evidence of foreign-government involvement is nugatory and circumstantial. Is it significant that Ramzi Yousef entered on an Iraqi passport and used "the Iraqi" as his alias? Still, the question of KSM's funding source is important, even today.

The head of the FBI investigation, James Fox, later told a former senior FBI official[23] that he had been ordered by the Clinton Justice Department to restrict his investigation "to the water's edge." (Fox is now deceased.) The FBI official he spoke with said the Justice Department instructions meant that he should not pursue any leads that would lead to foreign governments or even foreign terror groups. President Clinton was not looking to go to war.

Over the next decade, the FBI realized it was facing a new kind of terror organization. Usually, terror outfits were highly structured and centrally organized and had repeatable patterns of attack. On background, one senior FBI official said he never believed in the loose or ad hoc structure of Islamist terror networks. He kept thinking there had to be an East German–style apparatus hidden from view. "But I lost these arguments because I had no hard evidence" showing a hierarchical structure.[24]

For whatever reason, the Tradebom perpetrators were considered simply a group of friends who worshipped at the same mosque.[25] While Ramzi Yousef's arrival was seen as a catalyst, the Bureau missed that he had been a field commander for a foreign mastermind.

The key question: "How did a Pakistani teen-ager [Ramzi Yousef] come to know a cleric from Egypt who had transplanted himself to New Jersey? One thread seems to link them: Afghanistan. . . . Both of [Blind Sheikh] Abdel Rahman's sons fought in Afghanistan, as did Mahmud Abouhalima [the getaway car driver]."[26] And both Ramzi Yousef and KSM were in Afghan training camps at the same time as Abdel Rahman's two sons.

Bureaucratic rules made it hard for FBI special agents to investigate the growing Islamic network in their midst, on the American homeland. Department of Justice guidelines required agents to have clear evidence of a federal crime before an investigation could be opened. While FBI agents and New York federal prosecutors had plenty of suspicions about the Blind Sheikh, the "jihad office," and several members of the 1993 World Trade Center plot before the bomb went off, they didn't have legal authority to investigate. The disadvantage of treating terrorism as a law enforcement matter meant that, essentially, the FBI could investigate only after a bomb went off.

CIA director Jim Woolsey fumed. The agents in the FBI's New York office were not sharing any information with the CIA. "It was frustrating," Woolsey told me. "Nobody outside the prosecutorial team and maybe the FBI [New York office] had access" to information about the investigation into one of the largest terror attacks in American history.[27] Woolsey was interested in the prospect of foreign authorship of the bombing.

The lack of coordination was no accident. To the FBI, the bombing was a crime. In criminal cases, any information that left the immediate prosecutorial team had to be shared with the defense attorneys and their clients. Imagine giving sensitive intelligence documents to the representatives of a global terrorist organization. (It's a worthwhile concern, but easily fixed. Congress could pass a law saying that all federal agencies involved in intelligence collection are effectively part of the prosecution team. This would serve the public interest of giving the prosecutors the best information about terror links without hampering the legal defense of the accused.) Still, in 1993, the FBI was faithfully following Rule 6E of the Federal Rules of Criminal Procedure. "It is not that they [the FBI and CIA] don't get along—it's that they can't share information by legal statute" in these kinds of cases, said Christopher Whitcomb, an FBI veteran who worked on the 1993 World Trade Center bombing investigation.[28]

Rule 6E also kept the CIA's Counter-Terrorism Center from doing its job, which was to share information with every significant federal intelligence service. The Counter-Terrorism Center is the interagency team made up of CIA, FBI, Secret Service, and State Department officials who were supposed to cut through red tape to investigate the terror attacks. The CTC's deputy director was an FBI official whose principal duty was to enable the would-be rival agencies to pool information. But the CTC was kept in the dark.

As a result of giving the World Trade Center bombers a civilian trial, which made it difficult for the prosecution team to share or receive evidence from the intelligence community, both the CIA and the FBI overlooked the links between Ramzi Yousef, Osama bin Laden, and Khalid Shaikh Mohammed for years.

As the FBI investigation continued and the press coverage grew, Ramzi Yousef became a star.

Strangely, KSM stayed in the shadows, not emerging to take credit for one of Islamist terror's most spectacular attacks. Given his well-developed desire for attention, it is strange that KSM did not publicly take credit for the World Trade Center bombing until after his 2003 capture.

Bin Laden later told Western reporters that he hadn't met Ramzi Yousef before the 1993 bombing. "Ramzi Yousef, after the World Trade Center bombing, became a well-known Muslim personality, and all Muslims know him. Unfortunately, I did not know him before the incident," bin Laden told ABC News in 1998.[29] That certainly confirms Ramzi Yousef's rock-star status among jihadis.

Bin Laden's claim that he didn't know Ramzi Yousef (and by extension didn't know KSM) tells us something interesting about how careers were developed inside the terror network. After training, you were supposed to develop your own ideas, network to find your own funding, and lead your own team to implement your plan. If you succeeded big enough or often enough, you would win a place in the management of Al Qaeda. From that perch, you could take part in even larger attacks and have a role in shaping the next generation.

The entrepreneurial nature of midlevel players—the self-starters of terror who fund, recruit, and execute on their own—functioned as a kind of sorting process for Al Qaeda while creating intense competition that spurred innovative new lines of attack, like the 1993 World Trade Center bombing. KSM's time as a terror entrepreneur schooled him to become a terror mastermind in the next decade.

Was bin Laden telling the truth? It is impossible to know. While

Ramzi Yousef and KSM were in Afghanistan for at least two years prior to the World Trade Center bombing and knew many people (including Sheikh Sayyaf, Jamal Khalifa, Omar Abdel Rahman, and Abdurajak Janjalani) who knew bin Laden well, it is possible he had not actually met them. It is also possible that bin Laden hadn't heard of either of them. How many rock stars can name all of their roadies? Before the 1993 bombing, KSM and Yousef were decidedly seen as small-timers.

Besides, bin Laden may have had good reason to dissemble. His ABC interview occurred a few weeks after the August 7, 1998, bombings of two U.S. embassies in East Africa, killing 224 people (including twelve American diplomats). He may have wanted to keep the focus on his most current attack. Of course, bin Laden's published war doctrine specifically allows for *taqqiya,* or lying to advance the Muslim cause.

Both KSM and Ramzi Yousef had stayed at Pakistani safe houses paid for by bin Laden's network, even though neither was yet a member of Al Qaeda in the years after the World Trade Center bombing. Additionally, KSM seems to have received some money from funders of Al Qaeda for the World Trade Center bombing.[30]

All rock stars with a double-platinum hit have the same problem: What do we do for an encore? After his triumphant return from New York, Ramzi Yousef "brainstormed" with KSM about novel ways to strike Manhattan again.[31] KSM wanted to hurt the United States economically, and that meant again striking its commercial capital.[32]

Then Yousef reminded him about their mutual childhood friend Abdul Hakim Murad.

Murad, after attending four different flight schools in the United States, finally had a temporary commercial pilot's license. (Many of the schools that Murad attended would later be used by the 9/11 hijackers. KSM never seemed to overlook any useful tidbit.)

Murad was back in Kuwait, looking for work, Yousef explained.

"Send for him," KSM said.

Lured by the (wholly imaginary) potential of a pilot's job with Pakistan's national air carrier and a free airplane ticket, Murad quickly agreed to come.

He soon realized the real purpose for his summons. KSM quizzed him extensively about how pilots are trained, how difficult it is to fly a plane, how much fuel they carry, and so on.[33]

Why not use jets loaded with fuel and passengers and fly them into skyscrapers? This would increase the death toll by killing people both on the planes and in the buildings. Murad insisted, according to the 9/11 Commission Report, that the idea came from him, in 1993. But it didn't matter. The idea was KSM's now.

Meanwhile, Ramzi Yousef had been busy. Following his escape from New York in 1993, Yousef was involved in a series of bomb plots across Asia. In the spring, he had been in Bangkok as part of an ill-fated effort to blow up the Israeli embassy.[34]

Later, he journeyed deep inside Iran. Near Mashad, an Iranian border crossroads that had been welcoming caravans since the days of Marco Polo, there is an ancient shrine to the Prophet Mohammed's grandson, Reza. It is a sacred site in Shia Islam and has long been a place for pilgrimage. Ramzi Yousef and his family (including KSM) are Sunnis. Ramzi Yousef, with his father, Abdul Karim, and his brother, Abdul Muneim, bombed it.[35] Revering the Prophet's grandson was, for them, "idol worship," something forbidden in their understanding of Islam.

Naturally, Ramzi Yousef made the bomb. Blasting that piece of history into dust was the start of a trend among Salafi Muslim terror groups: a concerted war against the historical relics of other faiths. The Taliban later blasted the ancient Buddha statues near Bamiyan, Afghanistan.

Again, in the Bamiyan case, the real targets were Shia Muslims, in that they made their livelihood off of the trickle of backpackers and tourists who came to see the giant Buddhas.

Before KSM could make any further plans, Ramzi Yousef began to work on a plot developed by his father: killing the future prime minister of Pakistan.

Benazir Bhutto was campaigning to be prime minister of Pakistan in September 1993. (Her father was the prime minister who had cracked down on Baluchistan in the 1970s.) Her opponent was then prime minister Nawaz Sharif. Sharif had been elected in October 1990 with money and grassroots support supplied by Osama bin Laden, according to former Pakistani intelligence official Khalid Khawaja.[36] Sharif had narrowly defeated Bhutto in 1990. And now it seemed as if Bhutto would win this election.

The connections between KSM's clan and the Pakistani prime minister are indisputable. When Pakistani investigators raided the house of Zahid Shaikh Mohammed, KSM's older brother, they found several photographs of Zahid and KSM with top advisers to Prime Minister Sharif.[37] Pictures of bin Laden were also found. Other photos showed Zahid with the prime minister himself.

The raid also appears to be the first time that KSM came to the attention of Pakistani authorities and provides evidence of his early links to bin Laden and top-level Pakistani political figures.

But the raid did nothing to stop the plot to kill the prime minister's more liberal rival.

Ramzi Yousef had designed a trademark nitroglycerin bomb to kill Bhutto—and clear the field for Sharif's reelection as prime minister. Yousef asked his old friend Abdul Hakim Murad to drive while Yousef kept the bomb at his feet in the passenger side of the vehicle. As they approached the high walls of Bhutto's private home, a police patrol stopped them. After getting past the police, Yousef picked up the bomb to examine it. It exploded in his hands.

He was so badly injured that Murad took him to the Aga Khan Hospital, according to then information secretary Husain Haqqani.[38]

Yousef told hospital workers that he'd been injured when a butane lighter exploded in his hand. It seems unlikely that the hospital staff bought his story, but they treated him nevertheless.

KSM later visited Yousef in the hospital and appears to have played a role in funding the attack on the prime minister.[39] (The Pakistani government would not learn about the September 1993 attempted attack on Bhutto until March 1995, when the arrests of six men produced confessions.[40])

"I want you to know that we have now found out that Mr. Ramzi (Ahmed) Yousef was sent here in Karachi in 1993 to assassinate me," Bhutto told the Reuters news agency.[41] She said that Yousef had rented an apartment near her home.[42]

As it happened, Bhutto survived and was elected prime minister in 1993. Explaining both her appeal to the electorate and the threat she posed to the jihadis, Bhutto would say, "As a moderate, progressive, democratically elected woman prime minister of Pakistan, I am a threat to the fundamentalist zealots on multiple levels."[43]

Out of the hospital, Ramzi Yousef was recovering in the Embassy Hotel in Karachi when KSM came to him with an idea so big that its success would finally make them not just jihadi famous but world famous. It would involve airplanes, bombs, and a trip to the strip clubs of Manila.

5

The Plot to Kill the Pope, the President, and Four Thousand Americans

With a massive encore to Ramzi Yousef's New York Tradebom attack in mind, KSM flew into Manila International Airport on July 21, 1994. He handed the customs officer a Pakistani passport issued in Abu Dhabi. Interestingly, the passport featured his full legal name: Khalid Shaikh Mohammed Ali Dustin al-Balushi.[1]

KSM's use of truthful documentation wouldn't last. In the next few months, he would employ nearly a half-dozen aliases as he developed plots to kill President Clinton, Pope John Paul II, and nearly four thousand lesser-known people on eleven different commercial airplanes.

After scouting Manila's traffic-choked neighborhoods, he selected one of the wealthiest. Known as Malate, it's home to most of the capital's high-end Western-style hotels and has a large, transient Arab population.[2] It also has a seedy side, complete with go-go clubs and women for rent.[3] There was something in Malate to appeal to every part of KSM's expansive personality.

Meanwhile, with twenty-one different aliases of his own,[4] Ramzi Yousef also arrived in the Philippines sometime in November 1994.

After Ramzi Yousef moved into KSM's apartment in Malate, KSM began to build a cell to carry out his plan. Next, he reached out to Abdul Hakim Murad, who had finally gotten his commercial pilot certificate.

KSM, Ramzi Yousef, and Murad were fairly close. They had all grown up together in Kuwait and each of them had joined the youth wing of Kuwait's Muslim Brotherhood.

Then their paths diverged. But for a few key decisions, Murad might have become an ordinary commercial airline pilot. He wasn't a very good pilot, though. It was his fourth professional pilot's school that finally gave him a passing mark. That school, the now-defunct Coastal Aviation, was in New Bern, North Carolina—roughly 190 miles from KSM's alma mater in Greensboro. He accepted KSM's paid invitations to visit him in Pakistan. Maintaining his relationship with KSM, a seemingly simple enough decision to stay in touch with a childhood friend, would change Murad's life—and those of many other people.

Next, KSM recruited Wali Khan Amin Shah. Shah was, in a sense, already working for KSM. Like KSM, he was Baluch, though from the Afghanistan portion of Baluchistan. (KSM's family hails from the Iranian and Pakistani parts of Baluchistan.) Shah was working at Konsojaya, a Malaysia-based business that KSM had started with Mohammed Jamal Khalifa, Osama bin Laden's brother-in-law, and another man known as Hambali.[5]

Like the other plotters, Shah had many aliases,[6] including Azmiri.[7] That's how he was known to his close friend Saif al-Adel, who later became a U.S. government witness in a number of terror cases. Al-Adel provided the federal government with its first inside look at Al Qaeda in the 1990s, although it would be years before intelligence analysts would fully understand his value. Al-Adel provided important context for the events in Manila and beyond, including Shah's involvement in another KSM plot "to assassinate President Bill Clinton during a trip to Africa in 1998." Shah was apparently involved with both of KSM's plans to try to kill President Clinton, first in the Philippines and second in Africa.[8]

Now that KSM had the targets, the location, and the team, he needed money. Capital, as even terrorist-entrepreneurs know, makes everything else possible. He would need funds for plane tickets, hotels, and meals for his team, as well as for disguises, false documents, industrial chemicals, and so on.

KSM's own connections to Saudi and Gulf Arab sheikhs could supply some of the money. KSM controlled an account at an Abu Dhabi bank that acted as a funnel for moving money from princes, plutocrats, and bogus charities to his terror projects.

KSM's business partner in the Konsojaya Trading Company, Khalifa, also ran a humanitarian nonprofit called International Islamic Relief Organization. For KSM, the charity's main purpose was to relieve him of budgetary constraints. Khalifa allowed KSM to spend fairly freely from its accounts.

Khalifa largely escaped scrutiny by the authorities because his unusual transfers of money to charities and businesses were not technically crimes, at the time, in the Philippines. Khalifa's second wife (of four) is the sister of Osama bin Laden. (Khalifa tried to distance himself publicly from bin Laden. "Bin Laden is one of my 22 brothers-in-law, and I do not condone his terrorist activities," Khalifa told a Philippine newspaper in 2000. He also denied ties to the attractive tourism secretary of the Philippines. "You better correct that, or my wives would kill me," Khalifa said. His third and fourth wives are Filipinas who read the local papers.[9])

Khalifa often supplied money for KSM's operations, and KSM was often unhappy when the money was slow to come or insufficient. Philippine investigators later found a laptop that contained a letter from KSM to a man he referred to as "Brother Mohammed Alsiddiqi," who is believed to be Khalifa. The letter is bitter but reveals a lot about their relationship. "We are facing a lot of problems because of you. Fear Allah, Mr. Siddiqi, there is a day of judgment. You will be asked if you are very busy with something more important, don't give promises to other people. See you on the day of judgment."

"Still waiting," the letter was signed, "Khalid Shaikh, and Bojinka."[10]

Bojinka was the code name of KSM's operations in the Philippines.

Khalifa knew Ramzi Yousef as well, bringing him to the Philippines in 1991 so that Yousef could teach bomb-making techniques to members of Abu Sayyaf, the Philippine terror group named after Abdul Rasul Sayyaf, who ran the Afghan camps that trained many of the jihadis.[11] Ramzi Yousef was disappointed because the Abu Sayyaf organization was more interested in guns than bombs and had launched a series of kidnappings for ransom that made no broader ideological points. He left, disgusted.

The pending terror operations would be credited by KSM to Abu Sayyaf, even though the group had nothing to do with any of the plots. Somebody had to get the credit.

KSM's other partner in the Konsojaya front company, and its putative founder, was known by the name Hambali. The nickname is a play on words in Arabic and refers to the Hanbali school of Islamic jurisprudence, one of the four major Sunni schools of thought and considered to be the one that has changed the least since the seventh century. More formally, he is known as Riduan Isamuddin. He left his native village in Indonesia in 1985 to fight in Afghanistan, meeting KSM, bin Laden, and other key figures there. Hambali told family and friends that he had worked selling palm oil.

Hambali secretly married a Malaysian-Chinese woman named Noralwizah Lee Abdullah, whom he had met while visiting the school of an Al Qaeda affiliate. Both husband and wife were put on the board of Konsojaya.

KSM, who had known Hambali since their days in Afghanistan,[12] gave him some 95,000 ringgit, or about $33,000, to set up terror cells in Southeast Asia.[13]

With Konsojaya as a front company, Khalifa's bogus charity and his Abu Dhabi bank account, KSM was well stocked with money to carry out any attack he could dream up.

What he dreamed up was called Oplan Bojinka. In Serbo-Croatian, *oplan* means "operation," and *bojinka* means "loud bang."[14] (KSM had learned a few words in Bosnia.) Bojinka would be launched from

KSM's new base in the Philippines. U.S. federal prosecutors would later refer to it as the Manila Air plot.

Interestingly, KSM had three different plots in mind, although each would evolve in the coming months. He assembled the money and men before he had a fixed idea about what exactly to do with them. This is how he liked to operate.

The first plot involved killing President Bill Clinton, most likely with a bomb. After studying the president's planned route as reported in the local newspapers, KSM sent Ramzi Yousef to survey the ground. Even days before Clinton's arrival, Ramzi Yousef noticed the presence of armed security and bomb-sniffing dogs. Plus, it appeared that an advance team of U.S. Secret Service was already on the scene and Philippine police were mobilized and aggressive. Ramzi Yousef advised against an attack, citing security and the lack of time to prepare.

KSM moved to option two: killing the pope. The plan was for Murad to pose as a priest, approach the pope, and, when the pontiff extended his hand, trigger a bomb tucked under his priestly garments. The murder would give Murad fame and martyrdom and send shock waves around the world. The cell had acquired a photograph of John Paul II, a Bible, and a crucifix. Murad had even seen a tailor about getting a cassock made.[15] Only luck would save the pope.

The third and main plot was daring in a sinister sense: explode eleven jumbo jets over the Pacific nearly simultaneously, killing several thousand people. If it succeeded, it would be the largest terrorist attack in history. But first, KSM and Ramzi Yousef would need to solve a number of technical problems.

The airline plot required a bomb small enough to bring aboard a plane in carry-on luggage. Ramzi Yousef came up with a unique liquid-nitroglycerin design.

KSM and Ramzi Yousef tested their unique nitroglycerin bomb four times. For the first test, Ramzi Yousef put a bomb in the janitor's closet of a busy shopping mall in Cebu City. The bomb exploded on time and no one was hurt. Now they knew the bomb design worked.

The second test involved a bigger, more powerful version. Team member Shah was told to put the bomb under a seat in the Greenbelt Theater, a movie house in a Manila shopping mall, on December 1, 1994. Again, no deaths, but this time almost a dozen people were injured.[16]

Now sure of the bomb design, KSM began devising ways to get it on an airplane. Ramzi Yousef's brainstorm was to carry the components onto the plane and assemble the bomb in its tiny bathroom.

The hard part was getting nitroglycerin onto an airplane. Would airport security stop them? KSM had to prove to himself that he could get Ramzi Yousef's bomb onto an airplane. He carefully poured nitromethane into fourteen bottles of cleaning fluid for contact lenses. He packed thirteen bottles into his carry-on and gave one to Ramzi Yousef to bring onto a different flight. KSM flew from Manila to Seoul, South Korea, while Ramzi Yousef flew from Hong Kong to Taipei. They were not discovered and easily returned to Manila.[17]

Next, KSM had to test whether he could get the timer and the battery aboard a plane. The timer was a ten-dollar plastic Casio wristwatch. But a battery would be needed to send a strong enough electrical charge to detonate the bomb. The battery was the only metallic component of the bomb. KSM and Ramzi Yousef puzzled over how to get it through airport security and X-ray machines. Finally, he thought of hiding the battery in the hollowed-out heels of his shoes, which fall below the area the airport scanners cover. This is the same loophole the "shoe bomber," Richard Reid, used a decade later and why you now have to remove your shoes to go through airport security.

KSM came up with another clever test of the security system. KSM taped a small metal bolt to the arch of his foot, then covered it with a sock and shoe. "As expected, the metal detectors went off when KSM passed through it and he was asked to take off his shoes, but the police did not insist that he take off his socks," CNN's Maria Ressa notes.[18] He wasn't sent back through the metal detector. KSM had found another weakness in the airport security system.

Now a final test: Could they get the bomb components onto a plane, assemble them, arm the bomb timer, safely escape, and have the bomb explode? This time, KSM sent Ramzi Yousef on Philippine Airlines Flight 434 from Manila to Tokyo, which made a scheduled stop at the Philippine island of Cebu.

Once the seat-belt light was turned off, Ramzi Yousef rose and went to the lavatory. As planned, he combined the chemicals and made the bomb. He set the Casio watch timer for 11:43.[19]

Carefully, he packed the bomb into a brown sandwich bag and took it back to his seat. He was cautious to avoid bumping into anyone. The bomb might have exploded in his hands. He moved the life vest aside and secured the bomb under the seat. When the plane landed at Cebu City, he got off.

On the flight's final leg to Tokyo, a Japanese engineer, Haruki Ikegami, took Ramzi Yousef's seat.

Halfway through the flight, the tiny alarm rang, triggering a thunderous explosion. It cut in half the luckless Japanese engineer and smashed a hole in the thin skin of the airplane.

The man behind him, Yukihiko Usui, awoke howling in pain. The blast had seared his legs like a blowtorch. Nine other passengers were injured.

After forty harrowing minutes, the pilot made an emergency touchdown at Naha Airport on Okinawa.[20] As the plane came to a stop, the passengers spontaneously cheered.

Meanwhile, on Cebu, Ramzi Yousef calmly phoned the Associated Press office in Manila and claimed the bombing was the work of the Abu Sayyaf terror group.

Philippine investigators later found that the seat occupied by the hapless Japanese engineer had been previously used by "Amaldo Forlani." It was a name Ramzi Yousef had chosen from a list of Italian politicians.[21]

Now that they had a working bomb design and a sure method to get it past airport security, KSM began to think big. Why hit one plane when a team could strike almost a dozen simultaneously?

KSM studied the flight schedules of all aircraft leaving East Asia for the United States. These would carry the most fuel and passengers.

In the *Official Airline Guide*, he found at least eleven flights that would make a stop before crossing the Pacific Ocean. The stop was crucial; it allowed a terrorist to switch planes and deposit a second bomb on another flight, and then get off when the second plane made its scheduled stop before crossing the Pacific.

Here's how KSM wanted Oplan Bojinka to work: five men, eleven planes. Four men would get on two planes, leaving bombs on each. A fifth man, most likely KSM himself, would get on three planes and set three bombs. All the terrorists would be safely en route to Pakistan when the timers beeped.

While planning a series of bombings designed to create an Islamic superstate, KSM and Ramzi Yousef enjoyed a playboy life in the Philippines, at odds with Islamic law. They hung out nearly every night at strip clubs, where Arminda Costudio, a waitress, remembers KSM's "chubby" fingers and fat wads of cash.

Another favorite haunt was an alcohol-serving karaoke bar on A. Mabini Street in Manila. They enjoyed music and alcohol while watching the overhead television screen. Bin Laden would not have approved. KSM didn't care. He had his own financing and made his own rules.

Then an accident brought the party to a sudden end. While Ramzi Yousef was teaching Murad to make the nitroglycerin bombs in the kitchen of their shared apartment, the mixture started to smoke. Instinctively, Murad put the chemicals in the sink and turned the water on. The water accelerated the chemical fire.[22]

Panicked, Yousef and Murad ran out of the apartment, down the steps, and through the lobby. They holed up in a karaoke bar,[23] considering their options. The fire and police departments would almost certainly be called. When the authorities entered Apartment 603, they would find passports under various aliases, large piles of cash (mostly in U.S. dollars), bottles and beakers full of chemicals, and a laptop that detailed their future plans. Someone had to grab the incriminating evidence before the authorities did. Also, they needed cash to finance their escape.

But they couldn't decide who should take the risk and go. After an hour, they decided to go together. When they arrived, they found Philippine Police Captain Aida Fariscal and a uniformed policeman in the lobby.

A hotel clerk spotted Murad and pointed him out to the police. Murad ran, but a policeman tackled him. As he squirmed, he was cuffed. Murad was taken to a special facility used by Philippine intelligence, in Camp Crame, Quezon City.[24] He was interrogated for days.

Ramzi Yousef ran. Bounding through the crowds, he quickly lost the police. With advice and money from KSM, he left Manila quickly, disappearing into a series of safe houses and hotel suites across Asia.

While Ramzi Yousef was lucky to get away, so was the pope. The fire in the bomb-makers' apartment was roughly five hundred feet from the residence where the pope would be staying during his official visit. The resulting police investigation foiled the plot against the pontiff.[25]

Strangely, KSM stayed put. Boldly, he decided he was safe. He had cleverly insulated himself from any risk by moving out of the Dona Josefa apartments before Murad and Shah arrived. They knew that Ramzi Yousef was getting money and direction from elsewhere, but they only had a hazy idea of KSM's involvement, if any.

KSM was not immediately a suspect, and, he believed, Murad and Shah would not talk about him to their interrogators. You can't talk about what you don't know, KSM thought.

Plus, KSM was confident that investigators would not find any usable physical evidence linking him to the plots. He had worn gloves in every visit to Ramzi's apartment, something that his comrades thought strange in Manila's oppressive humidity. That meant that his fingerprints literally wouldn't be there.

He failed to realize how quickly his comrades would crack.

Murad started talking after being held for less than forty-eight hours. "Murad said Ramzi Yousef sought him out in New York City in 1992 . . . [and] asked him to survey New York City and find a target for a bomb that would produce maximum casualties. They said

Murad told them he suggested to Ramzi Yousef one place where thousands of people congregate every day: the World Trade Center in New York's financial district. Murad said he left for Pakistan almost immediately but that four months later, in February, 1993, he was surprised to hear . . . that terrorists had bombed the twin towers."[26]

A Philippine tactical interrogation report, written by Senior Inspector Eugenio H. Roxas on September 9, 1995, has Murad describing how the bombs were made and who was to put which bomb on which plane. He also detailed a plot of KSM's to bomb the New York City subway and told the police that he was to call the U.S. embassy in Oman and to claim credit in the name of the Fifth Battalion, the same fake terror group that Ramzi Yousef had named in the 1993 World Trade Center bombing.

Importantly, he also identified KSM.

Murad also explained KSM's idea to hijack planes and fly them into buildings in the United States, according to a January 20, 1995, Philippine police report:

> With respect to their plans to dive-crash a commercial aircraft at the CIA headquarters in Virginia, subject [Murad] alleged that the idea of doing same came out during his casual conversation with Abdul Basit [Ramzi Yousef] and there is no specific plan yet for its execution. What the subject have [sic] in his mind is that he will board any American commercial aircraft and pretending [sic] to be an ordinary passenger. Then he will hijack said aircraft, control its cockpit, and dive it at the CIA headquarters. There will be no bomb or any explosive that he will use in its execution. It is simply a suicidal mission that he is very much willing to execute. That all he need [sic] is to be able to board the aircraft with a pistol so that he could execute the hijacking.

Meanwhile, police arrested another terror-team member, Wali Amin Shah, on January 11, 1995. He, too, spoke freely to the police—perhaps in the hopes of shifting the blame. When Shah was taken into custody, he had "in his possession a detonating cord, mercury, a quartz timer, two sets of handcuffs, springs for a pistol and a firing pin. These items were to be used for the attempt on the pope's life."[27]

Shah, too, also tipped off Philippine police to the existence of KSM.[28]

In his own interrogation, Shah said he had met with a man named Adam Ali in Manila in connection with the plot to kill the pope. He recalled that he had been introduced to the same man in Karachi in 1992, under the name Abu Khalid.

In addition to interrogations, the police had a wealth of physical evidence. Ramzi Yousef's Toshiba laptop proved to be a gold mine. So did a handwritten notebook in Arabic: "It was like a cookbook with step-by-step instructions on how to make various bombs," said one Philippine official, adding that the FBI later found fingerprints on the notebook matching those of Ramzi Yousef.[29] Yousef was compulsive about writing out his bomb-making recipes.

Finally, Yousef's laptop revealed the other cell members, including clues leading to KSM. All five cell members were identified from photographs found on Yousef's computer. Though the computer file that contained the photographs had been erased, Philippine authorities were able to easily restore it.[30]

Inside the U.S. federal bureaucracy, identifying the KSM threat was a glacial process.

"I read the cable traffic as the operation against Murad, Shah, and Yousef unfolded," former CIA officer Melissa Boyle Mahle writes.[31] "It was complicated, with pieces coming in a bit at a time, in the most confusing of patterns. Khalid Shaikh Mohammed was just a blip on the screen. He would later become a major target on my screen."

Larry Johnson, the State Department's counterterrorism coordinator, got the call that finally put KSM in U.S. crosshairs from Philippine colonel Rodolfo "Boogie" Mendoza. After combing through the aliases and intricate patterns, a pointillist portrait was forming. At first, like bin Laden, KSM was seen as merely a terror financier. This is like describing a producer as simply a movie financier; some producers develop ideas, get scripts written, and bring movies into being. At the time, financial middlemen like KSM were competing to produce bigger and bigger terrorist blockbusters.

KSM also appeared on the screen of Mary Jo White, the diminutive, no-nonsense federal prosecutor for the Southern District of New York.

Mary Jo White was in a bureaucratic tug-of-war with the deputy attorney general in Washington, Eric Holder. Both wanted the chance to prosecute the "Manila Air" plot.

White had to phone Attorney General Janet Reno to get control of the case.

While Mary Jo White was preparing her case, the staff of the White House's West Wing was preparing the president.

The CIA and the FBI briefed the National Security Council's Richard Clarke. This was something too big to ignore. President Clinton himself had been one of the targets.

The briefing was extensive and detailed. Ramzi Yousef was the focus, as the alleged ringleader and World Trade Center bomber. But somewhere along the way, a financier named Khalid was mentioned. He wasn't given any special attention. Yet it was likely the first time U.S. officials outside the intelligence community had referred, even indirectly, to Khalid Shaikh Mohammed.

A manhunt for Ramzi Yousef began immediately.

6

Losing Ramzi

Ramzi Yousef was led by Ishiatique Parker, a South African Muslim he had met only a few months before, down Street 20 in the F-7 district of Islamabad, Pakistan. Snaking past the residence of the Iraqi ambassador, they soon came to number 31, the Su-Casa Guest House. The small structure had tacky Greek pillars, and a fake balcony loomed over the front door. Parker led the legendary fugitive into its white-marble-tiled lobby.

It was a strange neighborhood for a hideout. The streets were crowded with uniformed policemen and military officers, and the neighborhood was home to many of Pakistan's senior officials and diplomats. Parker explained that he lived diagonally across the street and that the neighborhood was "safe." But it wouldn't be safe for long: Parker was laying a trap for Yousef.

KSM was waiting for them at the guesthouse. We do not know when he left the Philippines or how, but, by February 1995, he was happily back in Pakistan.

With the Philippine plots in tatters, KSM was already working on his next attack, which involved placing high-tech explosives in remote-controlled toy cars.

For thirty-two days, the FBI, the CIA, Pakistan's ISI, and the Philippine National Police had been hunting Ramzi Yousef. Somehow, he had eluded a global dragnet.

Neither KSM nor Ramzi Yousef knew that Murad's interrogation in Manila had revealed that the cell's rendezvous point after the attacks was to be Karachi, Pakistan.[1] No one in the intelligence community thought that Ramzi Yousef was foolish enough to go to the "rally point" in Karachi once the operation was blown. This crucial bit of intelligence only gave investigators a place to start looking, a country and possibly a city to begin the search in. The Department of Justice distributed posters and matchbooks featuring Ramzi Yousef's face (see photo section). Below his name and face was a reward for $2 million. It was a shot in the dark. If the FBI was lucky, one of his acquaintances would turn him in.

KSM and Ramzi Yousef also did not know that they had acquired a powerful enemy: President Clinton's counterterrorism czar, Richard Clarke. Even the intelligence officers who privately complained that he was a bully would, in the same breath, say that he was a devoted and surprisingly effective career counterterrorism officer. From his office in the White House's National Security Council, in the area called the "rabbit warren," Clarke made finding Ramzi Yousef his highest priority. In one of the oddities of history, Clarke occupied Colonel Oliver North's former office. Indeed, Clarke made use of Colonel North's illicit second-story loft, which had been installed to provide space for additional staff.

Clarke relentlessly brought up Ramzi Yousef in his meetings with other intelligence officials. His favorite question was "Well, where is he?"

On the first Sunday in February 1995, Clarke arrived at his office shortly after 6 A.M. to read the classified cable traffic from the night before. Suddenly, he stopped reading.

Ramzi Yousef has been seen in Islamabad.

So the World Trade Center bomber was in Pakistan. . . .

Clarke knew enough to be cautious. There are many false dawns in a terrorist manhunt. The report could be false (the $2 million price on Yousef's head produced a lot of useless leads) or it could be a case of mistaken identity (a Ramzi Yousef look-alike).

The clock was ticking. The cable said Yousef was leaving in a few hours on a bus for Peshawar, on the border of Afghanistan. Clarke might not get another chance.

He phoned the FBI's counterterrorism section.

"O'Neill."

Clarke did not recognize the name of the new section chief. "Who are you?"

"I'm John O'Neill. Who the fuck are you?"[2]

It was the start of a remarkable partnership. O'Neill had been brought to Washington only days before, to helm the Bureau's anti-terror efforts; he had driven all night from Chicago and come into the office on a Sunday, a day before he was supposed to start work. O'Neill's gung-ho approach landed him a historic opportunity.

Clarke asked him to put together a team to capture Ramzi Yousef.

An overseas rendition—a kind of legal kidnapping—is a massive bureaucratic enterprise. O'Neill, operating out of the FBI's Strategic Information and Operations Center, had to make the bureaucratic wheels turn quickly—and on a weekend. The State Department would have to grant clearance for the FBI team to enter Pakistan and work with the Pakistanis. The CIA would have to pool its information with the FBI. The Air Force would have to supply aircraft, both a helicopter and a plane. (At Pakistan's insistence, the USAF had to repaint its helicopter as a civilian one.[3]) The National Security Agency would have to greenlight the use of its satellites, and so on. The to-do list was long.

And, on top of all that, both Clarke and O'Neill knew they would have to write themselves a bureaucratic insurance policy, in case the cable was wrong or Ramzi Yousef got away.

Inside the FBI, O'Neill found a fingerprint expert who could conclusively match the suspect (assuming he was captured) with a print lifted from a brown bottle of sodium azide[4] found in the Space Station storage unit, which had served as the New Jersey bomb-making factory for the 1993 World Trade Center attack.[5] O'Neill also found and dispatched a doctor, in case Ramzi Yousef was wounded in the capture.[6] The fingerprint expert and the doctor were bureaucratic insurance: if they captured the wrong man or wounded the right one, they had the capacity to mitigate the possible career damage.

Most of all, O'Neill needed an experienced capture team from the Bureau's New York office. Finally, O'Neill had to arrange for a midair refueling of the Air Force jet. He couldn't risk landing the plane in a third country; he feared that Ramzi Yousef would claim asylum if it touched down anywhere in the world. The operation would end up costing the military some $12 million.[7]

While one FBI team was readying to leave, O'Neill had to find federal personnel in Pakistan—right now!—to actually seize Ramzi Yousef before he fled by bus. There was only one FBI official in Islamabad at the time. O'Neill made more calls. He rounded up a strapping Drug Enforcement Agency official and several bruisers from the U.S. embassy's Bureau of Diplomatic Security. It would have to do.

The Bureau's source was Ishiatique Parker.[8] Yousef had tried to recruit him for a future terror operation over tea months before, but the $2 million reward had made him bold enough to turn in the world's most wanted terrorist.

The FBI wanted Parker to knock on Room 16 of the Su-Casa Guest House and make sure Yousef was there. Parker nervously realized that he was going to have to earn that $2 million.

Parker walked out of the door of the Su-Casa Guest House and lifted his skullcap. The capture team knew what that meant.

At approximately 9:30 in the morning local time, Pakistani Special Forces battered down Yousef's door. In seconds, the barefoot bomb maker was spread-eagled on the floor and handcuffed. Federal agents flooded into the small room, seizing and bagging all of Yousef's belongings as evidence. Investigators found photographs of Osama bin Laden posing with an AK-47 (which may have been meant as a gift for a friend or family member) and a business card from KSM among Ramzi Yousef's belongings.

Meanwhile, KSM boldly spoke to the press, saying he was also staying in the hotel and had seen the operation go down. The Associated Press reporter referred to him as "Khalid Shaikh," just an ordinary guest at the hotel.

"It was like a hurricane," KSM told the Associated Press. "They stormed in and left in less than five minutes."

KSM added, clearly enjoying his moment, that Ramzi had shouted, "I'm innocent, I'm innocent" as he was dragged away.[9] No other account records these words of Ramzi Yousef. It may have been KSM's feeble attempt to help Ramzi Yousef or to send him a message (assuming, of course, that he would be able to read the press coverage of his capture).

After the police and reporters left, KSM must have been devastated.

Ramzi Yousef was not only his closest friend, but his only friend. Since childhood, they had done nearly everything together. Even during the 1993 World Trade Center bomb plot, they were in touch several times per day. They had lived together, traveled together, risked their lives together. They were closer to each other than they were to their own wives. Now Ramzi was gone and the damage was irreversible.

KSM, for the first time in his life, was truly alone.

On the other side of the world, news of Ramzi Yousef's capture produced an opposite feeling: joy.

President Clinton's national security adviser, Tony Lake, was alone in his kitchen when the phone rang. Lake knew that 1 A.M. calls came with the job.

It was Clarke. He sounded excited. That was unusual. "We've got him."

Ramzi Yousef was in custody. Pinching the phone between his shoulder and his head, Lake clapped so that Clarke could hear it.

"Going after terrorists is usually a drawn-out, sometimes ambiguous process," Lake told me. "In brief moments of success, you get a surge of adrenaline and something like joy. And this was such a moment."[10]

After Ramzi Yousef was transferred to U.S. custody, he became talkative. FBI special agent Brad Garrett's initial interview is vividly captured in an internal FBI report:

> At approximately 10:37 A.M. on 2-7-95, Ramzi Ahmed Yousef, shortly after being arrested by Pakistani Military officials, was interviewed by FBI Special Agent Brad Garrett at a military station in Islamabad, Pakistan. Yousef was asked what his name is and he stated "I have many," but he stated he is presently using Ali Baloch, DOB [Date of Birth] 2-15-66. Yousef was asked if he is Ramzi Ahmed Yousef and he stated that he was Yousef and that the individual in the FBI wanted flyer is in fact him.
>
> Yousef was fingerprinted at the military station with a preliminary indication that his prints match Yousef. Yousef stated that his real name is Abdul Basit, DOB: 4-27-68 and that he was born in Kuwait. Yousef was verbally advised of his [Miranda] rights and then [the] SA [Special Agent] wrote out in longhand his rights and read them to Yousef. Yousef advised he understood his rights, does not want an attorney and will voluntarily talk.
>
> Yousef was asked if he committed the World Trade Center (WTC) bombing and he stated, "I masterminded the explosion." Yousef stated he purchased the materials to build the bomb from City Chemicals in Jersey City, NJ. Yousef stated the WTC bombing cost less than $20,000. Yousef stated he built the bomb used in the WTC bombing. Yousef declined to state who provided the money [he didn't want to trap KSM] but he stated the money partly came from friends in Pakistan. Yousef said that because of a lack of funds, the WTC was not as successful as he desired. Yousef stated he was hoping for a quarter million casualties but could not obtain the funds to complete the bomb to his satisfaction.

Yousef stated the reason for the bombings was because of the U.S. military, financial and political support of Israel. Yousef talked at length about Israel being an illegal state and that Israel is committing criminal acts against Muslims. Yousef stated that the American people would need to convince Washington of changing Israeli policy and this would happen by bombing various locations in the U.S. Yousef stated that he was most affected by a BBC report, where Israeli soldiers broke the hand of a Palestinian using a rock. Yousef stated he has no personal agenda with the U.S., only the U.S.-Israeli policy.

Yousef stated that he was born in Kuwait and lived there for 20 years until the Iraqi war [against Kuwait] when his family moved to Pakistan. Yousef stated that his family was originally from Pakistan. He attended high school in Kuwait and from 1986 to 1989 attended the West Glamorgan Institute of Higher Learning in the United Kingdom. Yousef stated he earned a Higher National Diploma in Electronics and the course was called Computer Aided Electronics. In 1989 he returned to Kuwait and worked as a communications engineer at the National Computer Center for the Minister of Planning. After Iraq invaded Kuwait in August 1990, Yousef then moved to Pakistan.

After moving to Pakistan Yousef stated he went to various training camps in Afghanistan for a period of six months. Yousef described these camps as "a place Arabs can get training" in explosives, defensive tactics, weapons use, etc. These camps are located at various sites in Afghanistan but Yousef declined to provide their locations or any specific information about their funding or manpower. Yousef stated that after training in Afghanistan, he returned to Pakistan and continued to read about bomb building.

Yousef stated that during World War II the U.S. dropped nuclear bombs on Japan to force Japan to surrender. Yousef advised the same logic applies to him setting off explosive

> devices at U.S. targets to force the U.S. to change their policy toward Israel. Yousef stated that this is an extreme approach but believes it is the only way to force the U.S. to withdraw its support of Israel.
>
> Yousef asked [the] SA [Special Agent] several questions about executions in the U.S. and asked the length of time before executions are carried out after receiving the death penalty. Yousef stated he believes that he will be executed in the U.S.[11]

During the final leg of Ramzi Yousef's transcontinental journey, he was shackled to the seat of a helicopter. He remained talkative throughout the long trip.

The two FBI agents with him were concerned that if Yousef saw them taking notes, he would stop talking. They took turns sneaking back into the rear seats to scribble down notes from Yousef's conversation.

Looming large in the front windows were the twin towers of the World Trade Center. The flight plan was no accident.

"You see that? They're still standing," one FBI agent said.

"They wouldn't be," Ramzi Yousef replied, "if I had enough explosive."[12]

The "helicopter notes" were revealing:

> [On February 7–8, 1995] Abdul Basit Mahmoud Abdul Karim [also known as Ramzi Yousef], hereafter referred to as "Basit," was interviewed aboard an aircraft en route from Islamabad, Pakistan, to the United States. Basit advised that he could fluently speak, read and understand the English language. He was advised of the official identities of the interviewing agents and was reminded that he was under arrest for offenses concerning the bombing of the World Trade Center (WTC) in New York City. He was, thereafter, advised of his constitutional rights by reading them and

having them read to him. Due to Basit's request, notes were not taken in his presence, but were summarized during breaks in the interview.

[Concerning Yousef's 1992 trip to New York prior to the World Trade Center bombing:] Upon entry at John F. Kennedy International Airport, in New York, Basit utilized an Iraqi passport in the name of Ramzi Ahmed Yousef. Basit explained that he had purchased the Iraqi passport for 100 U.S. dollars in Peshawar, Pakistan. He noted Peshawar is the easiest place to purchase Iraqi passports and further explained that these are genuine documents stolen by Iraqi rebels who raid passport offices in Northern Iraq. When presenting the Iraqi passport to U.S. Immigration Officials, Basit requested political asylum, and was processed and released.

Basit advised that in the fall of 1994 [after the World Trade Center attack], he had learned through various press accounts that President Clinton would be traveling to Manila in November. Basit claimed that he traveled to Manila a few days prior to the President's arrival. Once in Manila, Basit determined the President's planned itinerary through reported press accounts. Basit related that he thereafter traveled to each of the sites which the President would visit, in order to survey them for opportunities to attempt an assassination. He noted that the level of security which he observed at each of these sites was very high. Basit advised that the assassination attempt on Clinton was never carried out, due to the observations of high security, and his lack of time needed to plan and organize such an attempt.

The second option which Basit considered was a bombing attack of the Presidential motorcade while the motorcade was en route between sites in Manila. Basit indicated that he considered placing an improvised explosive device in a location along the motorcade route, designed to disable the lead car in the motorcade. He explained that by disabling the lead vehicle, the entire motorcade would be brought to a stop, enabling an explosive or poisonous gas attack on the Presidential limousine.

He related that he had considered using the chemical agent phosgene in the attack on the limousine, and noted that he had the technical ability to readily manufacture that substance. According to Basit, the phosgene, in a liquid form, could be placed in a metal container, which could then be opened with a charge of explosive, rapidly dispensing the substance as gas.

He related that his associates had [also] been interested in the Pope, but denied that the Pope was an assassination target. Basit attributed religious articles and photographs of the Pope, found in [his] apartment in Manila, to the general interest of his associates [in the Pope]. [This is almost certainly disinformation.]

He spoke of an incident which occurred in his Manila apartment in early January 1995, which had been reported in the media as a fire. He related that he had been demonstrating the burning of a mixture of [chemicals] when smoke produced by the burning began to fill the apartment. He was then questioned as to certain materials found in the Manila apartment which appeared to refer to U.S. airline flights. He noted that, if the incident at the Manila apartment had not occurred, there would have been several airline bombings within two weeks of that time [known to federal prosecutors as the Manila Air plot].

Basit asked the interviewing Agents whether the Agents knew how the person who had been arrested in the Philippines, and who had subsequently escaped, had effected the escape. In discussing [this] individual, Basit acknowledged that this individual was known as Wali [Khan Amin] Shah. Following Basit's descriptions of Wali as strong and intelligent, Basit was questioned as to whether Basit had been

> acting under the direction of Wali Shah. Basit would not further elaborate on that issue.
>
> When questioned regarding a business card in the name of Mohammad Khalifa [bin Laden's brother-in-law Jamal Khalifa], found in Basit's apartment in the Philippines, Basit stated that he did not personally know Khalifa, but that Khalifa's business card had been given to him by Wali Shah, as a contact in the event Basit needed aid. Basit acknowledged that he was familiar with the name Osama bin Laden, and knew him to be a relative of Khalifa's, but would not further elaborate.[13]

KSM would never see Ramzi Yousef again. Yousef was convicted for the World Trade Center bombing and sentenced to 240 years in the supermax maximum-security prison in Florence, Colorado.

KSM and other members of Ramzi Yousef's family soon got their revenge.

Exactly one month later, in Karachi, an unmarked white Toyota van from the U.S. consulate stopped at a red light. A taxi swerved alongside. Four masked men swarmed the trapped vehicle, spraying it with bullets. Two of the three American diplomats inside bled to death, and the third was severely wounded. Pakistani investigators would count seventy-six rounds of 7.62 mm ammunition that had sliced through the vehicle. They linked the gunmen to the SSP, a terror group in which Ramzi's father is a prominent leader.[14] The gunmen drove off in the stolen taxi. Clearly the shooting was retaliation for Yousef's arrest.

KSM knew he had to be careful. Ramzi Yousef had always promised him that he would never give authorities his name. But banking on that promise was risky. Besides, another cell member or stray computer file could give him away.

That interview after Ramzi Yousef's arrest was reckless. Bold, and even funny, but reckless. What if some curious intelligence analyst had decided to plug his name into one of their voluminous databases?

After Ramzi Yousef's capture, KSM went to Khartoum, Sudan, an intelligence official told me.[15] Most likely he was trying to meet bin Laden or one of his lieutenants there. We will never know.

The Sudanese intelligence agency, known as the Mukhabarat, knocked on his hotel door. He was told, politely, to move on. Sudan already had enough trouble from Western governments with its emerging reputation as a rest stop for terrorists. It didn't need any more wanted men in its capital city. He was given a few weeks to find a safe haven—outside of Sudan.

Sudanese intelligence later told a Cairo-based FBI legal attaché about KSM's visit to their country.[16] More important, Sudanese intelligence revealed the terrorist's next destination: Qatar.

By now the FBI knew who KSM was: one of the financiers of the 1993 World Trade Center bombing. The special agents did not know how important KSM was. He was just a name on an indictment.

CIA operations officer Melissa Boyle Mahle had been hunting KSM for months when a source tipped her off that he was living in Doha, the modern capital of Qatar.

KSM apparently had the use of an apartment owned by the then minister of religious affairs, Abdullah bin Khalid al-Thani. The minister had funded KSM's terror operations for years through a variety of Islamic charities, including Human Appeal International.[17]

Mahle was excited. Ramzi Yousef's trial was only months away. KSM "would be useful for the prosecution—plus there were lots of loose ends that needed to be tied," Mahle writes. Including stopping future terrorist attacks.

As Mahle prepared to capture KSM, the CIA and the FBI went to war with each other. "When the FBI was briefed, the Legat based in Rome moved in and tried to take over the operation without concern for CIA equities on the ground or Qatari political tendencies," writes Mahle.

The FBI official wanted a normal criminal investigation with all of the intergovernmental formalities that followed. The problem? Qatar's government could not publicly support an arrest without alienating political factions inside the country. "I was concerned that because of sympathies for Islamic extremists, Muhammad [KSM] would be warned off by Qatari officials and would flee. I cautioned strongly against the direct approach, instead proposing a snatch operation, luring Muhammad out of Qatar and interdicting him as he traveled. The FBI would still get their man. But the FBI was in a hurry, wanted to control the case and wanted to do it the 'FBI way.' It was pure vinegar and water when it came to the FBI special agent and me, with disastrous results," Mahle said.[18]

By October 1995, KSM was seemingly cornered. The CIA and the FBI had tracked him to an apartment building in Qatar. The special agents had even confirmed his presence by using an undisclosed "surveillance technology" and provided the government of Qatar with his street address and an apartment number, Clinton's counterterrorism coordinator, Richard Clarke, told me.[19]

The FBI agents were told to wait in a hotel until the extradition paperwork was complete.

FBI director Louis Freeh repeatedly phoned the head of state security in Qatar. But it seemed that Qatar's government was stalling.

KSM's arrest and transfer to an American prison should have been a legal formality that took only a few days. Qatar has a longstanding extradition treaty with the United States. But weeks went by. The Qatari authorities insisted on processing the formal extradition request as slowly as legally possible, one FBI agent personally involved in the case told me.[20]

Finally, the FBI agents received a valid extradition order. They raced over to KSM's apartment. It was empty. Indeed, it had been thoroughly cleaned. There wasn't even any dust.

How had he gotten away? Qatar's minister of religious affairs had tipped off KSM and provided him and a traveling companion with false passports, according to Robert Baer, a former CIA official.[21] Baer, who at the time was a CIA case officer working in the region, said that Hamid bin Jassim bin Hamad, a disgruntled member of the Kingdom of Qatar's ruling family, had told him about the arrangement.

"Because of an FBI-CIA sandbox fight," the CIA's Mahle writes, "Khalid Shaykh Muhammad escaped capture in 1996, leaving him footloose and fancy free to revamp his disrupted airplane-hijacking plan into the September 11 plot."[22]

He soon went to Afghanistan, looking for Osama bin Laden.

7

Meeting bin Laden

Mary Jo White, the diminutive, tough federal prosecutor for the Southern District of New York, smiled into her telephone.

On the other end of the phone was a federal prosecutor who had walked outside a Manhattan federal courthouse to call her. A grand jury, meeting in secret, had indicted Khalid Shaikh Mohammed for the "Manila Air plot."[1]

The indictment was a close-run thing. "There wasn't a lot of evidence" against KSM, she told me.[2] Just a few stray references on Ramzi Yousef's captured laptop computer and a few recollections of Abdul Hakim Murad and Wali Khan Amin Shah.

But White wasn't going to take any chances. Her prosecutorial philosophy was simple: "I knew these were very dangerous people. We had to cast a broad net" in order to save lives.[3]

The indictment was "sealed," or kept secret, so that it wouldn't tip KSM off that the United States was hunting him.

■ ■ ■

Capturing KSM was not made much easier by the secret indictment.

The music was loud at Bandido restaurant[4] in central Manila. KSM was back in the Philippines, once again posing as a Saudi businessman.

Philippine National Police and a small FBI team had set up a mobile command center to catch KSM a few blocks away. Just as they were beginning their surveillance, KSM stood up and backed away from his table.[5] Before the dragnet could encircle the restaurant, KSM bolted through a back door.

The Philippine police spread out in a broad search pattern. But the mastermind was gone.

Had he spotted an FBI officer? Or did he have a sixth sense? All that is certain is that another chance to capture KSM was gone. The ghost had walked through walls and vanished.

For the first time in his terrorist career, KSM had to run. His home base in Doha had been raided by the FBI, and he knew it wasn't wise to return to Qatar. Pakistan would be risky, too. Ramzi Yousef had been captured there, and KSM's older brother Zahid had said that his house had been searched by Pakistani police. KSM didn't know what the Americans knew about his plot to murder President Clinton, kill Pope John Paul II, or explode eleven commercial airliners over the Pacific Ocean, but he did know that three of his coconspirators had been arrested and could be talking.

He would have to turn to people he knew and trusted, people from the jihadi underworld. KSM's movements over the next year are hard to track due to his restless search for a safe haven. It appears that he visited people he knew from his Afghan days in Yemen, Malaysia, and Brazil.[6]

Brazilian and Argentine intelligence services deny that KSM ever visited Brazil's remote town of Foz do Iguaçu, which is the site of South America's largest waterfall and where the borders of Argentina, Paraguay, and Brazil come together. The so-called Tri-Border Region is a sparsely populated, humid jungle, dotted with private estates. It makes an ideal place to hide. The region is home to some thirty thousand people of Arab descent. On the far side of the bridge linking Brazil to Paraguay, the gold dome of a mosque flashes in the sun. The Brazilian magazine *Veja* claimed to have a twenty-eight-minute video of KSM's visit, but has so far refused to make it public or offer it to American intelligence officials.[7]

Using one of his more than fifty aliases, KSM returned to Karachi. There he saw his brother and his nephews, including Ammar al-Baluchi and Abdul Karim Mahmood Abdul Karim, who had attended North Carolina A&T with him. Both were rising stars in the Al Qaeda constellation.

As he talked his way through his situation—and people who knew him during his North Carolina days say that he liked to think by talking aloud—he began to realize that he could no longer operate on his own. His team of nephews and childhood friends from Kuwait had been arrested—including Ramzi Yousef, Abdul Hakim Murad, and Wali Amin Shah—or had drifted back to well-established terror networks that offered regular pay, housing, health care for pregnant wives and young mothers, and other benefits. KSM and his contemporaries were married, sometimes to multiple wives, and were responsible for their growing families. KSM himself had a wife and two sons. It was time to grow up and get something approaching a normal job, albeit one inside an Islamic terror network.

Part of him sensed that he needed to join or at least come under the protective umbrella of a large, well-funded terrorist organization in a secure location. Osama bin Laden was the obvious choice.

Still, KSM was torn. He had been a solo operator—a "terror entrepreneur" in the words of the 9/11 Commission—for almost ten years. That independence was hard to give up.

Very little is known about KSM's first substantive meeting with Osama bin Laden. It most likely occurred in 1995 in Tora Bora.[8] Tora Bora was a string of crude bunkers and warehouses hewn out of the dirt and rock of Afghanistan's White Mountains, using construction equipment that bin Laden had brought there in 1987. Bin Laden made his tea from a creek that ran nearby; the water was always cold, even in midsummer. Here, around a campfire at night or under a canvas awning by day, bin Laden liked to talk to new recruits about Islam and their commitment to jihad.

The Tora Bora meeting was the first time he had seen bin Laden since 1989, KSM later told his CIA interrogators.[9]

The two men certainly knew of each other, but how well is hard to say. Bin Laden knew that KSM was an uncle of Ramzi Yousef, whose 1993 bombing of the World Trade Center was seen in Al Qaeda circles as daring and bold. The two men also knew a good number of the same people, but they were hardly comfortable with each other.

Still, KSM got a measure of respect for the years he spent working and networking in jihadi circles. KSM had been an assistant to Abdul Rasul Sayyaf, a religious leader whom bin Laden liked and respected. KSM had also worked for Abdullah Azzam, bin Laden's mentor until his death in 1989. But bin Laden must have killed Azzam.

In Azzam's last moments, he was driving to *jummah* prayers on a Friday afternoon in Peshawar, Pakistan, with his father and his brother. He passed by a gas station, where there was a bomb hidden in the rubble of the road. Azzam's car disappeared in a flash of light and thunder. Its burning chassis left almost no human remains. Snaking away from the wreckage was a well-hidden detonation cord that disappeared into a sewer crawl space. The killer had watched for Azzam's car and triggered the explosion. Then he'd calmly crawled away.

At the time of his death, Azzam and bin Laden were arguing about the direction of the jihadi movement. Azzam wanted to consolidate their gains in Afghanistan and form a perfect Islamic state there. Bin Laden wanted to use the global network that the two men had established in the 1980s to drive unbelievers out of Muslim lands and even retake the lands in Europe and Asia that the Arabs had lost in the Middle Ages. Many suspect that bin Laden himself was behind Azzam's car's bombing. He is certainly the one who most benefited from Azzam's disappearance from the scene.

Differing views on Azzam were not the only thing that set KSM and bin Laden apart. The meeting must have been awkward, as the men could hardly have been more different. Lawrence Wright sums up the differences this way:

> Except for their hatred of America, Khaled Sheikh [sic] Mohammed and Osama bin Laden had almost nothing in common. Mohammed was short and squat; pious but poorly trained in religion; an actor and a cutup; a drinker and a womanizer. Whereas bin Laden was provincial and hated travel, especially in the West, Mohammed was a globetrotter fluent in several languages, including English.[10]

KSM, perhaps prodded by bin Laden's quiet questions, had no doubt told him about his exploits in the Philippines and elsewhere. Certainly KSM's plots seemed innovative and ambitious. . . .

After the small talk, KSM presented a battery of outrageous ideas to bin Laden: another plan to kill the pope, this time in Africa; a plan to hijack planes and fly them into buildings on America's two most populous coasts; plans for London, Paris, Singapore, Hong Kong, and on and on.

It was like a Hollywood pitch meeting, with KSM as the journeyman producer and bin Laden as the studio chieftain. KSM had ideas, many ideas, while bin Laden had oceans of money and a supporting cast of martyrs prepared to die, along with a technical staff of document forgers, money movers, communication encrypters, and so on.

And pitch meetings are structurally adversarial and unequal. One man was the beggar, the other the chooser.

Clearly, bin Laden had his doubts. Choosers always do. Sure, KSM was an "idea man." But could he be a team player? Could the terror entrepreneur be a terror executive, working with bin Laden's many committees and rules? After a few hours, bin Laden politely declined to back any of KSM's plans but asked him to join Al Qaeda and move his family from the Baluch region of Iran to Kandahar, Afghanistan.[11]

Now KSM had to make a choice. He had come to seek money and other aid to continue to act as a free agent, under bin Laden's protection. Instead, he was invited to join the official roster and follow orders. That meant hierarchy and a loss of independence. Bin Laden didn't want to be another of KSM's financial sponsors. He wanted to be the boss. Was KSM willing to be a subordinate?

After a respectful moment of silence, KSM turned bin Laden down, he later told the CIA.[12] It would be years before he joined Al Qaeda and swore allegiance to bin Laden. Apparently he wasn't ready to be managed, second-guessed, and made to ask permission. KSM knew there were other terror lords with money for an enterprising producer. He would travel and find another one. This is the only power a beggar has over a chooser—the ability to go to the competition.

Within months of turning bin Laden down, KSM was spotted traveling to South America again,[13] looking for money and men for his own operations.

He also returned to Southeast Asia, seeking out his old friend Hambali: "He, too, was cool to KSM's grand plans," the 9/11 Commission Report notes.

Next, KSM tried to link up with Ibn al-Khattab, who ran an Islamist terror group in Chechnya. Khattab was a Saudi-born militant who had disfigured his right hand while trying to detonate a homemade bomb in the Afghan war against the Soviets. He later fought in Bosnia, with the backing of Iranian intelligence, against the Orthodox Christian Serbs and Roman Catholic Croats. It appears that Khattab met KSM there.[14] Shortly thereafter, Khattab decamped to Chechnya, where Muslim locals were fighting for autonomy from the Russians who had ruled that territory for almost two hundred years. Khattab's Arab mujahideen fighters soon developed a reputation for both bravery and brutality.

KSM made several attempts to reach Khattab overland by going through Iran and the central Asian republics, but the Russians had effectively sealed the borders and the airspace. KSM had to turn back.

Striking out with Hambali in Southeast Asia and with Khattab in central Asia, KSM knew there was only one warlord left with the will and the wallet to help him realize his grand plans of large-scale destruction.

Back in Karachi in 1997, after more than a year of wandering, KSM had sought out his old friend Mohammed Atef, who was in charge of Al Qaeda's military wing. Atef agreed to set up another meeting with bin Laden. When the archterrorist renewed his offer to join Al Qaeda, KSM accepted. He later insisted that he did not swear an oath of allegiance, known as *bayat*, to bin Laden for many years, in order to keep the fig leaf of his vaunted independence.

Initially, KSM was given no fixed duties. He was simply supposed to hang around and try to be useful. Bin Laden was essentially testing KSM; he wanted to see if the man who liked to lead could also serve.

KSM began to seek out various Al Qaeda middle managers in 1997 and 1998, helping them fix their computers and advising them on press releases.[15] Over time, KSM gravitated to Al Qaeda's media outreach efforts, which were similar to the work he had done for Abdullah Azzam in the late 1980s.

"In early 1998, he [bin Laden] sent a signed letter to an associate in Pakistan telling them to increase payments to selected journalists. He wanted to see an increase in coverage of his statements and activities, he told his correspondent."[16] KSM seems to have been in charge of distributing some of these payments.

KSM had to learn to be patient, to continue to do what he undoubtedly saw as menial tasks, while bin Laden came to trust him.

Then on August 7, 1998, Al Qaeda effectively declared war on the United States, and KSM saw his chance to make history.

Prudence Bushnell, the U.S. ambassador to Kenya, had been annoying her superiors at State Department headquarters for more than fifteen months. She had sent numerous cables and memos begging for new security measures for the embassy building in downtown Nairobi. When visiting delegations of congressmen and senators would pass through Kenya's sprawling capital, the ambassador would pull them aside and relate how unsafe she felt. She continued to believe that a terrorist strike against her embassy building was only a matter of time. In December 1997, she even wrote a personal note to U.S. Secretary of State Madeleine K. Albright.[17]

The CIA was already gravely concerned about the security of U.S. embassies in East Africa. Working with Kenyan police in 1997, the CIA had interviewed Wadih el-Hage, an American citizen living in Kenya who had ties to Al Qaeda. In an August 1997 raid on el-Hage's Kenyan house, investigators found computer disks and paper files describing African cells of Al Qaeda and outlining potential targets for attack. Two other major terrorist threats were also formally investigated by the State Department. When General Anthony C. Zinni, the commander of U.S. forces in the Central Command, which includes the Middle East and East Africa, offered to send his own team to review security at the embassy in Nairobi, the State Department turned him down. Instead, three months later, the State Department sent its own team to assess security at the embassy. That team recommended that a new chain-link fence be installed around the parking lot.[18]

The State Department, despite the deadly 1983 attack on its embassy in Beirut by Islamist radicals and the 1979 takeover of its embassy in Tehran by Islamist radicals, did not see much of a threat to its embassies and personnel by Islamist radicals. In its 1998 budget request to Congress, it asked for security upgrades at only two embassies: Beijing and Berlin.

Ambassador Bushnell was attending a budget meeting with Kenyan officials on August 7, 1998, when she heard several popping sounds, followed by a loud thud. Then the roar of a massive explosion filled the room.

It threw her to the floor, where a wave of glass shards speared her. The ambassador and several Kenyan officials struggled their way down a narrow concrete stairway, crowded with smoke and people, with a metal banister "wet with blood."[19]

The blast shattered windows in every direction for three miles, raining down piranha-like chunks of glass that sliced into people on the crowded sidewalk below. As the acrid black smoke rose, survivors could see burning metal cars thrown into light poles and walls.

The secretarial college across from the U.S. embassy collapsed into a pile of concrete dust and twisted metal. Rescuers, many plunging their bare hands into the hot debris, desperately tried to dig out those trapped inside.

The rear of the embassy was an unsteady two-story mountain of jagged concrete chunks dangling from a twisted steel skeleton. Pipes sprayed water and sewage into a crater more than three feet deep.

CIA and FBI investigators learned that Al Qaeda had been patiently assembling the plot since May 1998. The massive two-thousand-pound bombs were delivered on the back of a Toyota pickup. When the two bombers in the truck cab were turned away from the main entrance and sent, like all other deliverymen, to the embassy's rear loading dock, they calmly followed instructions. When the uniformed Kenyan guard insisted that they had no notice of a scheduled delivery, one of the men threw a hand grenade at him. It exploded, while the second man in the truck opened fire with his pistol.

One of the bombers, Mohammed Rashed Daoud al-Owhali, ran from the bomb-laden truck as his comrade flipped the dashboard switch to detonate. Wounded in the blast, he would later be arrested in his hospital bed in Nairobi—lying alongside his victims.

Nine minutes later, at the U.S. embassy at Dar es Salaam, Tanzania, security personnel slid open the metal gate for the scheduled arrival of the embassy's official water truck. The guard noticed that the man behind the wheel wasn't the usual driver, but waved him in anyway. Once inside the compound, the truck exploded.

The two East African embassy bombs killed 212 Africans and a dozen American diplomats, while wounding upward of 4,500 Muslims who were simply standing on the wrong sidewalk at the wrong time. It was the largest terrorist strike in the history of East Africa.

At the time of the embassy bombings, the State Department's recommended chain-link fence had not yet been installed. It wouldn't have made a difference.

■ ■ ■

Strange as it may seem, the East African embassy bombings gave KSM some hope. The operation was large and ambitious. The two bombings occurred within nine minutes of each other, more than four hundred miles apart, thanks to careful planning. The death toll was satisfyingly large. Finally, the United States would realize it was at war.

KSM began to lobby Mohammed Atef for yet another meeting with bin Laden. He wanted to talk to him again about what had become known inside Al Qaeda as the "planes operation." The meeting was short and, apparently, not as memorable as its result. Sometime in the last few months of 1998,[20] bin Laden gave his approval for what became the September 11 attacks.

KSM was elated.[21]

BOOK III

THE PLANES OPERATION

BOOK III

8

September 11, 2001

For KSM, the planes operation was essentially a management problem.

KSM soon found he had to manage up as well as down. Bin Laden was a micromanager, and he liked to discuss every angle from different points of view, according to American intelligence officials who have evaluated reports from KSM's interrogations.

Mohammed Atef, the head of Al Qaeda's military wing, and other members of the *majlis*—Al Qaeda's senior management team, a kind of sounding board for bin Laden—were well accustomed to bin Laden's long, roaming conversations. Often it seemed as if bin Laden couldn't make a decision at all. At other times, the archterrorist would make a decision in seconds or minutes. Sometimes the most grave decisions (such as selecting key personnel) were made instantly, while less significant decisions would be talked about for days. The *majlis* as a body did not vote, and bin Laden was not bound to take their advice—even if they were unanimous. Bin Laden's management theory seemed to come from his understanding of the practice of the Prophet and the four Rightly Guided Caliphs, who were known to overrule their councils.

Bin Laden's management style caused some friction with KSM, who was a talker and a brainstormer. Once a course of action was chosen, KSM made decisions—quickly, even compulsively. KSM preferred to fix a poor decision after the fact, where bin Laden preferred to avoid making a mistake in the first place.

KSM would have to manage his interactions with bin Laden carefully, lest he offend him. And that, by itself, took discipline and work. KSM had more meetings with bin Laden than anyone else after 1998, according to French intelligence consultant Roland Jacquard. Jacquard said his assessment is based on a review of Al Qaeda documents collected by various branches of French intelligence.[1]

Bin Laden was often critical of KSM's ability to focus on one project at a time, even a project as massive as the future September 11 attacks. KSM proposed a number of other operations in 1998 and 1999. He sent Issa al-Britani, a British convert to Islam, to meet with Hambali in Kuala Lumpur, Malaysia, to explore the possibilities of terror attacks in the Far East.[2] That meeting later produced plans by KSM to bomb churches in the Molucca Islands and attack nightclubs in the Hindu-majority island of Indonesia. In the first months of 2001, KSM sent Issa al-Britani to Manhattan to photograph and evaluate various Jewish targets.[3] KSM also developed a plan to find a Saudi air force pilot to steal a fighter jet to strafe and bomb the Israeli resort city of Elat. "Bin Laden reportedly liked this proposal," the 9/11 Commission Report notes, "but he instructed KSM to concentrate on the 9/11 operation first."[4]

KSM also had to work to get along with colleagues. While he was generally described as "an intelligent, efficient, and even-tempered manager" his coworkers often found his ambition excessive. Abu Zubaydah later hinted to interrogators that KSM often stole the ideas of others and represented them as his own.[5]

The planes operation began as a series of long meetings. The plan continued to evolve. The original idea involved ten hijacked aircraft. Four would be driven into the tallest buildings in California and

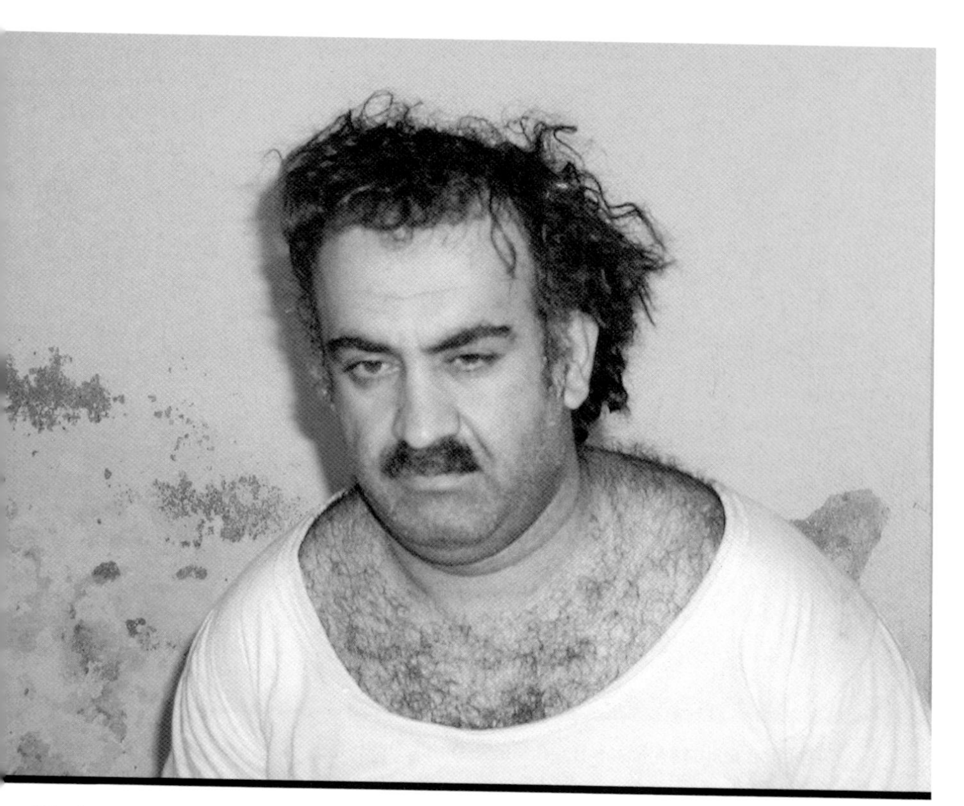

The famous capture photo of Khalid Shaikh Mohammed.

KSM posing for a Red Cross photographer in 2008 in a photograph that soon became a propaganda tool for Al Qaeda worldwide.

The house at 18A Nisan Road, Rawalpindi, Pakistan, where KSM was captured.

A courtroom sketch of KSM on trial at Guantánamo Bay. The trial was halted by President Obama, who campaigned promising a civilian trial for the mastermind.

A matchbook cover like this one persuaded Ishatique Parker to turn in Ramzi Yousef.

WANTED BY THE FBI

AIDING & ABETTING; IMPORTATION, MANUFACTURE, DISTRIBUTION AND STORAGE OF EXPLOSIVE MATERIALS

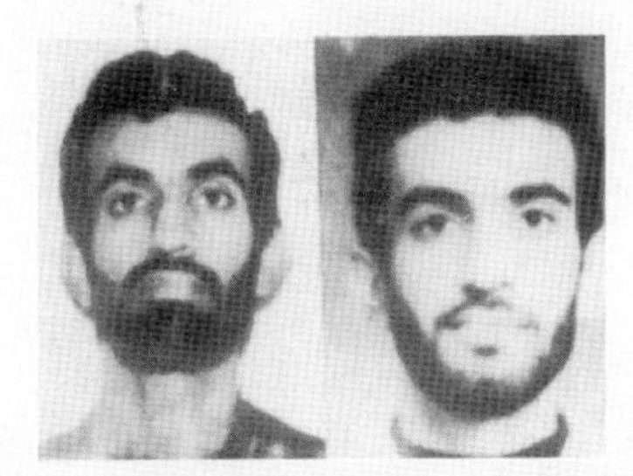

RAMZI AHMED YOUSEF

DESCRIPTION

Date of birth: May 20,1967; Place of birth: Iraq (also claims United Arab Emirates); Height: 6'; Weight: 180 pounds; Build: medium; Hair: brown ; Eyes: brown; Complexion: olive; Sex: male; Race: white; Characteristics: usually clean shaven; Social Security Number Used: 136-94-3472 (invalid SSAN);
Aliases: Ramzi Yousef Ahmad, Rasheed Yousef, Ramzi Ahmad Yousef,Kamal Abraham, Muhammud Azan, Ramzi Yousef, Rashid Rashid, Kamal Ibraham, Ramzi Yousef Ahmed, Abraham Kamal, Khurram Khan

CAUTION

YOUSEF ALLEGEDLY PARTICIPATED IN THE TERRORIST BOMBING OF THE WORLD TRADE CENTER, NEW YORK CITY, WHICH RESULTED IN SIX DEATHS, THE WOUNDING OF NUMEROUS INDIVIDUALS, AND THE SIGNIFICANT DESTRUCTION OF PROPERTY AND COMMERCE. YOUSEF SHOULD BE CONSIDERED ARMED AND EXTREMELY DANGEROUS.

A wanted poster for Ramzi Yousef, circulated in 2004 and 2005.

The "blind sheikh," Omar Abdel-Rahman.

Abdul Rabi Rasul Sayyaf, the tennis-playing founder of the first Afghan terrorist training camps.

Wall Street Journal reporter Daniel Pearl.

Garthe Faile, KSM's professor at Chowan University, who taught him Chemistry 102.

Parker Hall, where KSM lived at Chowan University.

The University of Dawa and Jihad, above the Jalozai refugee camps in Pakistan.

A close-up shot of the logo of Sayyaf's university. The English is for subcontinental and East Asian Muslims.

The Dona Josefa apartment building in Manila, Philippines, where KSM plotted to kill the pope and President Clinton.

Daniel Pearl while a hostage in Pakistan.

CONSPIRACY TO KILL NATIONALS OF THE UNITED STATES

KHALID SHAIKH MOHAMMED

Aliases: Ashraf Refaat Nabith Henin, Khalid Adbul Wadood, Salem Ali, Fahd Bin Adballah Bin Khalid

DESCRIPTION

Dates of Birth Used: April 14, 1965; March 1, 1964
Place of Birth: Kuwait
Height: Medium
Weight: Slightly Overweight
Build: Unknown
Language: Unknown
Scars and Marks: None known
Remarks: Mohammed is known to wear either a full beard or a trimmed beard, or he may be clean shaven. He has been known to wear glasses.

Hair: Black
Eyes: Brown
Sex: Male
Complexion: Olive

CAUTION

KHALID SHAIKH MOHAMMED IS WANTED FOR HIS ALLEGED INVOLVEMENT IN A CONSPIRACY PLOT, BASED IN MANILA, THE PHILIPPINES, TO BOMB COMMERCIAL UNITED STATES AIRLINERS FLYING ROUTES TO THE UNITED STATES FROM SOUTHEAST ASIA IN JANUARY OF 1995. HE WAS INDICTED IN THE SOUTHERN DISTRICT OF NEW YORK IN JANUARY OF 1996.

REWARD

The Rewards For Justice Program, United States Department of State, is offering a reward of up to $25 million for information leading directly to the apprehension or conviction of Khalid Shaikh Mohammed.

SHOULD BE CONSIDERED ARMED AND DANGEROUS

IF YOU HAVE ANY INFORMATION CONCERNING THIS PERSON, PLEASE CONTACT YOUR LOCAL FBI OFFICE OR THE NEAREST AMERICAN EMBASSY OR CONSULATE.

www.fbi.gov

Poster Revised June 2002

The FBI's most wanted poster that circulated in Pakistan seeking information on KSM.

REWARD
$2,000,000

KHALED SHAIKH MOHAMMAD

ALIASES: KHALED SHAIKH, SALEM ALI, ABU-KHUALA, ASHRAF REFAT NABIAH HENIM

1993-1994

October 1995

DESCRIPTION:
DATE OF BIRTH: April 14, 1965 or March 1, 1964
PLACE OF BIRTH: Kuwait or Pakistan
HEIGHT: 165 cm
WEIGHT: 60 kg
HAIR: Dark Brown/Black
EYES: Brown
BUILD: Slightly overweight to medium
COMPLEXION: Olive or Light Skinned
CHARACTERISTICS: Long shaped face, wears a full beard, a trimmed beard and clean shaven. Has been known to wear glasses.

On January 6, 1995, a fire broke out in an apartment in Manila occupied by KHALED SHAIKH MOHAMMAD. The information developed from the investigation into this small fire, ultimately saved the lives of thousands of people.

The investigation revealed that in August 1994 through January 1995 in this apartment and elsewhere, KHALED SHAIKH MOHAMMAD unlawfully and willfully conspired to bomb U.S. civilian airliners by placing explosive devices on twelve airliners flying over the Pacific Ocean during a two day period in January 1995.

Had any of these devices exploded, innocent lives would have been lost. People should not have to live under the fear of terrorism. KHALED SHAIKH MOHAMMAD has been indicted for his involvement in this deadly conspiracy and must stand trial for his crimes.

The United States is offering a reward of up to $2,000,000 for information leading to the arrest or prosecution of KHALED SHAIKH MOHAMMAD. If you have any information about KHALED, contact the nearest U.S. embassy or consulate. In the United States, you may call your local Federal Bureau of Investigation or contact the Department of State Diplomatic Security Service at 1-800-HEROES-1, or write to:

HEROES ■ Post Office Box 96781 ■ Washington, D.C. ■ 20090-6781 U.S.A.
www.heroes.net ■ e-mail: bsmith@heroes.net

The U.S. Department of State's rewards for justice poster.

Khalid Shaik Mohammed was a maste of disguises.

Washington State, while five others would be flown into the U.S. Capitol building, the Pentagon, and either the twin towers or the CIA and FBI headquarters buildings. The tenth plane would be piloted by KSM himself. He would kill all the adult males aboard and use the plane's radio to contact American broadcast media. After landing the plane at an American airport, KSM would deliver a blistering speech attacking American support of Israel and Arab dictators. Then he would magnanimously release the women and children and fly off to freedom. Bin Laden found the plan too bizarre and complex and asked for a smaller, more realistic idea. This grandiose scheme, the 9/11 Commission Report notes, "gives a better glimpse of his [KSM's] true ambitions. This is theater, a spectacle of destruction with KSM as the self-cast star—the superterrorist."[6]

Next came target selection. KSM met with Osama bin Laden and Mohammed Atef in bin Laden's compound in Kandahar, Afghanistan. These three alone would choose the targets of the September 11 operations.

KSM later discussed the targeting meeting with his CIA interrogators. The CIA reports of the discussion were provided to the 9/11 Commission investigators, who summarized the discussion vividly:

> Bin Laden imagined that America—as a political entity—could actually be destroyed. "America is a great power possessed of tremendous military might and a wide-ranging economy," he later conceded, "but all this is built upon an unstable foundation which can be targeted, with special attention to its obvious weak spots. If it is hit in one hundredth of those spots, God willing, it will stumble, wither away and relinquish world leadership." Inevitably, he believed, the confederation of states that made up America would dissolve.[7]

In short, bin Laden believed the United States to be as weak as most Arab dictatorships and concluded that its federal structure was similar to that of the United Arab Emirates.

Although he had traveled to Stockholm and London as a boy, bin Laden had no real sense of the deep structure of Western society. He didn't realize that in a crisis, in an instant, people organize themselves like heroes, rescuing the wounded and confronting the dangers. He simply couldn't anticipate the bravery of New York firemen or the passengers on United Flight 93. His only experience with authority was the kind that is consciously pushed down, not the kind that spontaneously wells up.

Bin Laden was clear that he wanted to strike the White House, the U.S. Capitol building, and the Pentagon. He wanted to destroy the centers of America's political and military power. (The White House was later taken off the list "for navigation reasons," KSM told Al Jazeera.[8])

KSM wanted to nominate what he thought was the locus of America's capitalist power: the World Trade Center.

He wanted to try the old target again. Perhaps he had Ramzi Yousef in mind. Rohan Gunaratna, a Singapore-based Al Qaeda expert, theorizes that KSM had developed a "losing and learning doctrine" in which Al Qaeda would return to favored targets.[9]

Bin Laden tentatively agreed.

Then came recruitment.

Selecting "martyrs" is a tricky business. The two most important qualities that KSM was looking for were a willingness of the recruit to die for the cause, and "patience." Operatives were generally "not pressured to martyr themselves," he said.[10] It wasn't necessary. There were many who wanted to die. Patience was vital because planning and prepositioning operatives for such a complex attack "could take years."[11] Many recruits were too desperate for action to wait. They would simply join another Pakistan-based Islamist outfit and martyr themselves in India, Israel, or the Far East.

Typically, terror groups plan and execute bombings in a matter of weeks. Many Al Qaeda "field operations" are performed this quickly. But operations run by headquarters (such as the 1998 embassy bombings) can take years. As a result, patience is prized. Mohammed Rashed Daoud al-Owhali, the would-be suicide bomber who ran from the bomb-laden truck in Nairobi and was captured in a hospital bed after the 1998 embassy bombings, testified that he had been forced at an Al Qaeda training camp to chant for hours: "I will be patient until patience is worn out from patience."[12]

Al Qaeda actually had a questionnaire for new recruits. The questions included: What brought you to Afghanistan? How did you travel here? How did you hear about us? What attracted you to the cause? What is your educational background? Where have you worked before?[13]

The application served multiple purposes, including detecting the potential spies (a persistent Al Qaeda fear) and spotting recruits with special skills, such as knowledge of engineering or English.

Those willing to be martyrs were first interviewed by Al Qaeda military commander Mohammed Atef.[14]

In turn, he would then pass on his recommendations to KSM.

Bin Laden played an active role. According to KSM, bin Laden delivered lectures at the training camps and later met with the recruits in small groups. Bin Laden, KSM told his interrogators, could screen people "in about ten minutes." Most of the 9/11 hijackers were initially approved this rapidly. If he spotted someone whom he thought outstanding, bin Laden would ask him to visit Tarnak Farms, the archterrorist's Afghan compound, outside Kandahar. There, over tea and dates, bin Laden would question the recruit more closely.

Once the recruits were approved by bin Laden, they were sent to KSM for evaluation and training. KSM had unique criteria for selecting the future hijackers. He did not necessarily want hardened jihadis who were well known to Pakistan's intelligence services or its Western counterparts. Instead, he sought out young recruits "with clean records" in order "to avoid raising alerts during travel."[15] It was a shrewd move.

KSM was recruiting two kinds of hijackers: "pilots" and "muscle."

Most of the muscle hijackers were veterans of the Afghan training camps and knew how to use automatic weapons and obey orders. Seven of the muscle hijackers had trained near Kandahar at the Al Farooq camp.[16] Two other "muscle" hijackers had trained at Khaldan, the camp originally established by Abu Sayyaf.[17]

All of the muscle hijackers were selected between the summer of 2000 and April 2001. Once selected, a recruit would be asked to swear to carry out an operation that would result in his own death and to obey the order of his emir and other commanders.

Once the oath of obedience and martyrdom was done, KSM was put in charge of the recruit's training. He usually asked them to tape a "martyrdom video" to be released after their deaths—this video was just one more means of exerting managerial control. If the recruit backed out, the video could be used to shame him or his family. Fear of shame can be an important motivator in the Arab world.

Next, the hijackers needed visas to enter the United States. KSM gave them each two thousand dollars and sent them to their home countries to get new passports and then on to Saudi Arabia, where the State Department was running an experimental Visa Express program that made it much easier for Saudis to get U.S. visas. Usually, the Saudis would not even be interviewed by a U.S. consular officer, and the majority of the process was done by mail. The United States did not have a similar visa program with any other country. The 9/11 Commission Report dryly notes: "The majority of the Saudi muscle hijackers obtained U.S. visas in Jeddah or Riyadh [Saudi Arabia] between September and November of 2000."[18]

Another peculiarity of Al Qaeda's tradecraft: it would order its operatives to report their passports lost or stolen and get genuine replacements from their country of origin. This way, it was believed, America or other target countries would have no way of knowing that an operative had visited Pakistan or Afghanistan—and, therefore, no reason to deny a U.S. visa. While this measure might work against Egypt or a similar country with limited use of computer databases, developed countries generally link travel records of old passports with travel records of new ones. The United States, for example, does not rely solely on the physical passport to track travelers.

Nevertheless, the 9/11 Commission Report found: "Fourteen of the 19 hijackers, including nine Saudi muscle hijackers, obtained new passports. Some of these passports were then likely doctored by the Al Qaeda passport division in Kandahar, which would add or erase entry and exit stamps to create 'false trails' in the passports."[19]

Once they had their visas, they were ordered to report back to Afghanistan.

In December 2000, Abu Turab al-Urduni began training ten muscle hijackers together as a group.[20] This was to build unity and confidence among the members. They were not told what the operation was or even what it was called. "To prevent any leakage of information, they [the muscle hijackers] were not informed of many details," KSM later told interrogators. "We told them that brother Abu Abdul Rahman [the codename for the lead hijacker, Mohammed Atta] would provide them with details at a later stage."[21]

The recruits lacked basic English-language skills and had no idea how to function in a Western society. KSM began to have doubts about the hijackers' ability to operate in the United States. These concerns were well-founded: among the belongings left in a rental car by one of the muscle hijackers was a handwritten note in Arabic carefully explaining the differences between shampoo and conditioner. KSM showed them videos of Hollywood blockbusters with hijacking scenes to get them used to the idea of taking over an aircraft and dealing with troublesome passengers.[22] KSM managed to buy an edition of the San Diego Pacific Bell Yellow Pages at a Karachi flea market and patiently showed the future hijackers how to use it.

While training his team, KSM also began to test airline security measures—just as he had with the aborted Manila Air operation. He sent Tawfiq bin Attash on flights from Kuala Lumpur to Bangkok and then on to Hong Kong. Bin Attash was instructed to carry a box cutter in his shaving kit and to fly on U.S.-owned air carriers. While airport security officials opened his carry-on bag and even his dopp kit, they raised no alarms and did not take the blade away from him. When bin Attash safely returned to Karachi, KSM knew that he had spotted a significant hole in airline security: box cutters could be safely smuggled onto an aircraft.[23]

Shortly thereafter, KSM ordered the muscle hijackers to train themselves with box cutters by butchering live sheep and camels. This was to get them used to the idea of using the box cutters as weapons and to overcome any aversion they might have to spilling blood.[24]

The pilots were harder to recruit and required more training. It would take KSM almost two years to get four pilots. The pilots would cause KSM heartburn—and almost wreck the 9/11 plot at least a dozen times.

But, in the beginning, all seemed to go smoothly. KSM found four students from Hamburg, Germany, who seemed to make ideal pilots for the planes operation: Mohammed Atta, Ramzi bin al-Shibh, Marwan al-Shehhi, and Ziad al-Jarrah.[25] One of them would eventually be replaced.

From the start, Mohammed Atta, a middle-class Egyptian studying urban planning, stood out, as Lawrence Wright notes: "His black eyes were alert and intelligent but betrayed little emotion. 'I had a difficult time seeing the difference between his iris and his pupil, which in itself gave him the appearance of being very, very scary,' one of his female colleagues recalled. 'He had an unusual habit of, when he'd ask a question, and then he was listening to your response, he pressed his lips together.' "[26]

Atta was selected as the overall group leader.

KSM told the four Hamburg men that they should distance themselves from known Islamic extremists in Germany and adopt a more Western-style appearance. Atta shaved his beard and avoided the radical mosques he had previously frequented. Ziad al-Jarrah also shaved his beard and, according to his girlfriend, "acted much more the way he had when she first met him."[27] Meanwhile, Marwan al-Shehhi went to the United Arab Emirates for his own long-delayed wedding feast. A friend said it was good to see al-Shehhi "acting like his old self again."[28]

By March 2000, three of the four pilots received visas to travel to the United States. Ramzi bin al-Shibh's visa application was rejected. A new pilot would have to be found—and fast.

Once they were in the United States, KSM had limited ability to manage his team. He could only await reports from the field. The reports were full of problems.

Most of the problems came from Khalid al-Mihdhar and Nawaf al-Hazmi. They had fought in Bosnia, Afghanistan, and Chechnya but couldn't figure out how to get an apartment in Los Angeles. Flying in from Bangkok, the pair could barely find their way out of LAX.

KSM gave the two operatives special permission to contact members of the American Muslim community, starting with the King Fahd mosque in Culver City, California. The mosque is named after a Saudi king and receives substantial funding from the Saudis.

The mosque contact soon went sour when a mosque-goer talked his landlord into allowing al-Mihdhar to assume his lease. Al-Mihdhar put down a $650 deposit and signed a lease. A few weeks later, al-Mihdhar suddenly demanded a refund of his deposit, saying he found the apartment unacceptable. The landlord refused, and that, he remembers, set al-Mihdhar to "ranting and raving" as if he were "psychotic."[29]

Over the next twenty months, they would have several avoidable run-ins in two states, get publicly drunk in Las Vegas casinos with half-naked dancers, and blurt out secret information to American Muslims they had met only hours before.

The 9/11 Commission later documented ten "operational opportunities" that might have stopped the attacks on New York and Washington; eight of those ten opportunities concerned al-Mihdhar and al-Hazmi.[30]

When al-Mihdhar learned from his wife, back in Yemen, that she had given birth to their first child, he couldn't stay in Southern California any longer. He flew to Yemen on June 9, 2000.

When he learned that al-Mihdhar had stranded his partner and flown back to Yemen, KSM was inconsolably angry. He thought the planes operation was compromised and would have to be shut down. His masterpiece was ruined by incompetence.

Bin Laden insisted that the plan go ahead. At the very least, KSM insisted, al-Mihdhar should be dropped because he had broken operational security and endangered the objective and the other participants.

Bin Laden overruled him, and al-Mihdhar stayed.[31] Ultimately, he would be on board Flight 77 when it crashed into the Pentagon.

By September 2000, Mohammed Atta and Marwan al-Shehhi had enrolled in Jones Aviation, in Sarasota, Florida. There they were also the source of many problems. A Jones instructor later told the FBI that "the two were aggressive, rude," and sometimes even fought with him to take over the controls during their training flights.[32]

After both Atta and al-Shehhi failed an instruments exam, they left Jones Aviation in disgust. They returned to Huffman Aviation, another pilot training institute where they had earlier tried to pass their pilots' exams. But their angry and aggressive conduct marked them out—compromising the secrecy of the plot.

By July 2001, KSM had run into another problem with the "pilots." This time it was Ziad al-Jarrah. He had made hundreds of phone calls to his German girlfriend, Senguen Ayzel, and had diverted from returning from an overseas trip to see her in 2000. Earlier in 2001, she had come to stay with him for ten days. He was deeply in love with her and started talking about backing out of the plot. Meanwhile, al-Jarrah was arguing with Atta. Senguen bought him a one-way ticket to Dusseldorf. When he arrived in Germany on July 25, Ramzi bin al-Shibh met him at the airport. Al-Jarrah refused to talk to him and insisted on seeing his girlfriend as soon as possible. A few days later, bin al-Shibh and al-Jarrah met again, and this time he was talked into completing the mission.[33]

KSM must have been tearing his hair out.

Atta used an Internet chat room to communicate with bin al-Shibh. Atta, pretending to be a student visiting America, wrote to "Jenny" in German.

Sometime on September 6, 2001, Atta called Ramzi bin al-Shibh in Germany. The date Atta had chosen was passed along in a coded message that bin al-Shibh later recalled: "A friend of mine gave me a puzzle I am unable to solve, and I want you to help me out."

Still, the "couple" used a code. The World Trade Center was "the faculty of town planning," the Pentagon was "the faculty of fine arts," and the Capitol building was "the faculty of law."[34]

Bin al-Shibh said to him, "Is this time for puzzles, Mohammed?"

"Yes, I know," Atta said, "but you are my friend and no one else but you can help me."

A moment of silence filled the international phone line.

"Two sticks, a dash, and a cake with a stick down. What is it?"

Bin al-Shibh asked, "You wake me up to tell me this puzzle?!"

Bin al-Shibh quickly translated the code. The two sticks? The number 11. The dash? A dash. The cake with a stick down? The number 9. "11-9" is the way Europeans would write September 11.

He passed the message on to KSM, who in turn told bin Laden.[35]

In Afghanistan, the 9/11 attacks began at 3:48 in the afternoon.

The training camps and safe houses were on high alert. The buzz among the "brothers" meant that a major operation was unfolding, but only bin Laden, bin al-Shibh, and KSM knew what to expect.

By four, they were crowded around the television set, which was replaying reports that a plane had struck a World Trade Center tower. The brothers shouted, *"Allahu akbar!"* and were deliriously happy, according to bin al-Shibh. The Al Qaeda members thought only one plane was involved.

We said to them: "Wait, wait," bin al-Shibh told his interrogators. "Suddenly our brother Marwan [the pilot] was violently ramming the plane into the Trade Center in an unbelievable manner! We were watching live and praying: 'God . . . aim . . . aim . . . aim . . .'"[36]

BOOK IV

HUNTING KSM

BOOK IV

9

The Daniel Pearl Murder

Four months after the September 11 attacks, KSM was living in luxury in an air-conditioned house in the Baluch section of Karachi. He had grown fat on American fast food, favoring buckets of the Colonel's Kentucky Fried Chicken.[1] He spent his days playing with his two small sons (then seven and nine years old) and planning elaborate atrocities.

In the front room of his Karachi house, over tea and small cakes, he met with a stream of Al Qaeda operatives. He discussed plots to bomb the Panama Canal, kidnap famous drivers from the Paris-Dakar road rally, and kill sun worshippers at Israel's Red Sea resorts. KSM's ideal terror target had high symbolic or strategic value and a large death toll that would trigger a tsunami of media attention.

In February 2002, he began work on what he thought would be his masterpiece. In a plot never before reported in the United States, KSM schemed to kill tens of thousands of spectators packed into stadiums during the World Cup soccer games hosted by Japan and South Korea in 2002. The attack was to be in retaliation for the handful of Japan Self-Defense Forces members who went to Iraq to rebuild schools and hospitals. Later that year, he would spend three months in Japan, studying targets and trying to put together a network to make and plant the bombs.[2] But eventually he would give up, when he couldn't find enough Muslims in Japan to work with.

While he calmly received visitors in his Karachi house, most of Al Qaeda's senior leadership were on the run in the unforgiving mountains of Afghanistan. KSM didn't share bin Laden's savage asceticism, and therefore he didn't share his suffering at Tora Bora in December 2001. Many Al Qaeda leaders had died in the constant aerial bombardment of their subterranean bunkers, while bin Laden narrowly escaped with his life. Dr. Ayman al-Zawahiri, Al Qaeda's number two, had lost his wife in the foolish showdown with American and allied forces. KSM hadn't even lost a night's sleep.

Nevertheless, his star continued to rise. When a predator drone aircraft killed Mohammed Atef in November 2001, KSM was promoted to the number-three position in Al Qaeda and given the title "chief of external operations."

With this new role came new responsibilities. With President Pervez Musharraf leaving on February 12 for his first-ever visit to the United States,[3] KSM would have to bring the Daniel Pearl situation to a swift conclusion. The *Wall Street Journal* reporter had been held captive for nearly a month—now it was time for action.

Daniel Pearl joined the *Wall Street Journal* in 1990 and quickly developed a reputation for careful articles that refused to accept the official line on foreign affairs.[4] He was especially effective at challenging the U.S. government's version of events when it concerned Muslims. Tariq Ali, a Pakistani journalist, praised Pearl's questioning U.S. policy in Kosovo—where Muslims were fighting Orthodox Christian Serbs—and to Pearl's clear-eyed account of President Clinton's cruise-missile strike on an "aspirin factory" in Khartoum, Sudan. The president had claimed the facility was used to make biological weapons. Pearl's reporting showed otherwise.[5]

The September 11 attacks had forced the *Wall Street Journal* from its flagship offices across the street from Ground Zero and driven Pearl to investigate the miasma of Pakistani politics. He quickly came to believe that Pakistan's intelligence services, military, and mafias were interconnected with Islamist terror groups, including the Taliban, Al Qaeda, and a welter of smaller terrorist groups that carried out attacks inside India. The deeper he dug, the more he discovered, and the closer he came to the fateful trip to Karachi.

Pearl's tragic journey began the day after the September 11 attacks,[6] with a phone call to Mansoor Ijaz, who ran a New York–based global investment fund that specialized in energy production and exotic technologies with military applications. Ijaz's father, a nuclear scientist who worked in a classified federal laboratory in Virginia, had trained the people who built Pakistan's atomic bomb. On his deathbed, Ijaz's father begged him to "save my country."[7] He meant Pakistan.

Ijaz initially set up schools in the countryside, but he soon realized that the real threat to Pakistan was not rural ignorance but urban indoctrination. Radical groups, with a dizzying array of acronyms, had sprung up to promote jihad against India, Israel, the United States, and other infidel governments. Naively, Ijaz met with many of their leaders in the hopes of talking them out of terrorism. He believed that his special standing as a Muslim American gave him a unique opportunity to build a bridge with extremists. It didn't work. But Ijaz developed a broad network of contacts among jihadi groups. So Daniel Pearl had good reason to phone Ijaz.

At first, the financier didn't want to help. "I thought it would be too dangerous for a Jewish reporter," Ijaz told me.

Daniel Pearl made a tempting target. Kidnapping a reporter from a major American newspaper would generate a tremendous amount of publicity and would be a strike against the "Jewish business interests" that KSM believed controlled American politics—meeting two of KSM's criteria for authorizing terror operations.

Seizing Pearl would have other geopolitical benefits. Inside Pakistan, it would send a signal to President Musharraf that jihadis would punish him if he cooperated too closely with the Americans. It would embarrass Pakistan at a key moment in the country's war on terror. Within Pakistan's military and intelligence superstructure—particularly the internal intelligence organization, the ISI—the kidnapping would boost the morale of Al Qaeda's secret sympathizers. On the heels of losses in Tora Bora, the Pearl operation would let the world know Al Qaeda was alive and active. The kidnappers would also have a helpfully chilling effect on Western journalists. By silencing one over-inquisitive journalist, perhaps KSM could silence them all. (Interestingly, both the kidnappers and President Musharraf used the same adjective to describe Pearl: "over-intrusive."[8] While Pakistan has a handful of brave investigative journalists, most members of the press are in one way or another controlled by the government. Terrorist groups including Al Qaeda have been known to make payments to journalists as well. As a result, news articles that carefully document the shadowy connections between Pakistan's intelligence service, its military, and its mafias and assorted terror groups are not welcomed, but feared and punished.)

Finally, the Pearl operation would burnish KSM's image. It would show that the man known to his associates as "the fat man"[9] was still capable of decisive action.

Pearl's next phone call was to Robert Baer,[10] a former CIA case officer who had served in Lebanon and northern Iraq. Baer's career had come to a sudden end, and he later emerged as a bestselling author and vocal critic of the agency. He is believed to be the first person to mention Khalid Shaikh Mohammed to Pearl and speculated that he was most likely the author of the September 11 attacks. He also told Pearl that from 1992 to 1996 KSM had a no-show job with the government of Qatar and that that government had hampered American efforts to arrest KSM there in 1996. Ever the diligent reporter, Pearl had called the foreign ministry of Qatar for information about KSM.

By December 2001 Pearl was breaking a series of investigative articles about Pakistan's intelligence service and its purported links to terrorist organizations. Pearl seemed most interested in a little-known "humanitarian organization" known as Ummah Tameer-e-Nau, which some analysts believe was involved in passing Pakistan's nuclear secrets to Osama bin Laden.[11]

As he continued to work the story, Pearl struck up a friendship with Hamid Mir, the only journalist to interview Osama bin Laden *after* the September 11 attacks. Mir agreed to share his contacts with the enterprising *Wall Street Journal* reporter.[12]

Meanwhile, Ijaz put Pearl in touch with Khalid Khawaja, who was linked to Pakistan's military intelligence agency, Osama bin Laden, and the Taliban.[13] He joined the Pakistani air force as a pilot in 1971. In 1985 he was transferred to the ISI, where he was tasked with working with radical Muslim groups. He quickly developed relationships with Abdullah Azzam, Abdul Rasul Sayyaf, and Osama bin Laden. He cemented these ties by fighting alongside the jihadis against the Soviets in the battle of Jaji, in the White Mountains of Afghanistan, southeast of Tora Bora, in 1987.[14] "Khawaja, in short, was a source to kill for and Danny charmed him," Ijaz said.

Khawaja told Ijaz that he found Pearl to be a "competent, straightforward" journalist who didn't ask "inappropriate questions."[15]

Ijaz thought that he had helped a reporter with a valuable story and didn't know that his December 26, 2001, phone call with Pearl would be his last.[16]

Pearl continued to give Pakistani officials headaches. Reporting from Bahawalpur, Pearl visited the headquarters of Jaish-e Mohammed, a terror group that the Pakistani government had told the U.S. government had been shut down. Pearl found that the Jaish-e-Mohammed offices were still open for business and that its bank accounts, far from frozen, were active. "If Danny hadn't been on the ISI's radar scope before," Robert Sam Anson wrote in *Vanity Fair*, "he was now."[17]

Pearl was also investigating two other stories that were likely to complicate the relationship between the United States and Pakistan. One concerned Dawood Ibrahim, a figure connected to one of Pakistan's mafias as well as several jihadi groups.[18] The other, equally explosive story focused on Sheikh Mubarak (also known as Mubarak Ali Shah Gilani). Gilani, two of whose four wives are African American women, may be linked to efforts to indoctrinate black Americans, train them for jihad in camps in Pakistan, and return them to the United States to carry out bombings and other attacks.[19]

At this point Pearl was most likely under active ISI surveillance, according to *The Guardian*, a British daily.[20] Pearl was also pulling on a third thread: the alleged link between Richard Reid, the British-born "shoe bomber" who tried to down an aircraft over the Atlantic Ocean, and another Pakistan-based terror organization known as al-Fuqra, according to the *Boston Globe*.[21]

The *Globe* story deepened Pearl's interest in Gilani. Pearl believed that Gilani was connected to al-Fuqra and went to see his star source, Khalid Khawaja. Khawaja tried to talk him out of seeking an interview with Gilani. "Don't try," Khawaja said. "You will not be able to do it."[22]

But Pearl kept trying. Eventually Pearl was put in contact with Ahmed Omar Saeed Sheikh, who was operating under the alias Chaudrey Bashir.[23] Pearl met Sheikh at the Akbar International Hotel in Rawalpindi, a city just south of Pakistan's capital. "It was a great meeting, we ordered cold coffee and club sandwiches and had a great chit-chat," Sheikh said. "We had nothing personal against Daniel. Because of his hyperactivity, he caught our interest."[24]

The two men exchanged contact information, and Sheikh agreed to set up a meeting with Gilani.

In a series of e-mails following the Rawalpindi meeting, Sheikh, still as "Bashir," pretended to organize a sit-down with Gilani, who said he was looking forward to meeting Pearl. He told Pearl that a Gilani contact would meet him at the Village Garden Restaurant, next to the decrepit Metropole Hotel.[25]

In the taxi en route to his fateful rendezvous, Pearl phoned his wife, Mariane. They had just learned that their unborn child was a boy. Both were very excited and planned to celebrate with friends later that evening. He said he would be back around 8 P.M.[26]

Clearly, Pearl was worried about the meeting. He next sent a text to the man who'd first introduced him to "Bashir": "Give me a quick reply. Is it safe to see Gilani?"[27]

The sun was setting as Pearl's taxi arrived outside the restaurant.

The taxi driver saw Pearl shake hands with a young bearded man and climb into a white Toyota Corolla.[28]

What Pearl didn't know was that the young bearded man was actually Mansur Hasnain, who had been involved in the 1999 hijacking of India Airways Flight 814.[29] Nor did he know that Hasnain's hijacking had been undertaken to free Omar Sheikh from an Indian prison where he was serving time for kidnapping and killing. The trap, which had been carefully laid for the past several weeks, snapped shut. Pearl was now a prisoner.

Within an hour, his wife realized something was wrong. A flurry of phone calls revealed that Pearl's cell phone was off and that he had not called to check in with editors, as previously arranged.[30]

Pakistani police opened an investigation, and they were soon joined by the FBI, which had more than a dozen special agents working inside Pakistan at the time.[31]

Four worrisome days passed before CNN and Fox News received e-mails from a group calling itself the National Movement for the Restoration of Pakistani Sovereignty. The group's name was a typical KSM touch: a fictitious group making outrageous demands, just as the imaginary "Fifth Battalion of the National Liberation Army" had taken credit for the 1993 World Trade Center bombing. Claiming that Pearl was a CIA spy, the missive demanded better treatment for prisoners held at Guantánamo Bay, Cuba, or else Pearl would be killed.[32] Ominously, attached to the e-mail were several photographs of Pearl. In one, he was holding up a newspaper showing the date, and in another there was gun at his head.

The originating e-mail address also showed a trace of KSM's bitter humor. It was from "KidnapperGuy@hotmail.com."[33]

Back in New York, the *Wall Street Journal*'s managing editor, Paul Steiger, had been reviewing reports from U.S. government agencies, the embassy of Pakistan, and the paper's own team of reporters in South Asia. Steiger, working from the *Journal*'s temporary offices in midtown Manhattan, had to make a hard decision. Should he publicly call for Pearl's release, or would doing so enrage the kidnappers and worsen Pearl's situation?

The demanding e-mail tipped the balance. Steiger decided to issue a public appeal. The open letter went through a number of drafts, with the last edit made by Steiger, an old-school newspaper editor.

Now all he could do was wait to see if his words could do what, so far, the Pakistani police had failed to do: free Pearl.[34]

Ijaz collapsed into a chair at my table in a midtown Manhattan steak house. He ordered a Diet Coke and seemed dejected. I asked him what was wrong. He told me he had phoned Steiger and other officials at the *Wall Street Journal*, offering to help. After all, he had helped set up Pearl's fateful meeting, and his network of sources might be able to persuade the kidnappers to release the journalist. He didn't like the *Journal*'s response. "They told me to stay out of it," he explained, and told me he felt stung by their suspicion of him.

Ijaz was not the only one frustrated that he could not influence Pearl's fate. Though he had organized and carried out the journalist's kidnapping, Omar Sheikh soon lost control of his operation to KSM.

And he was not happy about it.

"Basically it was like a hostile takeover because he [Omar Sheikh] was upset. His mood started to change when he spoke about this 'umbrella group' [Al Qaeda as led by KSM]," said Ty Fairman, the FBI special agent who interviewed Omar Sheikh in Pakistan. "He was a little upset that his authority was superseded."[35]

Omar Sheikh spoke in detail about the way authority usually works in Al Qaeda and other Pakistan-based terror operations. Essentially, the authority of the person who originated and commanded the mission was absolute. Even higher-ranking members of the terror group that authorized the operation could not overrule the commander, Omar Sheikh explained to his FBI interrogator. Sheikh said that the "fat man is the only one who could supersede his authority."[36]

The "fat man" was the code name for KSM.

As the deadline for the $2 million ransom demand to the U.S. embassy came and went, a car rolled through the gates of the property where Pearl was being held. From the car emerged Saud Memon, the wealthy garment manufacturer who owned the property, and three Arabic-speaking men. One was KSM.[37]

When they entered the house, it was clear that the short, fat man was in charge. KSM told all but one of Pearl's captors to leave. The only guard permitted to stay was Fatal Karim, an employee of Memon.[38] Karim's account is the sole reliable eyewitness testimony we have of what happened next.

KSM began to speak to Pearl in a language that Karim did not know. It was not English, but it might have been French.[39]

Anger spread across Pearl's face, and he began arguing with KSM in the same language.[40]

One of the Arabic-speaking men turned on the video camera as KSM, still off camera, began asking Pearl questions in English. Pearl tried desperately to win his captors' sympathy. Calmly answering their questions, he talked about his Jewish upbringing and expressed sympathy for the detainees held at the American facility at Guantánamo Bay, Cuba. He seemed unaware that death was seconds away.[41]

At a prearranged signal, Karim and one of the Arabic-speaking men rushed Pearl, forcing his shoulders to the floor. One of the Arab men blindfolded him, while Karim held down his legs.[42]

The five-foot-four KSM charged Pearl, landing on top of Pearl, who was more than six feet tall. As Pearl squirmed and struggled, KSM rode his chest, then sawed into his throat. Pearl screamed and writhed, but KSM kept relentlessly slicing away.

When Pearl was dead and nearly decapitated, KSM was angry to discover that the "brother" in charge of videotaping the execution had accidentally hit the pause button. The camera had not recorded the full slaughter of Pearl. KSM and his band grimly put Pearl's head back on his body and reenacted the whole gruesome scene again for the benefit of the videotape.[43]

Triumphantly, KSM held Pearl's head up before the camera.

Omar Sheikh turned himself in to a former Pakistani general on February 5 and was in turn handed over to a team of Pakistani police and American investigators on February 12,[44] timed to coincide with President Musharraf's visit to the United States.[45]

On the day he turned himself in, Sheikh phoned the man who

he believed was holding Pearl captive. He used a prearranged code phrase for Pearl's release: "Shift the patient to the doctor."

The man on the other end of the line used a code in return: "Dad has expired. We have done the scan and completed the X-rays and postmortem."[46]

Omar Sheikh understood that to mean that Pearl had been videotaped, killed, and buried.

Hamid Mir, the Pakistani journalist who had befriended Pearl, had good sources inside the interrogation room who heard Sheikh's confession.

> During interrogations, Omar told the members of a joint team of American and Pakistan officials that he was an ISI agent who had been operating from Lahore since his December 1999 release from prison in India.
>
> During interrogations, Omar reportedly named two officers of Pakistan Army's Special Services Group—Subedar Mohammad Saleem and Subedar Abdul Hafeez—as his trainers in the use of guns, rocket launchers, grenades and other explosives. Omar is said to have volunteered to describe his role in the explosion outside the Jammu & Kashmir state assembly building in October 2001, the attack on Indian Parliament in December 2001 and the January 2002 American Centre hit in Calcutta. . . . [T]he FBI investigators stationed in Pakistan just exposed the continued level of interaction between the ISI and Omar before and after the Pearl kidnapping. Alarmed at the interrogation results, the ISI high-ups had to intervene to obstruct these investigations. In fact, in the beginning of March 2002, the Karachi police bosses were ordered to stop Omar's interrogations.[47]

The videotape of Pearl's grisly murder was soon offered for sale to Karachi-based journalists. Shortly thereafter it appeared on a jihadi Web site. The ISP address indicated that it had been uploaded from an office in Riyadh, Saudi Arabia.[48]

Mariane Pearl made many calls to Internet providers to keep the video off the Internet. American broadcast networks, which the following year would spend hours showing still photographs and videos from the Abu Ghraib prison in Iraq, declined to air the gruesome moments of KSM's murder of Daniel Pearl.

Pakistani president Musharraf later wrote of Pearl's life and death: "War correspondents share something with soldiers: when they opt for this profession, they know the dangers."[49] He did not sound very sympathetic.

For years during his rise in Al Qaeda, KSM had been known as "the Brain," or, in Arabic, Mukhtar. He was the originator of ambitious plans, including the September 11 attacks. But until the Pearl murder, he had never been personally involved in killing. The "fat man" had shown that he wasn't weak, lazy, or spoiled by luxury. "The Brain," too, had a bloody right hand.

Certainly he was proud of killing the defenseless Pearl even years later. He boasted at his 2007 Guantánamo Bay status hearing: "I decapitated with my blessed right hand the head of the American Jew, Daniel Pearl, in the city of Karachi, Pakistan. For those who would like to confirm, there are pictures of me on the Internet holding his head."[50]

10

Explosions in Paradise

Little more than a month after killing Daniel Pearl, KSM was at dinner with another American, a man we now know as José Padilla.

Around the table was a perfect rogues' gallery of Al Qaeda leaders: Ammar al-Baluchi, a nephew and lieutenant of KSM, and Ramzi bin al-Shibh, another key KSM lieutenant. Both of these men had worked with KSM on the September 11 attacks, and now they were having a celebratory dinner with Padilla to plot their next attack against the American heartland.

After the lamb and rice and tea, KSM pulled out a wad of American dollars. With his fat fingers he counted out five thousand dollars and passed the pile to Padilla. Later, Ammar al-Baluchi gave him another ten thousand dollars in cash and a GSM cell phone to stay in contact with KSM's lieutenants in Pakistan. "Al-Baluchi instructed Padilla to leave on his mission through Bangladesh," according to U.S. Department of Justice reports.[1]

KSM thought that Padilla, as a U.S. citizen, would be able to easily slip into the United States and carry out a plot to kill hundreds of

Americans living in apartment towers in New York or Washington, D.C. KSM likely did not know Padilla's bizarre life story—or how it would compromise his mission.

José Padilla was born in Brooklyn into a Pentecostal Christian family. By the time the family moved to Chicago, the innocent boy had become a street thug. While drinking at the age of fourteen, he and an older friend decided to rob a pair of Mexican immigrants. The immigrants fought back, and Padilla's older friend stabbed one of them to death. Padilla kicked the victim in the head as he lay dying. The two young thieves got nine dollars and a cheap watch. Ultimately, Padilla received a five-year sentence in juvenile detention. If Padilla didn't have a violent temper, his victim might have survived the mugging, and he might not have spent his high school years behind bars.

Shortly after his release, at age nineteen, he got his girlfriend pregnant and soon abandoned her to raise their son, Joshua, on her own. He fled to south Florida, where he met Cherie Maria Stultz, a Jamaican immigrant working at a Burger King. Improbably, she fell in love with him.

Padilla still had a problem with anger. On a Broward County, Florida, highway, he cut off another car, and when the man honked his horn, Padilla brandished his revolver. When the outraged driver followed Padilla, Padilla fired a single shot in the air. Padilla was charged with three felonies and sent to Broward County Jail. While in custody, Padilla's anger got the better of him again, and he assaulted a uniformed guard.

When Stultz went to visit him in jail, he promised to change his ways. He told her that he'd had two dreams: in one, a mysterious man in a turban sits calmly in the desert, and in the other, a beautiful woman stands at the end of a dark passage. Behind her glows a "crystal, loving light."[2]

She bought his story. "Those two dreams made him change his way of life," Stultz said.[3]

When he was freed, Stultz helped Padilla get a job at a nearby Taco Bell, where he met Muhammed Javed, the restaurant's night manager and cofounder of the Broward School of Islamic Studies. Both Stultz and Padilla converted to Islam and studied the Koran with Javed's family. Eventually, they gravitated to a local mosque.

Padilla seemed at peace. "He is the type of person where he needs a dominant thing to keep him from going astray," Stultz said.[4]

Two years after their January 1996 marriage, Padilla told Stultz that he wanted to move to the Middle East to deepen his study of Islam. Just prior to his departure, Padilla ran into Javed at the mosque. When Padilla told him that he was going to teach English in Egypt, Javed was surprised. "I was baffled, thinking 'you yourself don't speak proper English,' but I said 'okay Jose, more power to you.' And then José disappeared from the scene."[5]

At first he called his wife regularly from Egypt, but then he met a man at a mosque who had a nineteen-year-old daughter. Over a few lukewarm Pepsis, her father agreed that she would be Padilla's bride.

Stultz begged Padilla not to marry the Egyptian girl. "He said I should go ahead with my life. I was sad. I was not going to get married again. There was a bond between us."[6] She filed for divorce.

While on hajj (pilgrimage) to Mecca and Medina, Padilla met a Yemeni man who is described simply in Justice Department documents as "The Recruiter."[7]

The Recruiter paid for Padilla's trip to Sana'a, Yemen's modern capital. Eventually Padilla was introduced to a man whom Justice Department documents refer to as "The Sponsor," who gave him a letter of introduction to terrorist training camps in Afghanistan.[8] The Sponsor accompanied him and helped him fill out the "Mujahideen Data Form/New Applicant Form." At the top of the form, a notice appears in Arabic:

"Top Secret: In the Name of God, the Merciful, the Compassionate: Brother Mujahid, this form includes questions pertaining only to you. We request that you answer these questions clearly. We pledge to you that no one will have access except those officials who need to know."[9]

Padilla's application was later "recovered by the FBI in Pakistan in a box containing a binder of over 100 such applications," according to U.S. government reports.[10] The form is similar to the ones that KSM had the September 11 hijackers fill out. On the form, Padilla called himself Abdullah al-Muhajir.[11]

Padilla was sent to the Al Farooq training camp in Afghanistan in September 2000. There he learned to fire a number of automatic weapons, including the AK-47, the G-3, and the M-16. He also learned to work with explosives, including land mines, dynamite, and C-4. After three months of training, Padilla was dispatched as an armed guard to protect a Taliban outpost near Kabul.

While still at the Al Farooq training camp, Padilla met Abu Hafs al-Masri, a legendary Egyptian-born Al Qaeda commander better known as Mohammed Atef.[12] Atef seemed fascinated that Padilla was an American and asked him about his commitment to Islam. After a series of meetings with Atef, he advanced Padilla some money to visit his family in Egypt, with the understanding that he would come back to Afghanistan for further training and a new assignment.

When he returned to Egypt, he discovered that his wife had given birth to a son named Hussein. Padilla was delighted, even if his American family was not.

Padilla returned to Afghanistan in June 2001. He found Atef at a safe house in Kandahar. Atef had developed a plan to seal up apartments in the United States, flood them with natural gas, and then detonate them using an explosive timer. He selected Padilla for the operation. He quickly agreed.

As Padilla continued his explosives-and-detonator training, he stayed in the same compound in Kandahar as Atef. There he watched the September 11 attacks on television. When, in November 2001, a drone aircraft fired a Hellfire missile at Atef's house, killing the terror leader, Padilla helped dig out Atef's body.

On the run with other Al Qaeda operatives, Padilla needed to link up with KSM's organization if he was going to carry out his apartment-bomb plot in America. Near the Pakistan border, Padilla met Abu Zubaydah, a key KSM lieutenant.

What Zubaydah remembered most vividly about José Padilla was his impatience to carry out a major bombing. He said he was tired of waiting.

Meeting with Abu Zubaydah in Faisalabad, Pakistan, he told the Al Qaeda leader about his "plan."[13] He wanted to detonate an atomic bomb inside America. (Zubaydah later told his CIA interrogators that Padilla's plan was harebrained; he said he had gotten the plans for the nuclear device from a Web site.)

While Zubaydah might have eventually used Padilla for one of his own operations, he realized that Padilla was fixated on his own plan and was too impatient.

Zubaydah was skeptical, but he gave Padilla a letter of introduction to KSM and some money for travel to KSM's hideout. Zubaydah, in his note to KSM, suggested modifying Padilla's plan to make use of Al Qaeda's store of radioactive hospital waste. It could be used to make a "dirty bomb," a conventional explosive that disperses radioactive material—contaminating an area for years.

Padilla arrived in Karachi in mid–March 2002.

He was led to a safe house in Karachi by Ammar al-Baluchi. There he met KSM, who was as rotund and cocky as ever. As Al Qaeda's number three, he was now the chooser and Padilla the beggar. KSM thought the dirty bomb idea "too complicated," and he wanted to "resurrect the apartment building operation originally discussed with Atef."[14]

This plot would involve selecting "as many as three high rise apartment buildings, which had natural gas supplied to the floors. They would rent two apartments in each building, seal all the openings, turn on the gas, and set timers to detonate the buildings at a later time."[15]

At first KSM wanted Padilla to detonate as many as twenty buildings at once, but even Padilla thought that was impractical.

They also discussed target cities. While KSM favored hitting New York City again, Florida, Washington, D.C., and the American Southwest were also discussed.

After a lengthy celebratory dinner, Padilla was sent on his way, and perhaps the most unusual terrorist plot in American history was set in motion.

In the wake of the September 11 attacks, the CIA was desperate for "bodies" to work against Al Qaeda. Along with dozens of others, Deuce Martinez was drafted into the worldwide anti-terror effort. (Deuce is a nickname, and since his full name has not been made public, I won't reveal it here.) Martinez, a CIA career man like his father, had spent the past decade tracking the movements of money and men linked to the South American drug cartels. He didn't speak Arabic or know much about Islam. To his dismay, he was sent to Pakistan to join the hunt for "high-value targets." It was his first trip outside of the United States.

The CIA's new command center in Islamabad was not much to look at. In the basement of the U.S. embassy building, office supplies had been cleared out and folding tables had been set up. Phone lines and power cords were duct-taped to the floor and the concrete-block walls. Phone calls were often interrupted by the loud rush of toilet water sluicing through the pipes overhead.

As veteran CIA operators looked on with increasing puzzlement, Martinez patiently filled one of the basement walls with a chart listing phone numbers and connecting lines. Every time a phone called one of the phones the CIA was monitoring, it was tracked, too—and added to Martinez's chart. It grew to billboard size and looked like a bizarre spider's web.

After a few weeks, Martinez said, "I think I know where Abu Zubaydah is."

Zubaydah was one of KSM's key deputies. If he could be captured, he would be the highest-ranking Al Qaeda official to fall into the CIA's grasp and potentially a fountain of information about future plots.

Pakistani Special Forces and CIA special-activity officers swarmed a large house on Canal Road in Faisalabad, Pakistan, known as Shabaz Cottage. It was a charmless, gray, three-story structure ringed with high walls and crowned with barbed wire and electrical lines.[16]

Elsewhere in Faisalabad and Lahore, other teams of Pakistani police and American intelligence officials were prepared to pounce. But Shabaz Cottage was the main event.

Pakistani police, using armored vehicles and patrol cars, quietly surrounded the target building. By 3 A.M. the police commander had ordered his men "to capture the suspects alive at all costs."[17] The ISI passed out photocopied drawings of Abu Zubaydah, the prime target. Only weeks before, he was freely meeting with KSM and Padilla. Now he was cornered.

No one thought capturing him would be easy. He and his associates were expected to be armed with machine guns and bombs.

Zubaydah, born into a Palestinian family living in Saudi Arabia's scorching capital, spent his life as a terrorist. Starting in the Gaza Strip at eighteen, working for Egyptian Islamic Jihad, he gravitated to Afghanistan in the 1990s, where eventually bin Laden put him in charge of a network of martyrs' safe houses along the Afghanistan-Pakistan border. There he sifted and selected the recruits to go to the training camps bin Laden had taken over from Abdul Rasul Sayyaf. Later, he ran a training camp near Jalalabad, Afghanistan. By 1998 he was a rival to KSM and deeply involved in the planning of the August 7, 1998, embassy bombings. He was also linked to the "millennium plots," which included Ahmed Ressam's attempt to explode the control tower at Los Angeles International Airport and gun down Christians at the place on the Jordan River where John the Baptist baptized Jesus.

By 2001 Zubaydah was working for KSM and was charged with supervising plots to blow up U.S. embassies in Paris and Sarajevo. Posing as a cotton buyer, he was using his house in Faisalabad to gather the jihadi diaspora that had fled Afghanistan and redirect them to Al Qaeda safe havens and staging areas.[18]

With rubber-handled clippers, police cut the electric lines running atop the cottage walls. Several policemen scaled the walls and silently surprised the guards. Running across the walled compound, two policemen slowly opened the creaking front gates.

The police swarmed in, breaking down the front door. As it broke open, four Arab men grabbed piles of money and passports and ran up the central staircase. The police ran after them. On the roof, one of the fugitives made a spectacular jump, some twenty-four feet, and tumbled onto the roof of a neighboring building.

Four Pakistani police were waiting on the roof for him. Zubaydah was furious, saying in English, "You're not Muslims!" "Of course we are," an officer said. Zubaydah shot back, "Well, you're American Muslims."[19]

Back on the ground, police had all four Arabs in custody. As they were herded to a police van, one of Zubaydah's comrades tried to wrestle away a policeman's AK-47. Bullets sprayed wildly. Three officers were wounded, while another one of Zubaydah's companions was shot and another killed. In the confusion, Zubaydah was shot in the leg, stomach, and testicles.

At a local hospital, CIA official John Kiriakou was told by the doctor in charge of Zubaydah that he would probably not live.

Zubaydah was bleeding and dying, and his Pakistani doctors could only stabilize him for a while, not save his life.

The CIA was now in the strange position of fighting to save the life of one of the men who had helped kill some three thousand Americans. If Zubaydah died now—and, in his condition, he easily could—more Americans would die in the future. Somewhere, locked in Zubaydah's now anesthetized brain, lay the looming plots against America and her allies and the locations of Al Qaeda's top leaders, including KSM and bin Laden.

The CIA station chief made a secure call to agency headquarters in Langley, Virginia. Zubaydah could die. The Pakistanis might not have the skill or the will to save America's first major Al Qaeda capture.

Out in the Baltimore suburbs, a phone rang in the middle of the night. A highly recommended surgeon from Johns Hopkins Medical Center answered. Would he be willing to fly to Pakistan to save a life? A military plane was waiting, and a car would pick him up within the hour.

Only after he arrived in Pakistan was the surgeon told who his extraordinary patient was.

After hours of surgery, the doctor walked out to meet the nervous CIA officials. The operation was a success. Zubaydah would live.

In weeks, Zubaydah was healthy enough for interrogation. CIA officials were hoping for a "river" of information to flow from him. Instead, they got a trickle.

The CIA's "best interrogators were just breaking their lance against the guy," one told me.

Kiriakou was one of the first to question Zubaydah, in a secret prison near Bangkok. He hit a brick wall.

Then orders came from Langley: waterboard him. After thirty-five seconds, Zubaydah crumpled. "It was like flipping a switch," Kiriakou said.

While Zubaydah began to talk—letting the CIA learn for the first time of KSM's key leadership role in the September 11 attacks—controversy erupted. FBI special agents, as well as some CIA officers (including Kiriakou), questioned the use of waterboarding.

A fissure opened in the intelligence community. The divide over the use of "enhanced interrogation techniques" (such as waterboarding) was not along partisan lines, but generally by agency and function.

FBI special agents feared that such techniques would taint any evidence needed for trial and likely cause that evidence to be thrown out by a federal judge, ruining any case against terrorist leaders. They were law enforcement men, long habituated to think in terms of trials and convictions.

Ali H. Soufan, an FBI special agent from 1997 to 2005, also interrogated Abu Zubaydah—without using waterboarding or any other special measures. Through Soufan's coaxing, Zubaydah revealed KSM's role in the September 11 attacks. Soufan soon became a vocal critic, pointing out that in two thirds of cases, no coercion was used or needed. We need smarter interrogators, he said, not meaner ones.

CIA officials, who were given the lead by President Bush in stopping attacks, were generally less concerned with making cases than saving lives. And, they pointed out, Soufan got Zubaydah to talk *after* waterboarding, not before.

Finally, a senior official asked Martinez to give it a try. "You found him," he said. "Now you make him talk."

For the first time in his career, Martinez was not an analyst solving a complicated puzzle. He was sitting across a small table from a killer. Somehow he would have to persuade this stranger to betray his cause and his comrades—before the next bomb went off.

His number-one question: Where is KSM?

After some time, Martinez seemed to make progress. Zubaydah said, "The code name for that chief was Mukhtar."[20]

Mukhtar. That word had appeared on numerous National Security

Agency intercepts, including ones linked to the September 11 attacks. It means "the Brain" in Arabic. But who was Mukhtar?

There were hundreds of mentions of Mukhtar in millions of phone calls, texts, and e-mails intercepted by the NSA and other federal agencies. Now each of them would have to be found and studied. Simply monitoring a phone in Yemen—used by the bombers of the U.S. warship the USS *Cole*—had yielded more than 260,000 phone numbers around the world. Perhaps Mukhtar was a more important player than the American intelligence community had realized.

Zubaydah eventually revealed that Mukhtar's real name was Khalid Shaikh Mohammed.[21]

Meanwhile, the CIA document-exploitation teams examined Zubaydah's laptop and other computer equipment. Those, too, gave up their secrets.[22]

Zubaydah's interrogation led to a change in outlook inside the American government. For the first time, intelligence officials knew who planned and directed the September 11 attacks. Now all they had to do was find the missing mastermind. "The Brain" was out there somewhere.

After meeting with KSM, Niser bin Muhammed Nasr Nawar, a twenty-four-year-old Tunisian man, agreed to go home to die. KSM had renamed Nawar—Nizar Seif Eddin al-Tunisi, or Tunisia's Sword of the Faith—in anticipation of his "great victory."[23] When Nawar returned to Tunisia, he recruited his uncle to join the plot. Together, they welded a gas tank into the bed of an Iveco pickup truck, pressurized the tank, and patiently filled it with propane gas. By ten o'clock on the morning of April 11, 2002, Nawar was wending his way along winding roads on the Tunisian island of Djerba. His target: the oldest synagogue in Africa.

As he drove toward his death, Nawar phoned a Muslim convert he had met in the training camps of Afghanistan, Christian Ganczarski. "Don't forget me in your prayers," he said. "Don't forget."[24] Ganczarski had dined with bin Laden and knew the members of the Hamburg-based September 11 cell.

That call was intercepted by Germany's version of the FBI, the Bundeskriminalamt.

Nawar's next call was to KSM. He explained to KSM how he had spent the twenty thousand dollars that KSM had given him. German and French intelligence were able to trace this call to Karachi, Pakistan, French counterterrorism judge Jean-Louis Bruguière told me. Bruguière prosecuted the case against Nawar's accomplices.

German intelligence has released a fragment of that conversation.

"I am the saber," said Nawar, referring to his new identity.

"What do you need?" asked KSM.

"Only the blessing of Allah," said Nawar.

KSM directed him to go ahead, wishing him good luck.

At about 10:20 A.M., a busload of German tourists pulled into the open-air parking lot beside the Djerba synagogue. As the Germans filed in, they passed another bus, this one packed with French tourists, also on their way into the historic synagogue.

Paul Sauvage, a French tourist, slowly climbed the steps of the main entrance of the synagogue. Because of his age and disability, he told his wife and two children to run ahead. They did. He slowly began to take off his shoes and placed a kippa on the crown of his head.

Nawar's truck barreled through the whitewashed archway of the synagogue. An accomplice, believed to be his brother, jumped from the vehicle.[25] The accomplice's role may have been to keep Nawar from losing his nerve. Whatever the accomplice's purpose, as usual in Al Qaeda attacks, terror is a family affair.

Seconds later, Nawar pressed a detonator button rigged to the dashboard. The electric current raced down a looping wire to the pressurized natural-gas tank. It exploded.

An oval blot of light suddenly expanded outward from the truck in all directions and disappeared. After the blinding flash came the boom, the vibratory roar of displaced air. Nearly two dozen people were instantly on fire. As they rolled and writhed to extinguish the flames, others cried out in German and French. They had been sliced through by nearly molten metal—pieces of fuel tank—moving at bullet speeds.

Paul Sauvage's family was protected by the ancient synagogue's sloping stone walls, but he was caught out in the open. He died in minutes.

Over the next few weeks, twenty other people—German, French, and Tunisian—succumbed to their wounds and died.

The Islamic Army for the Liberation of the Holy Sites took credit for the attack.[26] As in KSM's previous attacks, the group claiming credit was fictitious. Unlike 1970s terror organizations, it did not use bombings to establish its bona fides for negotiation with governments. It only wanted to hurt those connected, if only symbolically, with the governments it opposed.

The government of Tunisia, an Arabic-speaking country south of Sicily on the North African coast, made it clear that it did not condone the anti-Semitic attack. Tunisian intelligence worked closely with their French and German counterparts, sharing physical evidence, witness interviews, and other leads.

The damage to the synagogue was rapidly repaired. The shattered skeleton of the truck was hauled away within hours of the attack. Synagogue president Perez Trabelsi said that the government supplied almost one hundred men who worked for fifteen days to repaint the scorched walls and repair the wounded synagogue. "We are very grateful," Trabelsi told *The Guardian*.[27]

Back at a secret CIA facility outside of Bangkok, Thailand, Abu Zubaydah's interrogations continued. He knew nothing about the attack in Tunisia, but he surprised his interrogators by talking about a plot to detonate a conventional bomb wrapped in radioactive material. The so-called dirty bomb would contaminate an area for years and, Al Qaeda operatives hoped, provoke a wave of panic among the American people.

Zubaydah was not immediately forthcoming about the dirty bomber's name. He had been drugged and waterboarded and possibly no longer remembered it. Alternatively, since the dirty-bomb plot was an ongoing operation, the KSM lieutenant might not have wanted to endanger its success.

Zubaydah did describe Padilla's physical appearance and said he was a "Latin American man who went by a Muslim name."[28]

After combing through commercial, police, and intelligence databases, CIA and customs officials found a probable match: José Padilla. A photo of Padilla was shown to Abu Zubaydah, who confirmed that he was the dirty bomber.

By April 2002, American intelligence officials were actively searching for Padilla under a number of different aliases. They tracked his exit from Pakistan at Karachi International Airport, through Zurich, and then on to Cairo. He stayed with his Egyptian wife and sons for more than a month. In his absence, his wife had given birth to a second son, this one named Hassan.[29]

In early May, he left his wife with a stack of money and said he was going to America. As he changed planes in Zurich on May 8, 2002, he didn't realize that American and Swiss intelligence agents were joining him on the flight.

When he landed at O'Hare International Airport, he was met by FBI agents at the gate. He was arrested on a "material witness warrant" related to the September 11 attacks.

As a U.S. citizen arrested on U.S. soil, Padilla posed a considerable legal problem for the Bush administration. If he were put through the normal legal channels and tried as a criminal defendant, he would have access to a defense attorney and presumably all of the government's evidence against him. That meant that the federal government would have to disclose what it had learned from Abu Zubaydah and other operatives and under what means that information had been gleaned. Given the rules of evidence in criminal procedures, it is likely that the account supplied by Zubaydah and other detainees would be thrown out of court on the grounds that the information used to arrest Padilla had been unlawfully gained. It would also reveal the government's interrogation techniques. Additionally, Padilla would be entitled to bring Abu Zubaydah and others into a federal courtroom as witnesses for his defense—posing immense logistical and security problems. The resulting police overtime payments would be costly and the public might well object to blocked streets and the risks of bringing known terrorists into their midst. Foreign intelligence agencies, which often supplied information used in the interrogations of Abu Zubaydah and others, could also be made to testify—most likely ending their cooperation with the U.S. government. Pakistan and various Arab governments, while covertly aiding the United States, feared the domestic political problems—including terror attacks against their government buildings and citizens—that would be caused if they were publicly seen to be helping America. All of these reasons argued against what federal officials refer to as the "law enforcement option."

On the other hand, as a U.S. citizen held on U.S. soil, Padilla had certain inalienable constitutional rights, including the right to trial by a jury of his peers and the right to confront witnesses and evidence brought against him. He also had a constitutional right to a speedy trial and could not be held indefinitely without charge.

The debate over Padilla's fate ultimately reached the White House, with President Bush designating Padilla an "enemy combatant" who could be held in a U.S. military brig in South Carolina more or less indefinitely.

In 2004, a panel of three judges found that Padilla could be lawfully held as an enemy combatant for an indefinite period, citing the U.S. Congress resolution authorizing the war on terror following the September 11 attacks and various other federal court precedents. After years of legal wrangling, Padilla was tried in a federal court and found to be guilty of conspiring to carry out terrorist attacks against the United States.

Meanwhile, KSM, working from his safe house in Karachi, continued to plan and plot.

Sometime after the summer of 2002, KSM, acting at Osama bin Laden's direction, transferred money to his old associate known as Hambali, who ran the Southeast Asian terror organization Jemaah Islamiyah, which is affiliated with Al Qaeda.

By September 2002, the FBI had learned from a captured Al Qaeda operative, Mohammed Mansour Jadara, that Al Qaeda and

Jemaah Islamiyah had shifted from targeting hotels and embassies to going after "soft targets," including bars, restaurants, and open-air areas crowded with Western tourists.[30]

Australian and American intelligence officials were anticipating an Al Qaeda–Jemaah Islamiyah attack on October 7—the one-year anniversary of the start of the Afghan war against the Taliban. That year, October 7 fell on a Monday, and nothing happened.[31]

On Saturday night, October 12, the nightclubs in the Kuta district of Bali were crowded with backpackers, bikers, and tourists.

The beach bar Paddy's Pub was a favorite for Australians and Americans visiting Bali, a peaceful piece of paradise in the island archipelago of Indonesia. Here surfers and sunbathers gathered to watch the sun set into the Indian Ocean.

Few noticed the young man with the heavy backpack working his way through the crowd.

Less than a hundred yards away, a white Mitsubishi L300 van was idling outside the Sari Club, a popular nightspot. Inside the van, the mission commander, a thirty-one-year-old Sumatran known as Idris (also known as Joni Hendrawan),[32] instructed the second bomber to get behind the steering wheel. The bomber had only learned to drive in a straight line, but that day he would not have to drive very far.

Idris got out of the van and mounted the back of a brand-new Yamaha motorcycle driven by an accomplice. As they sped away, Idris dialed the number of a cell-phone detonator attached to a bomb hidden at the U.S. consulate. It exploded, injuring one person and damaging the consulate's outer gates.

By now the backpack bomber had waded deep into the crowd at Paddy's. No one heard him say "*Allahu akbar*," but hundreds heard the explosion that followed. Shrapnel from the backpack bomb raced outward at a rate of more than thirty-two feet per second, tearing into merrymakers and soaking the concrete in blood and beer.

Panicked survivors at Paddy's emptied into the street, unknowingly heading for the white van.

The van lurched forward, heading toward the Sari Club. Inside, twelve filing cabinets were filled with potassium chlorate, powderized aluminum, and a sulphur-TNT concoction. It was wired together with 450 feet of detonating cord and linked to ninety-four RDX electronic detonators. The bomb weighed 1.12 tons.

As the crowd surged toward the van, the van exploded—sending out a wave of flame and shrapnel into the crowd.

Lives ended in midsentence.

Two hundred and two people died immediately or quickly succumbed to their wounds, including eighty-eight Australians, thirty-eight Indonesians, twenty-four Brits, and seven Americans.

The survivors hobbled into the nearby Bounty Hotel with glass and metal etched into their faces and bodies. Many were severely burned, with the outer layers of their skin hanging off like carbon paper.

Local hospitals were ill equipped to treat the flood of victims and soon ran out of skin-graft material. Burn victims were put into nearby swimming pools to ease their throbbing pain, and many were flown more than a thousand miles to emergency units in Australia.

It was the deadliest attack in the history of Indonesia.

Three of the surviving perpetrators (including Idris) were tried, convicted, and executed by firing squad in 2008.

Imam Samudra was the overall commander of the Bali bombing. He had fought in the Afghan war against the Soviets, where he met and grew to admire Osama bin Laden. He later named his son Osama, in honor of the archterrorist.

When investigators seized his laptop computer, they found a wealth of evidence showing connections to Al Qaeda as well as hours of pornographic images of Barbie-doll-like women downloaded from Western Web sites. "Samudra insisted those files had been planted."[33] Another similarity between KSM and Samudra.

At the end of the trial of one of the perpetrators, Samudra was confronted by Jan Laczynski, a Melbourne man who had lost five friends in the Sari Club bombing. He held up an Australian flag decorated with the faces of the eighty-eight Australians killed. "We are proud to be Australians. Take a look at the people who have been killed," he said.

Samudra, startled by the flag and the man, yelled, "Calm down, infidel!"

"He wasn't too happy," Laczynski dryly told the *Sydney Morning Herald*.[34]

Mombasa is a humid city on Kenya's tropical southern coast. It is to the Israelis what the Caribbean is to many Americans, an affordable and exotic vacation destination that is less than four hours away by plane.

In November 2002, KSM funded and directed an operation to turn that bit of Eden into hell.

The traditional Kenyan dancers had just finished their welcoming routine for some two hundred mainly Israeli tourists in the lobby of the Paradise Hotel when a green sport utility vehicle crashed through the hotel's outer gate and rushed toward the lobby. At the same time, a man with a suicide vest ran into the lobby. Then, the SUV exploded.

Next, the suicide bomber detonated himself.

In seconds, sixteen Israeli tourists, including three small children, lay dying. The lobby was lit by the orange glow of flames as people screamed in Hebrew and in English.

Rescuers carried the injured out of the burning lobby and laid them gently on wooden chaise lounges near the beach.[35]

Meanwhile, on the runway of Mombasa's Moi International Airport, an Arkia Israeli Airlines jet readied for takeoff. In the weeds and scrub bush in nearby Changamwe, a team of Somali and Arab men crouched, readying their rocket launchers. As the plane climbed upward, two Strela-2 missiles were fired at the departing commercial jet. Both missed.

The Arkia flight landed safely at Ben Gurion International Airport, in Tel Aviv.

KSM had struck again. If the two attacks had succeeded, hundreds of Israelis and Kenyans would be dead, and KSM could celebrate another grim achievement.

CIA and FBI agents saw a building wave of attacks launched by the terrorist mastermind throughout 2002. One question kept being asked, with increasing urgency: Where is he?

11

"Recognize Us Yet?"

"Recognize us yet?" asked Khalid Shaikh Mohammed. Then he laughed.

Yosri Fouda, a senior correspondent for Al Jazeera, stood dumbstruck. His blindfold had just been removed. He blinked, suppressing disbelief, as he scanned the two men and the bare-walled apartment of a Karachi safe house.[1] It was April 19, 2002.

"They say you are terrorists," Fouda said.

"They are right," KSM responded. "That is what we do for a living."[2]

Fouda recalls KSM's tone being "firm and matter-of-fact." He was proud of it.

Fouda noticed that when it was time for the final prayers of the night, KSM did not lead the prayers. Usually, in circles of Arab men, the older or more experienced man leads. Instead, Ramzi bin al-Shibh, eight years younger than KSM, took charge of the prayers.[3] Fouda concluded that KSM was "not a man of religion" but "very much a man of operations, a man of action, he is very restless."[4]

"He likes being on top of a certain operation, directing people here and there, thinking of targets and stuff," Fouda writes. "It's in a sense also a game. He puts it in a religious context." As if to confirm Fouda's impression, KSM told him, "We like to terrorize unbelievers."[5]

The prayer was telling, too. Bin al-Shibh said: "Our words shall remain dead, like brides made of wax, still and heartless. Only when we die for [our words] shall they resurrect and live among us."[6] In that time and place, it was a decidedly jihadi prayer.

In the spring of 2002, Fouda was hosting a prime-time *60 Minutes*–style series on Al Jazeera, called *Top Secret.* Just as he was starting to think about doing something special for the first anniversary of the September 11 attacks, the phone rang. A mysterious caller invited him to Pakistan. Without telling his superiors, he soon left for Pakistan in hopes of meeting KSM.

In exchange for an exclusive interview, KSM insisted that he would supply the camera, the videotape, and the camera operator. Furthermore, he insisted that Fouda pledge not to reveal the location of the interview nor how KSM or Ramzi bin al-Shibh appeared. Fouda was made to swear to all conditions on a Koran. He did so.

What exclusive would Fouda get in return? Good journalists realize that they sometimes must bargain, not just accept gifts.

The mastermind did not disappoint—he had a scoop for Fouda.

KSM smiled and said, "I am the head of the Al Qaeda military committee and Ramzi is the coordinator of the 'Holy Tuesday' [9/11] operation," KSM said. "And yes, we did it."[7]

For the next few months, Fouda would keep his explosive secret as he waited for the videotape to arrive from KSM. While he waited, he knew he had to talk to his boss at Al Jazeera. That led to an extraordinary series of meetings inside the television network—and ultimately reached the ears of the CIA director.

The Diplomatic Club in Doha overlooks the beach and a long line of oil tankers slowly moving down the Persian Gulf to the open sea. It was June 14, 2002, and Yosri Fouda was at lunch with his Al Jazeera boss, Mohammed Jasmin al-Ali.

Patiently he laid out the extraordinary story, from months earlier, of the mysterious contact, the summons to Pakistan, the blindfolded trip to a safe house some five miles from the Karachi International Airport, and the strange meeting with Khalid Shaikh Mohammed, the 9/11 mastermind, and his lieutenant Ramzi bin al-Shibh.

When he was done, al-Ali stared at him in wide surprise and said, "No way!"[8]

After lunch, the two men worked their way up the Al Jazeera hierarchy, closing office doors and quietly relaying the incredible news. No one could believe that Al Jazeera now had the biggest scoop in the war on terror.

Wars can *make* television networks. CNN vaulted into the forefront of cable news outlets with its coverage of the first Gulf War. Fox News Channel became the number-one cable news network on the back of its coverage of the September 11 attacks and the American liberation of Afghanistan in 2001. This scoop, on the one-year anniversary of the attacks on New York and Washington, could make Al Jazeera the dominant Arab-language news provider in the world.

Over tea the next morning, Fouda and al-Ali met with Sheikh Hamad bin Thamer al-Thani, who was the chairman of the satellite network. He was also the first cousin of the emir of Qatar, the ruler of that desert kingdom.

After again telling his incredible tale, the sheikh cut Fouda off. Al-Thani was bursting with questions. "The tapes! When are you going to get ahold of them?"

Fouda explained that KSM's lieutenants would be sending him the tapes, perhaps through a series of dead drops.

Dead drops, which are used by both intelligence services and terror organizations, are places, usually in public areas, where a document or a tape can be hidden. At a pre-agreed time, a courier goes to the location, retrieves the package, and takes it to yet another dead drop. Then another courier picks it up from that place and takes it to still another. Often the couriers have no idea what they are transporting, and since they do not know who taped it to the bottom of the trash bin or park bench, they don't know who has dropped it off.

"How many people know about this so far?"

Fouda thought for a moment and said, "Only the people currently in the room."

"Keep it quiet and take no chances," Sheikh Hamad said. "If you need any special arrangements for your security, just let me know."[9]

What happened next is shrouded in mystery and may never be known. It seems likely that the head of the Al Jazeera network briefed his cousin, the ruler of Qatar. Then, somehow, CIA director George Tenet was tipped off.

In the CIA's Langley, Virginia, headquarters, Tenet took the elevator down to the secure conference room in the Counter-Terrorism Center, known inside the agency as the CTC. He walked in on its daily 5 P.M. meeting. He looked unusually excited. "I'm going first today," he said. "What I have today will be the only thing we're going to care about."

Tenet felt the interest level in the room quietly climb.

"As you know," Tenet said, "we've had our differences with our friend the emir [of Qatar]. But today he gave us an amazing gift."

Tenet explained that Al Jazeera had an impending scoop that could lead the agency to Ramzi bin al-Shibh and perhaps even KSM himself.

Tenet smiled. "In other words, the fat fuck came through."[10]

Gulshan e-Iqbal is one of Karachi's wealthiest neighborhoods and one of its most Westernized. In the hours before sunup on September 11, 2002, armored police vehicles rolled past a darkened McDonald's restaurant, a Toyota dealership, and a strip of Internet cafés and video stores, turned past the gates of one of the district's three universities, and crept toward a block of luxurious apartment buildings. Bin al-Shibh was the target.

Riding along with the Pakistani police were a handful of FBI and CIA officers. As part of the deal struck between CIA director

George Tenet and the emir of Qatar, the raid would have to occur before Al Jazeera's September 11 anniversary special aired later that night. That way the network could credibly deny that it had tipped off the CIA.

Al Jazeera wasn't solely responsible for pinpointing Ramzi bin al-Shibh. The terrorist himself played a supporting role. In 2001, nine out of ten calls intercepted between suspected European operatives and people in Pakistan funneled to a single city there, Peshawar. By 2001, almost 50 percent of those same calls were directed to Karachi.[11] With at least one careless satellite phone call, Ramzi bin al-Shibh gave himself away. Al Jazeera had given the CIA a clue: which Pakistani city to focus on. Bin al-Shibh's call revealed what floor of what apartment building was his hideout.

First, the police ringed the villa, then a "breach team" burst into the apartment building lobby and arrested two men. As a larger police force surged into the building carrying automatic weapons, other men opened fire from the balcony overlooking the lobby. Some threw hand grenades. In the initial volley of shots, two terrorists were killed and six policemen wounded. Slowly, the police battled their way up the stairs to a fourth-floor apartment.

The police could get to the front door of the apartment, but no further. The automatic-weapons fire was just too fierce. So, over the next few hours, the police repeatedly launched tear-gas canisters inside.

Bin al-Shibh and two others were holed up in a windowless kitchen, apparently using water from the sink to soak cloths to protect their eyes and noses from the roiling clouds of gas.

Finally, using a bullhorn, a police officer ordered the men to surrender.

Someone shouted back, "Bastard!"

Then one of the men hiding in the kitchen charged forward and was instantly gunned down by the police.

In a burst of courage, the police charged the kitchen, seizing the two remaining terrorists. Throwing punches, bin al-Shibh tried to snatch one of their guns. As he was held down, he screamed in Arabic, "You're going to hell."[12]

Ramzi bin al-Shibh, the man originally slated to be the twentieth hijacker in the September 11 attacks, and KSM's right-hand man, was in custody. With any luck, his interrogation would lead them to KSM himself.

It took almost seven months, but in March 2003, Pakistani police were in the Westridge district of Rawalpindi, 170 miles south of Pakistan's crowded capital, about to make an even bigger capture than bin al-Shibh. The journey to this place had followed a serendipitous path.

As strange as it might seem, "walk-ins" usually get very little respect inside the CIA. A typical walk-in is a foreign national who enters a U.S. embassy and asks to speak to someone in intelligence. His first few meetings are usually with consular-affairs officers or other State Department employees, who are simply screening him.

Typically the walk-in is treated with suspicion, not welcomed like a savior. He is asked to repeat his story several times, and any contradictions, or seeming contradictions, are immediately pounced on and pointed out to him. Once embassy personnel are persuaded that he is not a nut, a spy, or a foreign intelligence officer who is simply trying to identify who the CIA personnel inside the embassy actually are, he might be introduced to someone inside the American intelligence bureaucracy. Or, likely as not, he will be shown the door. The history of Cold War intelligence and counterintelligence is littered with examples of bona fide Soviet intelligence defectors being turned away.

But in late February 2003, at one of the CIA's largest overseas stations, in Islamabad, a young walk-in cleared all of the embassy interviews. He turned out to be a midlevel Al Qaeda official who was interested in betraying his comrades in exchange for a sizable financial reward. He reeled off a list of names of various Al Qaeda officials whom he had dined or traveled with—and the names checked out. What caught the attention of the intelligence officer interviewing him was the walk-in's claim that he had recently met KSM and expected to see the mastermind again at dinner that night.

That was different. People who volunteered to become American intelligence sources rarely promised quick results. They often hoped to string the Americans along to collect what benefits they could.

The walk-in was given a phone number to call if he happened to meet KSM. When the walk-in exited the embassy, one intelligence officer looked at the other and arched his eyebrow. Would anything come of this?

They would soon see.

At roughly 10 P.M. on March 1, in Rawalpindi, Pakistan, the walk-in rose from the dinner table and went to the bathroom. Closing the door behind him, he furiously typed out a text message to the number he had been given earlier that day: "I am with KSM."

Then, around midnight, he phoned the contact number. He claimed he had been sitting beside KSM at dinner for several hours and then joined the mastermind in a car that had dropped him off in a well-heeled enclave of Rawalpindi.

An American intelligence agent picked him up and asked the walk-in to lead him to the address where KSM had been dropped off earlier. That was a problem. He didn't know the address. The two men would spend the next frustrating hours snaking through Rawalpindi's better neighborhoods, looking for any buildings that the walk-in might have seen in his earlier trip with KSM. It was well after 2 A.M. when the walk-in spotted an apartment tower. "That's it," he said.[13]

Within the hour, a band of Pakistani police pulled up at 18A Nisan Road. They were outside the two-story town house of Dr. Abdul Qadeer Khan, a prominent microbiologist. The doctor's elderly wife was a local leader of Pakistan's largest Islamic political party. They were wealthy and politically wired; fortunately for the police, they were also out of town at a wedding in Lahore.

At 3:30 A.M., a flood of more than twenty police officers roared through the front door. Family members were pushed against the walls and held at gunpoint as other officers searched the adjoining rooms.

In one room, snoring on a mattress on a floor, they found a short, fat man in a long, loose white shirt. Hands grabbed his arms and pulled him into the light. There, dazed,[14] Khalid Shaikh Mohammed glared back at them. He said nothing. With his hair still askew, they snapped his picture—an embarrassing image that would soon make its way around the world.

The September 11 mastermind had been captured without a shot being fired.

Subsequently, the Pakistani authorities arrested Khan's uncle, Pakistani army major Adil Quddus Khan.[15] KSM, it seemed, had good, high-ranking contacts inside Pakistan's military and political establishments.

It was past midnight in northern Virginia. CIA counterterrorism chief John McLaughlin was trying to sleep when the phone rang.

"Son of a bitch—we got him!" It was Tenet.

"Sometimes, it's good to be lucky," McLaughlin said.[16]

Then national security adviser Condoleezza Rice told President Bush that KSM was in custody. Bush was excited, saying, "That's fantastic!"[17]

BOOK V

INTERROGATING KSM

BOOK V

12

KSM and Obama: The Mastermind's Last Laugh

KSM's life is redacted, blacked out, deleted from his March 2003 capture in Rawalpindi to his September 2006 arrival in Guantánamo. Blindfolded, chained, and drugged, he was never told where he was, nor was he allowed to see any clocks or calendars. All we can say with confidence is that he vanished into a series of "special-access facilities" jointly run by the CIA and foreign intelligence services, most likely near Bangkok, Amman, and Warsaw.

While we do not know where he was in this forty-one-month period, incredibly, we have a pretty good idea what he was thinking. KSM was trained to turn the tables on his interrogators and the mastermind diligently followed his training.

Fortunately, American intelligence officials had a copy of KSM's playbook.

On a high plateau about two hours east of Kandahar, U.S. Special Forces teams walked carefully amid the ruins of Al Qaeda's training camp.

At one time, hundreds of terror trainees had come through this ramshackle collection of low buildings to learn how to make bombs and poison gases. Bin Laden triumphantly visited the camp several times a month, John Walker Lindh (the so-called American Taliban) told his CIA interrogators.[1] Many Al Qaeda videos were shot here, showing terrorists scrambling through obstacle courses and firing automatic weapons. Now, in mid-February 2002, the camp was bombed and emptied. It looked more like a garbage dump, with pits and piles of debris. The relentless desert wind scattered the burnt embers of its remains.

After securing the perimeter and checking for explosive booby traps, the special forces teams spread out to sift the piles of charred wood and shattered glass. They were looking for maps, code books, computer hard drives—anything that might reveal Al Qaeda's future plans or capabilities.

In one mound they found a seam of muddy, wet papers written in Arabic and other languages. They didn't stop to examine them and stuffed the entire collection into black garbage bags.

The bags were flown to Bagram Air Base, outside of Kabul. There they were handed to the U.S. Army document-exploitation team, known in military circles as DOCEX.

Receiving garbage bags full of dirty, wet captured documents was routine for DOCEX. The team dumped a bag on the table and began sorting through the filthy papers.

Working conditions were hard. DOCEX labored in a long rectangular tent, whose frame would whine in the heavy wind. Sometimes a fuse would blow and the space heaters would go cold. But morale was high. Everyone considered their job to be war-winning work. And today they would be right.

A U.S. Army interrogator at Bagram at the time, who calls himself Chris Mackey, described what happened next:

> "Hey, look at this thing," one [DOCEX] team member said.
>
> It was a stack of paper, about sixty pages, with two binder holes on one side. It had coffee stains and was rippled from

moisture. Big chunks of it were handwritten, but it had clearly been photocopied. The top page had a rather surprisingly elaborate Al Qaeda symbol on it and the ubiquitous "in the name of Allah." Beneath that script was a handwritten note in Arabic:

"Brothers, this is the book about prisoners."

At first everyone thought it was a book about what Al Qaeda would do to their prisoners. But as we thumbed through it we realized that it was the Al Qaeda guide for resisting interrogation if they were taken prisoner.

All hell broke loose when the command realized what had been found. Interrogations stopped, and anybody who could read Arabic was thrown into translating the manual. We spread it over every flat surface in the ICE [compound] and had the whole thing translated by the next day.

It was unbelievable. Here, laid out in neat Arabic print, was every tactic we interrogators had encountered in Afghanistan: the passive resistance, the blatant lies, the cognitive fog that shrouded every name or meaningful landmark in a prisoner's travels.

The book taught captives never to give away "another brother's name" and advised them to use *cunyas* [aliases]. Prisoners were told to confuse their interrogators by using the Islamic calendar. It taught them to remain silent for a few days, then tell stories out of sequence, dribbling out erroneous information "in circles."

There was an entire section on the West. It showed a remarkable understanding of the American system. Hold out on providing any information for at least twenty-four hours, it said, to give "brothers" enough time to adjust their plans. The Americans "will not harm you physically," the manual said, but "they must be tempted into doing so. And if they do strike a brother, you must complain to the authorities immediately." It added that the baiting of Americans should be sufficient to result in an attack that leaves "evidence." You could end the

> career of an interrogator, maybe even prompt an international outcry, if you could show the Red Cross a bruise or scar.
>
> America's aversion to torture was presented as a symbol of American weakness. The West didn't have the stomach for such things, the book said, "because they are not warriors." Throughout, the tone is condescending. "Brothers, they will not understand our reasons [for fighting], and you must contrive to exploit their ignorance."[2]

In short, the Al Qaeda training manual taught its operators how to use American interrogation rules, designed to safeguard detainees, as a weapon to attack their interrogators.

One weapon detainees were taught to use was the false allegation of mistreatment. Here is one example: A detainee, held for killing, burning, and hanging four American contractors from a bridge in Iraq, inflicted a superficial wound on himself. It was enough to start the criminal courts-martial of the four members of the SEAL team that had apprehended him. Each of the SEALs was eventually acquitted.[3]

Another example: Sergeant Alan J. Driver was subject to court-martial for allegedly beating a senior Al Qaeda figure on the buttocks with an empty plastic water bottle. No marks were left. Sergeant Driver was eventually acquitted.[4]

Not all alleged abusers have been acquitted. Other U.S. servicemen have been sentenced to years of detention in military prisons for comparatively minor mistreatment of detainees. Even those who have been acquitted have had to spend money and months defending themselves—an agonizing experience when one is simply trying to serve one's country. Wielding false accusations works even when it doesn't kill a military career. An accusation alone is a permanent blemish on a military record.

As an interrogator in Afghanistan, Mackey has seen prisoners use every technique mentioned by the Al Qaeda manual:

> The most infuriating thing about the Al Qaeda manual was that its core diagnosis was dead-on: the Americans would

> keep you in a cage eating halal MREs and giving you showers a couple of times a week. But when it came down to it, you could lie to them, refuse to talk, switch your story from one session to the next, and there wasn't anything they could do about it. In the long run, that was our strength. But at the time, it felt like a weakness.[5]

The Al Qaeda manual correctly predicted that prisoners of the Americans would be well treated. But it didn't matter. To KSM and other Al Qaeda members, detention and trial would constitute the climax of their careers—a chance to fight one on one with bona fide representatives of the Great Satan.

Far from being passive victims caught in the machinery of their American interrogators, Al Qaeda detainees see themselves as warriors and the interrogation process as simply another field of battle. Lying about physical abuse or torture is simply one weapon. Claiming a Koran has been abused or a prayer interrupted is another kind of weapon. Indeed, the whole panoply of prisoner protections, once properly scrutinized, is an armory for any creative detainee. And no Al Qaeda captive has been more creative than the 9/11 mastermind himself.

Since his capture, KSM has carried on his one-man war against American interlocutors. We can cautiously assemble some shards of information to get a sense of that war.

KSM's captivity and his war against his captors can be divided into two phases: his detention at a series of "black sites," from March 2003 to September 2006, and his years in Guantánamo, from September 2006 onward.

In the first phase, KSM was essentially alone with his captors. He saw no other detainees and had no third-party allies, such as ACLU lawyers or Red Cross officials. He had no access to media, even indirectly. KSM was utterly dependent on the CIA and other U.S. government officials. His war was private, and, as we shall see, that without outside help it was short-lived.

Later, in the second phase of his captivity, at a U.S. Navy facility in Guantánamo Bay, his war became public as he used the Red Cross, human-rights lawyers, mainstream journalists, and members of both major American political parties as his unwitting allies. Even President Obama and Attorney General Holder played starring roles. With the encouragement of these allies, KSM's war was public and endless.

Regarding the first phase of KSM's captivity, intelligence officials make a distinction between "interrogation" and "debriefing."[6]

Interrogation is the period in which a subject's resistance to revealing information is eliminated and he begins to talk freely and truthfully. The interrogation period can last minutes, weeks, or, in extreme cases, months. Research and experience have taught intelligence officials the world over that eventually everyone "breaks" and decides to talk.

In July 2006, White House speechwriter Marc Thiessen, a national-security veteran who physically resembles the actor John Cusack, met with two CIA interrogators, one of whom had been KSM's lead interrogator. Here is how those two officials explained to Thiessen the initial interrogation process: "Two-thirds of those brought into the CIA program did not require the use of any enhanced interrogation techniques whatsoever—what critics loosely call 'torture.' Just the experience of being brought into CIA custody—the 'capture shock,' the arrival at a sterile location, the isolation, the fact that they did not know where they were, and that no one else knew they were there—was enough to convince most of them to cooperate."[7]

For the roughly one-third who do not cooperate immediately, intelligence officers have learned that there are two key periods in which a detainee will usually break: the first forty-eight hours, during which his largely imaginary fears will prey on him, and the end of the fourteenth day, when sheer exhaustion sets in. A handful of detainees, like KSM, "demonstrated extraordinary resistance."[8] He apparently defied his interrogators for more than fourteen days.

As a result, KSM was subjected to what the Bush administration described as "enhanced interrogation techniques," eventually including waterboarding. Only two other Al Qaeda captives were waterboarded.

Despite his "extraordinary resistance," KSM began talking shortly after waterboarding. He had held out for less than a month.

Once KSM began to talk honestly, all coercive (even psychological) techniques were withdrawn. In intelligence parlance, interrogation ended and debriefing started. Debriefing can provide useful information quickly. By the end of March 2006, KSM had "provided information on a plot to fly airplanes into London's Heathrow Airport."[9]

Debriefing KSM would pay real dividends. In the end, the information gleaned from KSM helped stop several Al Qaeda plots. What follow are two examples, both of which will be new to readers.

The Paris-Dakar Rally

Under KSM's direction, Al Qaeda, operating from bases in southern Algeria, plotted to kidnap drivers from the famous off-road race across the Sahara, from Dakar to Paris. The race, over more than four thousand unforgiving kilometers of deserts and mountains, is televised across Europe and the Middle East. It can take weeks to finish, and many two-man teams fail to make it. Engine fires, burst tires, and crashed vehicles are common. Trapped or stranded drivers would be heartbreakingly easy to take hostage.

Hostages can be a lucrative business, as Al Qaeda's experience in North Africa has taught them. European governments paid ransoms totaling some $18 million between 2002 and 2003. That sum enabled Al Qaeda to recruit, train, and equip an army of almost a thousand fighters.

KSM's information led to the deployment of a U.S. Navy SEAL team in "Operation Aztec Silence" and the capture of a key Al Qaeda leader. Eventually the leader of Al Qaeda's North Africa affiliate, then known as the GSPC (Groupe Salafi pour la Predication et le Combat), was cornered in the boulder-strewn high country of Northern Chad. After a drama with an allied desert tribe and some covert payments, the Al Qaeda leader was turned over to a mixed unit of U.S. Special Forces.

The racecourse was rerouted to avoid a region in Mali where Al Qaeda had tribal confederates waiting to seize hapless competitors.

The Singapore Plot

Encouraged by KSM, Al Qaeda's East Asian affiliate planned an all-out war on American embassies in the Far East. Al Qaeda teams were within days of bombing the U.S. embassies in Kuala Lumpur and Singapore, as well as a nearby U.S. naval base.

Again, information from KSM allowed investigators to thwart the plots in the nick of time.

For almost a week, U.S. Ambassador Frank Lavin went about his daily routine, trying not to reveal to his staff, his children, or the outside world that he knew his life was in danger.[10] If he did, the terrorists might flee before they could be arrested. When I met with him later, in his walled Singapore compound, Ambassador Lavin coolly told me that he had just been doing his duty. In fact, he'd been brave in a way few diplomats ever get credit for. He risked his life to ensure that Al Qaeda's Singapore network was smashed—saving hundreds of lives in the bargain. The unraveling of the Singapore plots is a dramatic tale of the quiet surveillance of several cells followed by the lightning-fast arrests of nearly forty terrorists.

These are just two of the plots thwarted thanks to information obtained from KSM. Former intelligence officials tell me that there were other—perhaps many other—examples of terror strikes that were halted as a result of the covert questioning of the Al Qaeda mastermind. The full details of these plots have not yet been declassified.

When weighing the merits of enhanced interrogation techniques, it is wise to consider the benefits as well as the costs.

One of KSM's main interrogators explained the value of the CIA's program in blunt terms: "It is the reason we have not had another 9/11."

During both the interrogation and debriefing phases, KSM's interlocutors were far less spontaneous than those on the TV show *The Closer* or even real-life policemen. Every interrogation and debriefing session was strictly governed by a written plan that required officials to receive approval for each procedure in advance and in writing. They were not allowed to make it up as they went along.

There were many procedures put in place to prevent abuse. A board-certified doctor was on hand at all times to guard the detainee's health and safety. In addition, a translator was usually present, providing another eyewitness. This made abuse even more unlikely.

Nor were KSM's CIA interrogators young or inexperienced. The median age of CIA interrogators is forty-three, and each has at least 280 hours of specialized training.[11]

In addition, each interrogator suffers through each and every enhanced interrogation technique himself, including waterboarding. Interrogators are well aware of the discomfort they are inflicting because they have endured it themselves. This, too, acts as a natural check on abuse.

Once a subject like KSM agrees to cooperate, interrogation ends and a new person enters the subject's life—the debriefer. The debriefer is usually cordial, even friendly. He has studied the detainee's dossier and those of his comrades. He knows what the detainee should know and expertly and patiently draws it out of him.

One of KSM's best debriefers is known as Deuce Martinez. He was no Grand Inquisitor, no sadist unleashed to terrify his charges. Mild-mannered and personally opposed to waterboarding, he wasn't a tough guy from central casting. While he was a veteran CIA man, he was not one of the larger-than-life "operators" who worked with dangerous men in far-off places. He was an analyst. Until 9/11 he had never left the United States. In fact, he had rarely left the Washington area and then only to visit family. He joined the CIA because his father had worked there in the technical division. It seemed like a safe and interesting job.

Nor was he initially a terrorism expert. Martinez spent his career in a largely unnoticed corner of the CIA, helping the agency fight narcotic flows from South America. Those who know him say that he knew little about Islam or Al Qaeda before the 9/11 attacks. He still doesn't speak Arabic.

Yet he had a gift for making terrorists talk. As a negotiator, a seducer, and an enforcer, he ruled the world inside what debriefers call "the room." He did it largely through charm, intelligence, and self-discipline.

Like sex, interrogation creates a kind of sustained intimacy that can lead to either betrayal or redemption. Clearly KSM enjoyed the parry and thrust. (He would tell the International Committee of the Red Cross in 2008, "I gave a lot of false information in order to satisfy what I believed the interrogators wished to hear.") This is most likely double-talk or empty bravado. All of his statements were carefully checked. False statements meant the withdrawal of "privileges," such as favorite foods.

KSM's words were compared against other evidence—captured documents, phone intercepts, the testimonies of other detainees—and against reason and common sense.

Truth was rewarded. Lies were not. Soon enough, KSM learned to either tell the truth or plead ignorance.

Eventually the pair developed a surprising rapport. They had long, rambling talks comparing Islam with Roman Catholicism. KSM even wrote poetry extolling Martinez's wife, whom he never met.

"Can't we get along?" KSM asked.

"Isn't it a little late for that?" Martinez said coolly.[12]

To strike the right balance between lifesaving information and humane treatment, both sides of the political controversy over interrogation must first be honest enough to admit that there is a trade-off between these two goods. You cannot have both goods in equal measure. Make the detainee too comfortable and you learn nothing. Press the detainee too fiercely and the information may be worthless or nonexistent.

And, of course, mistreating prisoners offends America's moral sense of itself. Habituating government officials to police-state tactics ultimately threatens the civil liberties of us all. A careful balance must be struck.

Inside a secret facility near the Szymany airport, outside of Warsaw, Poland, the CIA maintained a small "black site" interrogation center known as "the room."

In "the room," the CIA used a carefully calibrated series of punishments, ranging from open-fingered face smacks to humiliating belly slaps to "walling," which involves throwing a prisoner against a false, collapsible wall. When the wall moves back six inches or so and makes a loud noise, the detainee imagines he has been substantially harmed. Each of these punishments had to be approved in writing at least twenty-four hours before they could be administered.

With KSM, the CIA started with air conditioning. For a man used to the warm, wet air of the near tropics, the cold, dry blast was a torment. But he still wouldn't talk.

Harder measures would be needed. The CIA gradually moved up a staircase of increasingly adversarial measures, such as "walling."

Before the end of March 2003, KSM had been waterboarded. Critics make much of the fact that he was waterboarded 188 times. In reality, he was doused with water that many times, all within a single session. While defenders of enhanced interrogation techniques say that military personnel are waterboarded in escape-and-evasion training schools, rarely, if ever, are American soldiers and sailors doused more than a dozen times, let alone 188.

Still, waterboarding is not lethal and leaves no physical injuries. It is merely uncomfortable, perhaps enough so to compel conversation. And to a proud man like KSM, it would be humiliating.

Is it torture?

Not unless you torture the commonsense meaning of the word *torture*. What sets torture apart from mere harsh treatment is a permanent change in the subject's well-being: dismemberment, branding, broken bones, and so on. Every modern or medieval practice that is universally understood to be torture has this element of permanence. Waterboarding, walling, and other "enhanced" measures do not. Therefore, KSM was not tortured.

If every unpleasant or even psychologically painful experience visited on a prisoner is said to be torture, then the term "torture" loses its moral force. It becomes harder to call out regimes that gouge out eyes or electrify genitals. After all, everything is torture.

Torture, like pornography, is too often defined by the passions of partisans. For some, torture is any act or omission that makes a detainee uncomfortable. A delayed meal or a homophobe's contact with a gay soldier would qualify. Humans have long realized that making other people tell the truth requires some degree of discomfort. Suspects in big-city police stations are routinely made to feel uncomfortable. So mere discomfort alone cannot be the defining element that makes an action torture—it would include too many everyday things that are plainly not torture, but merely unhappy situations.

Again, for torture to have any meaning at all, it has to mean an irreversible, permanent, and negative change in a person's well-being.

Indeed, it seemed that critics of President Bush's interrogation policy hoped to short-circuit a debate over striking the proper balance between lifesaving information and humane treatment by deploying the word *torture.* Instead of two opposing views about how to balance two competing goods, we are left with one side calling itself "anti-torture" and labeling the other side "pro-torture."

In an effort to address its critics' concerns, the Bush administration devised an absurd system that is as dangerous for the interrogator as for the detainee. Let's examine it in detail.

Ask any CIA interrogator and he will tell you that there are two worlds: the world inside "the room" and the world outside.

Inside the room, interrogators duel with terrorists. It is a duel with at least one loser. If the interrogator gains the upper hand and the terrorist betrays his cause and his comrades, hundreds of innocent lives will be spared. If the terrorist is skillful—and many, like KSM, are trained to be—he can evade and extend, giving his compatriots valuable time to carry out their lethal missions. Hundreds could die.

As a duelist, the interrogator is at risk, too. If he loses his temper or his sense, he could cross some invisible line and break the law. The law is very complex, and designed to protect the prisoner more than the interrogator. In less than a minute, the interrogator could commit an act that might cost him his house, his pension, his reputation, and his freedom. Democracies imprison lawbreakers just as they do terrorists. "It is a dangerous game," a former U.S. Army interrogator told me. "I think it is even riskier for the asker than the asked."

Inevitably, the duel is seen differently outside "the room." Outside, politicians, the press, and the public debate a serious philosophical question, with enormous real-life repercussions, in safety and in ignorance. They don't have to live with the consequences of their ideas. The interrogators do.

It is also important to remember what a determined killer KSM is.

Aside from perhaps Osama bin Laden, Khalid Shaikh Mohammed is the most dangerous man of our generation. He was involved in virtually every major terrorist attack against the Western world, from the 1993 World Trade Center bombing to the September 11 attacks. He personally sawed Daniel Pearl's head off and swung it in the air triumphantly. He planned and plotted to kill the Pope and President Clinton and took part in schemes to murder ambassadors and detonate passenger planes over two oceans.

KSM single-handedly increased the lethality of Al Qaeda. From the moment he joined the organization, in 1996 (without swearing an oath of allegiance or *bayat* to bin Laden for several years), Al Qaeda went from killing dozens to murdering hundreds, then thousands, of people at a time.

Consider the pre-KSM era. Al Qaeda's first attack on Americans, in December 1992, targeted hundreds of U.S. servicemen living in two hotels in Yemen. While the bombs went off, no American military personnel were harmed. Two people died, including one Austrian tourist.[13] Al Qaeda's next attack was in Somalia, in an incident that Americans know as "Black Hawk Down." Al Qaeda–trained rocket-launcher teams and mortar crews—combined with Somali militiamen—cut down eighteen American soldiers.[14] The 1995 attack on the Saudi Arabian National Guard headquarters, in Riyadh, slew seven, including several American military trainers.[15] The 1996 truck bombing of a U.S. Air Force barracks in Dhahran, Saudi Arabia, killed twenty-three Americans.[16]

Now consider the KSM period. The two U.S. embassy bombings in 1998 murdered 224 people, including twelve American diplomats.[17] The 2000 "millennium plots" were thwarted before anyone inside the United States was killed; also prevented was the imminent attack on pilgrims at the Jordan River, near where Christ was baptized by John the Baptist. The millennium attacks would have killed thousands if they had succeeded.[18] The attack on the USS *Cole*, an American warship refueling in Yemen's Aden harbor, killed seventeen Americans.[19] The September 11 attacks slew nearly three thousand.[20] The Bali bombing in 2002 erased 202 lives.[21] The Madrid train bombings killed almost the same number.[22]

Next, consider Al Qaeda's post-KSM period. There have been no successful attacks on American soil since 2001 and no major attacks on American embassies or military installations since 2004. The handful of attacks that have occurred against American consulates or buildings owned by American corporations have been largely limited to Iraq and Pakistan. The death tolls in those attacks have reverted to the pre-KSM pattern of killing tens, not hundreds, at a time. While Al Qaeda continues to attempt aircraft attacks and bombings inside America, these have been thwarted, partly with the help of KSM's interrogations and partly by taking KSM out of the Al Qaeda decision-making process. The London train bombings on July 7, 2005, took more than fifty lives, not hundreds or thousands.[23] And let's not forget the stopped plots to explode aircraft over the Atlantic, the attempt to ignite the underwear bomb on a U.S.-bound flight, and the botched truck bombing of New York's Times Square. If KSM were still in command, these murderous efforts might have succeeded.

While Al Qaeda may someday succeed again in inflicting mass casualties, in the absence of KSM, it has yet to do so.

Clearly Al Qaeda's ability to kill large numbers in a single blow depends on the quality of its management. Without KSM, the organization is far less deadly, at least so far.

Those who contend that Al Qaeda's managers are easily replaced should carefully consider the rise and the fall in the death tolls following KSM's recruitment and his capture. No wonder Congressman Porter Goss, then-chairman of the House Intelligence Committee and later director of the CIA, said of the capture: "This is a very huge event. This is the equivalent of the liberation of Paris during World War II."[24]

Osama bin Laden has weighed in with a threat to kill more Americans if KSM is executed.[25] The archterrorist didn't make a distinction between an execution following a civilian trial and one resulting from a military commission. Nor did he get into whether waterboarding was torture or not.

These debates absorb America and her allies—but not Al Qaeda. It is too busy planning the next attack.

It is a strange feature of contemporary American politics that the evidence of KSM's crimes is clear, but the details of his confessions are not.

It is admittedly hard to independently evaluate the effectiveness of the CIA program. I have spoken to a number of government officials who interrogated KSM or who were responsible for evaluating the results of those interrogations. No two accounts agree.

There are several reasons for this. For one, the FBI and the CIA have different approaches to interrogation and color their accounts to vindicate their agencies' cultural preferences. More important, following the 2006 elections, which handed control of the U.S. Congress to the Democratic party, and the 2008 presidential election of President Barack Obama, career intelligence officials feared that they would face criminal prosecution for the conduct of those interrogations. Thus, every account seems to be sloped to avoid legal liability or endangering a career.

While it may seem like an overreaction to an outsider, the spy agency's internal culture has a long memory. Many of the CIA's senior managers began their careers just as the CIA received its first serious political attack.

America's intelligence agencies (especially the CIA) have yet to recover as institutions from the hearings launched by Senator Frank Church in the mid-1970s and the actions taken by President Carter's CIA director, Stansfield Turner.

A liberal Democrat from Idaho, Church was a self-proclaimed "dove" who opposed the Vietnam War. When the war ended with U.S. withdrawal in 1973 and the invasion of South Vietnam in 1975, Church set his sights on the CIA. As chairman of the Senate Foreign Relations Committee from 1976 to 1981, Church held a series of hearings, treating the CIA as if it were an ongoing criminal enterprise that routinely violated the constitutional rights of Americans at home and foreign nationals abroad in the name of a "paranoid" anticommunism.

The effect on the culture of the CIA was devastating. Since its creation in the 1940s, the clandestine service had always been treated with respect, even reverence. Now some senators saw it as run by potentially mentally unstable people engaged in a pointless anticommunist crusade. The stab of betrayal was immediate and deep. Those who didn't find their careers ruined, retired. The remainder vowed to take no risks.

Even the definition of risk changed. Formerly, a risk was defined as being caught by a foreign government; now it was defined as being caught by your own.

The next body blow came from inside the CIA. In 1978, Admiral Turner, as CIA director, gutted the agency's directorate of operations, firing more than eight hundred veteran operators. These were the people the public thinks of as spies, people who developed personal networks of sources in foreign lands and collected secret documents.

Instead Turner wanted to replace so-called human intelligence (known inside the agency as HUMINT) with signals intelligence and technical intelligence (known as SIGINT and TECHINT). This move touched off a thirty-year trend inside the intelligence community that preferred spy satellites and phone intercepts over tips and documents from well-placed sources. As a result, the agency became very good at photographing the tops of people's heads and very poor at understanding what was going on inside those heads.

In fact, it wasn't the intelligence community that was paranoid, but its critics. They believed that the CIA, the FBI, and other agencies were run by lawless thugs who would use any pretext, or none at all, to peer into the private lives of others.

Nevertheless, the legal landscape changed. Senator Church sponsored and Director Turner supported the Foreign Intelligence Surveillance Act of 1978, which required American intelligence investigators to receive a warrant from a special "FISA" court in order to listen in on the phone calls of anyone inside the United States—including officials of foreign governments or other foreign nationals. Other 1970s-era restrictions made it essentially illegal to bribe foreign government officials for information or to subject foreign nationals to adverse treatment in the hopes of gleaning valuable intelligence.

Thus, an intelligence culture of risk aversion and a welter of restrictive new laws set the stage for the intelligence failures in the run-up to the September 11 attacks and the political debate that raged throughout the Bush years.

This history shaped the internal debates over what to do with KSM and other "high-value" detainees. Outside the intelligence community, both President Bush's domestic critics and Al Qaeda detainees knew this history—and how to manipulate it.

Under a tropical night sky, KSM was led in shackles down the ramp of an American military cargo plane. The tarmac was hot and stank of diesel fuel. It was September 2006 and he had just arrived at Guantánamo. He and several other detainees were herded to a staging area just off the runway.

Next, a U.S. Navy vehicle took KSM to a small boat to ferry him across a choppy tidal bay to an American prison built on an old golf course. KSM was destined for Camp 7, the most restrictive. His biggest battle was about to begin.

Days later, to thunderous applause, President Bush walked rapidly through the door of the White House's East Room and climbed onto a small temporary stage. It was September 6, 2006, and the president was about to make a surprising announcement about KSM.

The East Room is usually reserved for state dinners, signing ceremonies, and other momentous events. It is known for its formal elegance. Gilbert Stuart's famous 1797 portrait of George Washington, which was rescued just as British troops burned the White House, hangs prominently over a red marble mantel. The windows are hung with long, custom-made gold silk drapes, specially designed under Laura Bush's direction.

As the television cameras zoomed in, President Bush announced that every high-level Al Qaeda leader in custody, including KSM, had recently been transferred to an American prison facility in Guantánamo. Al Qaeda's captive leaders were now held in public view, where reporters, lawmakers, and lawyers could contact them. A new front in the war on terror had opened.

President Bush's speech—and the major policy change it signaled—had been secretly in the works for months.

By the spring of 2006, senior Bush administration officials had realized that they could not continue with the current CIA interrogation program without exposing the president to political risk and CIA officials to legal jeopardy.

In Congress, Senator John McCain had shamelessly used his own experiences of severe torture in a North Vietnamese prison to push the Detainee Treatment Act of 2005. Senator McCain knew he had the major television networks and the editorial pages of *The New York Times* and *The Washington Post* at his back when he confronted President Bush, the man who had defeated him in his quest for the Republican nomination for president in 2000. Whether motivated by high ideals or bitter revenge, it didn't matter. The Detainee Treatment Act attracted crowds of Republicans in both houses of Congress. McCain's law made it virtually impossible for President Bush to hold KSM and other high-value detainees incommunicado in secret locations. Instead KSM and other detainees would win many of the rights of prisoners of war, including visits by the Red Cross and the right to send and receive letters from family members. Virtually all "enhanced interrogation techniques," including waterboarding, were essentially outlawed.

Once the act passed Congress, CIA Director Porter Goss informed the White House that he was stopping all interrogations of high-value prisoners including KSM. The CIA director didn't believe that his officers had "adequate legal protection."[26]

History played a silent part in Goss's decision. He had served in the CIA in the early 1970s and knew several CIA officers whose careers were sidelined by Senator Church. He wasn't going to let himself or his agency fall into the hands of Senator McCain.

Meanwhile, the United States Supreme Court was also limiting the president's options. In June 2006, the high court had handed down its decision, in *Hamdan* v. *Rumsfeld*, requiring the president to win congressional approval before trying Al Qaeda detainees before military commissions. To secure congressional support, the president would have to press his case before the press and the public. In short, Congress and the Supreme Court had forced the president's hand. The secret CIA program would have to end.

The new CIA director, Mike Hayden, was in the midst of a grueling internal review to design interrogation techniques in compliance with the 2005 Detainee Treatment Act when the 2006 Supreme Court decision forced the spy agency to put those efforts on hold. Clearly there was nothing the CIA could do until Congress adopted new legislation. Questioning high-value detainees had been suspended since the middle of 2005. There was no hope of restarting them now.

Inside the Bush administration, a high-octane debate flared. Every agency involved brought its own lawyers and its own legal opinions. No one knew who was right and who was wrong, because they were now in uncharted constitutional territory. From the time of George Washington until 2005, there were essentially no limits on the president's ability to hold and question enemy prisoners, except for the gentlemanly "laws of war" and the treaty obligations under the various Geneva Conventions. Since neither Al Qaeda nor Afghanistan was a signatory to the Geneva Conventions, and violated them at every opportunity, some administration officials contended that the conventions did not limit the president's constitutional authority in this case. Others pointed out that Congress had just limited the president's powers to hold and question prisoners. The Supreme Court, after *Hamdan* v. *Rumsfeld*, was unlikely to support the view that Congress's encroachment on the president's prerogatives was unconstitutional. A solution had to be found that would maximize the CIA's ability to extract lifesaving information from Al Qaeda detainees within the confines outlined by Congress and the Supreme Court.

CIA Director Hayden was eager to transfer all of the detainees out of CIA custody and into the hands of the U.S. Navy. He was shrewdly shifting responsibility from his agency to the Department of Defense. When Defense officials objected, insisting that the CIA could still produce vital information from those detainees, Hayden was ready with his counterblast: "The intelligence value is never zero. But I'm willing to concede that the intelligence value of the remaining people in our custody is such we no longer need to hold them in these circumstances. So let's move them on."[27]

Secretary of State Condoleezza Rice agreed with Hayden. She knew that the CIA's secret prisons were becoming a major impediment to U.S. diplomatic efforts with its Western European allies and were hurting public perception of America around the world. Then she made a moral argument—and a prudent political one. She stressed that, for the 9/11 families and for the nation, KSM and the other terrorists responsible for the 9/11 attacks needed to be brought before the bar of justice and held accountable for their crimes. She also realized that the legacy of presidents is determined not just by their actions but by the actions of the presidents who follow them. "Sooner or later there was going to be a new president and you don't want to have a new president suddenly lift the lid and say, 'Ooh, what have we in here,'" she said.[28] In short, they needed to develop a policy that would make it difficult for the next president to prosecute either CIA officers or senior Bush administration officials. Rice's insight caught the attention of everyone in the room.

The debate about defending the CIA's interrogation was over.

Senior officials had given up trying to save the current CIA interrogation program—they were now trying to save themselves.

By July 2006, President Bush agreed with CIA Director Hayden's plan of "disclosing the program in order to save it."[29]

Throughout the summer, in a series of meetings between President Bush, Secretary of State Rice, CIA Director Hayden, Defense Secretary Donald Rumsfeld, and others, the president decided that all prisoners (including KSM) currently held in secret prisons around the world would be transferred to Guantánamo before any public announcement was made. The president and other officials feared that announcing any transfer in advance would invite Al Qaeda attacks designed to rescue the prisoners.

As the Labor Day weekend approached, the president and his senior advisers were still debating how much of the CIA's secret interrogation program should be made public. The concern was that waterboarding and other techniques would be labeled torture. With his characteristic directness, the president brought the debate to a halt: "You know, if anyone asks me 'did you water board KSM?' you know what I'll say? Damn right."[30]

The Camp 7 guards looked at the passes proffered by the men in suits from Washington, D.C., and waved them in. Drawn from several agencies, including the FBI and the Department of Justice, these men were the "clean team." Their job, which would take them more than a week, was to question KSM without using any coercive techniques that might taint his testimony. The government lawyers would have to persuade KSM to admit to everything that he had said in the previous three years without once directly referring to his prior admissions. They had to act as if they were friendly observers who knew nothing about KSM's confessions to the CIA. It was part of a deliberate legal strategy.

Their aim was to get a complete record of KSM's crimes that could be presented in court, either civilian or military, without giving defense attorneys an opening to have KSM's admissions excluded on the legal grounds that they were improperly obtained (i.e., the result of "torture").

The clean team was in for two surprises. The first was KSM himself. He freely admitted that he had planned and supervised the 9/11 attacks and was responsible for at least thirty acts of actual or attempted mass murder. He was proud of his crimes.

The second surprise would take a few years to emerge. Nothing the clean team accomplished would stop KSM or any of his various advocates from claiming that his testimony should be thrown out on the grounds that it was wrung out of him by torture. In a better world, the clean-team effort would have been seen as a good-faith attempt to present and preserve evidence for timely administration of justice. Instead, it was a waste of time.

The U.S. Navy facility at Guantánamo Bay is not the gulag that some imagine. Detainees are entitled to eight hours of uninterrupted sleep every day and cannot be woken up for questioning. They are served three halal meals per day and their guards eat the very same food. Nor are the detainees starved. They receive more than three thousand calories of food per day. They are free to pray five times a day, without interruption, and may set their own prayer schedule. As a result, there are almost as many prayer schedules as there are prisoners. This is no accident; it allows detainees to confuse or fool their guards. And, of course, the timing of daily prayers is often changed, sometimes every other day. In practice, prayers are used as a "get out of jail free" card to get a detainee out of any activity he doesn't like—including questioning by intelligence officials.

Every detainee is entitled to a minimum of two hours of outdoor recreation per day, with the U.S. government supplying shoes for basketball, soccer, and volleyball. If they are injured playing soccer, U.S. Navy doctors treat them free of charge.

Detainees receive better treatment than American citizens convicted of crimes in the United States. At Guantánamo, doctors and dentists performed almost a hundred surgeries and five thousand dental operations between 2002 and 2006. A hundred and seventy-four pairs of eyeglasses were passed out in the same period. At least twenty-two detainees have prosthetic limbs supplied to them by the U.S. Navy.[31]

Interviews with detainees do not involve the rubber hose or even the "third degree." Sessions are limited to four hours and usually run less than half that. Usually, interviews are interrupted by prayers, often at the spontaneous suggestion of the detainee.

As a result, interrogators are often forced to act like a kindergarten teacher trying to coax her reluctant pupils. One interrogator baked cookies for her detainees, while another bribed them with sandwiches from Subway and McDonald's. Both fast-food franchises are available on base. Filet-O-Fish is an Al Qaeda favorite, one Guantánamo interrogator told me.[32]

But while the detainees are treated well, the guards are not. Between July 2005 and August 2006, there was an average of 8.8 attacks on the guards per day. Almost anything can be sharpened or shaped into a weapon. Springs were taken from the insides of faucets and rubbed on concrete to make knifelike blades. Ceiling-fan blades have been smashed and fashioned into impromptu swords. Detainees even use broken fluorescent light tubes as daggers. Rear Admiral Harry B. Harris Jr., who commanded the Guantánamo facility in 2006, told me: "These folks are McGyvers."

The Combatant Status Review Tribunal met in a temporary building roughly the size of a double-wide trailer, ringed by chain-link fences and topped with razor wire. The meeting was a hearing to determine whether KSM should be officially classified as an "enemy combatant." It was March 10, 2007, and KSM was just beginning to turn America's legal procedures into a propaganda theater.

When KSM was called to address the tribunal, he alternately spoke in broken English and accented Arabic. He confessed to masterminding the 9/11 attacks as well as thirty other terror plots. He clearly wanted the credit.

The Department of Defense's official finding, issued on August 9, was hardly a surprise. KSM was now officially an "enemy combatant" of the United States. That was but step one in a long process mandated by Congress. If anything, KSM was pleased. He would have years to torment Americans using their bizarre legal process.

By June 5, 2008, it was clear that holding KSM accountable for the murder of three thousand people on September 11 was taking longer than the plot itself. He had been formally charged in February 2008 with carrying out the attacks, but legal delays and procedural questions were continuing to slow the process.

KSM himself seemed to have two goals: To maximize each public hearing for its propaganda value and to drag out the process enough to punish President Bush and other American officials. Perhaps he sensed that he might get a better deal from the next president of the United States.

Surprisingly, KSM would be aided by an odd alliance of former Clinton officials, liberal activists, and camera-chasing lawyers.

Clinton's former attorney general, Janet Reno, agreed to headline fundraising efforts for the American Civil Liberties Union, a liberal Washington-based individual-rights group that has been at the center of legal fights over political issues for more than fifty years. In April 2008, the ACLU announced that it had raised a war chest of $8.5 million to provide a free legal-defense team for the more than three hundred detainees held at Guantánamo. While each of the detainees who had been formally charged, including KSM, already had military lawyers to provide a free legal defense for them, the ACLU was funding civilian lawyers who would attempt to bring legal claims on behalf of detainees in civilian courts and to provide research and support for military-defense lawyers. The ACLU's fund went to cover legal research costs and to defray the travel expenses of attorneys shuttling between the American mainland and the American base in Cuba.

The ACLU had allied itself with the National Association of Criminal Defense Lawyers and a clutch of U.S. military lawyers.

ACLU Executive Director Anthony Romero said his organization was interested in defending KSM because "he appears to be the government's top priority in this prosecution. And whether or not they are able to convict Khalid Shaikh Mohammed under these rules may well determine the fates of the almost three hundred other men who are detained at Guantánamo."[33] In other words, the ACLU saw its legal effort as stymieing the government's case against the confessed 9/11 mastermind and upending the Bush administration's efforts to try captured terrorists in military courts.

The ACLU called its legal-defense team "the John Adams Project." Adams, as a Boston attorney, had defended eight British soldiers accused of killing colonists in the so-called Boston Massacre of 1770. (Of course, the men Adams defended were innocent and six were acquitted. The other two received minor sentences, having a brand placed on their thumbs.)

Another lawyer waiting in the wings was Jennifer Daskal of Human Rights Watch. She, too, believed in a vigorous defense of KSM. She told the press: "The only way to protect the system from being a complete sham is to make sure that they have a good defense."[34] She would later play a key role making detainee policy in the Obama Justice Department.

While the ACLU and Human Rights Watch talked about putting on a strong defense, KSM was thinking about putting on a good show.

On June 5, 2008, KSM and four co-defendants—Ramzi bin al-Shibh, Walid bin Attash, Ali Abdul Aziz Ali, and Mustafa Ahmed al-Hawsawi—were brought before the military tribunal in Guantánamo.

It was supposed to be a simple arraignment—a hearing in which the defendants would plead guilty or not guilty and various procedural issues would be decided. Instead it was a circus.

When Judge Ralph Kohlmann asked KSM whether he agreed to be represented by the lawyers present, KSM objected. Because he recognized only Sharia law, he would not have any lawyer who would invoke any other legal code. Instead he wanted to represent himself—much as he had in Greensboro, North Carolina, in 1985.

It was the first time the public had a look at KSM since his 2003 capture. He appeared very different than the furry fat man in bedclothes. In his years in captivity, he had grown a long gray beard, which was brushed straight for his moment in court. He looked visibly older and thinner and wore military-issue eyeglasses. He had carefully cultivated his appearance; it was as if he were an extra from *Lawrence of Arabia* rather than a globetrotting twentieth-century terrorist. He wanted to appeal to viewers of the Arab television networks, which were in Guantánamo alongside their American counterparts.

When Judge Kohlmann warned him that he faced execution if convicted, KSM couldn't have been happier: "Yes, that is what I wish. I wish to be martyred. I will, God willing, have this, by you."[35]

KSM immediately made the claim that he had been tortured, knowing full well that that would touch off a media feeding frenzy. "All of this has been taken under torturing," he said. "You know this very well."[36]

What this claim completely ignores is that KSM confessed again to the "clean team" in September 2006—and those confessions had been extracted without any coercion at all, let alone torture.

KSM's nephew Ali Abdul Aziz Ali spoke for the other defendants in declining legal assistance, saying, "The government is talking about lawyers free of charge. The government also tortured me free of charge all these years."

When Judge Kohlmann advised him that representing themselves was unwise, Ali shot back, "For me, this proceeding in its entirety is unwise."[37]

Only one of the five defendants, Mustafa Ahmed al-Hawsawi, had agreed to work with his military defense team. Yet when Hawsawi entered the courtroom, KSM heckled him, joined by bin al-Shibh, saying, "What, are you in the American army now?"

Hawsawi's lawyer, Major Jon Jackson, said his client changed his mind on the spot, telling the judge, "I want to defend myself, by myself."[38]

KSM and his co-defendants were clearly having a great time on the first day of their trial. Though the judge tried to keep the proceedings moving, KSM and his lawyers created constant distractions and delays. ACLU lawyers asked for time to talk to the defendants to persuade them they needed legal representation. KSM sang verses from the Koran, mocked the Arabic skills of the tribunal's interpreter, denounced "evil laws" in America about gay marriage and American law in general, saying it was "not the laws of God." He called the hearing "Inquisition Land."

KSM even demanded to see the courtroom sketch of him, claiming that the Geneva Conventions gave him the right to approve any images of himself before they were made public. Ultimately, he rejected the sketch because he didn't like how the artist had drawn his nose.[39]

KSM couldn't help smirking throughout the proceedings and was often seen chatting with his four co-defendants. The trial was likely the first time since 2003 that KSM had seen Ramzi bin al-Shibh, who'd served as a liaison between KSM and the 9/11 hijackers. It was also likely that this was the first time he had seen Walid bin Attash.

Through a soundproof window, some sixty journalists watched KSM and his co-defendants having a good time. The journalists and human-rights observers in the gallery occasionally laughed at KSM's antics,[40] yet reported his wild allegations in a neutral tone, as if the 9/11 mastermind had as much credibility as the president of the United States. These objective observers couldn't possibly say who was right and who was wrong.

The 9/11 families, who were seated alongside the journalists, were far from amused by KSM or the shameful behavior of the press.

When it came his turn to make mischief, Walid bin Attash asked Judge Kohlmann, "Will we be buried at Guantánamo or will our bodies be returned to our countries?" No one bothered to point out that Al Qaeda had done nothing to help return the bodies of victims of the 9/11 attacks to the 108 countries (besides the United States) that they'd come from. Doubtless, Judge Kohlmann thought that pointing this out would raise questions about his impartiality.

The circus atmosphere continued when the judge turned his

attention to Ramzi bin al-Shibh and advised him that execution was a likely outcome of a guilty verdict. Bin al-Shibh said he had wanted to pilot one of the 9/11 planes, adding, "I have been seeking martyrdom for five years! If this martyrdom happens today, I will welcome it."

He began to shout, "God is great! God is great! God is great!"[41]

The trial date was set months in the future in order to give the judge time to consider the various procedural motions raised by the accused and their civilian lawyers.

Shortly after, as KSM preened before cameras in Guantánamo and mocked his own trial, Eric Holder climbed onto a hotel podium. He was there to address the American Constitution Society, the liberal lawyers' alternative to the Federalist Society. In a wide-ranging speech, he dismissed the idea that there was a need to balance the rights of detainees against the right of the public to know about future terrorist plots. Instead, the future U.S. attorney general contended that providing increased rights and protections for the detainees would lead to increased safety for the American public. He criticized some of the measures that the Bush administration had taken as "excessive and unlawful." He added: "We owe the American people a reckoning."[42]

Apparently, Holder did not see any problem with KSM's media circus in Guantánamo. KSM had taken an arraignment, which usually takes minutes in civilian courts, and made it last hours. Yet there was nothing in Holder's speech to indicate that he had revised his view at all. He had his mind made up, and new evidence wasn't going to sway him.

Following his arraignment, KSM began to prepare for his upcoming trial. Prosecutors had pushed for a September 2008 court date,[43] but KSM and human-rights lawyers did everything they could to delay its start.

KSM's strategy turned on accusing the judge of "bias," based on his military record.

Ultimately, a new military judge would be appointed.

With the help of ACLU-supported counsel, KSM made a number

of other pretrial requests. These requests provided Judge Ralph Kohlmann with a real-world test of Eric Holder's idealism. KSM argued that he and other detainees were entitled to computer laptops to prepare for their own defense and at least twelve hours per day of battery power. He also demanded the right to access the Internet, a request that was denied on security grounds.[44]

Colonel Stephen Henley was the next judge to face KSM. When the December 8, 2008, hearing was called to order, Judge Henley read aloud a letter he had received from KSM. In the letter, KSM said he wanted to plead guilty. Henley accepted KSM's guilty plea. Next he ruled on a motion from defense attorneys, which contended that two of the defendants were not mentally competent to stand trial. When Henley ordered mental-competency hearings, as the procedure required, KSM objected. He wanted to withdraw his guilty plea until all defendants could plead together. The smirking mastermind had sprung his legal trap.

But KSM's antics did not stop there. KSM complained about the slow responses to his written requests. Then he dismissed his military lawyer, who was simply serving as a legal adviser, as KSM was still representing himself. Nevertheless, KSM said he could not abide the military lawyer, because he had served in Iraq and had therefore "killed Muslims." Of course, KSM himself was responsible for the deaths of hundreds of Muslims during his time in Al Qaeda, from the 1998 embassy bombings to the Bali bombings in 2002. Again, in the interest of impartiality, no one bothered to point this out.

For Maureen Santora, it was supposed to be the day on which she, at last, got justice for the loss of her son, New York City firefighter Christopher Santora. She had received special permission from the U.S. Department of Defense to travel to Guantánamo to watch the trial.

With President Obama's inauguration looming, both civilian lawyers and military prosecutors were seeking to slow down the military commission trying KSM and four other defendants—putting them at odds with the families of 9/11 victims.

Family members became increasingly irate that the military commissions might stop in the middle of the trial. "Though the wheels are grinding, they are turning here and this place must remain open and justice must be served," Andrew Arias told the Associated Press. Arias's brother Adam had been killed in the 9/11 attacks.[45]

The 9/11 families were shocked that the military prosecution team would be the ones seeking to delay the proceeding. But that is what happened.

Colonel Steven Henley said he would rule on the prosecution's motion to suspend the proceedings after seeking guidance from the chain of command—meaning Defense Secretary Robert Gates and ultimately the president of the United States.

KSM himself did not want the trial to be halted. "We should continue so we don't go backward," he told the judge.[46]

The Obama administration didn't agree.

They didn't just go backward; they went round and round.

On his first day in office, President Obama signed Executive Order 13491, which immediately halted all military commissions—including the trial of KSM.

In fact, it seemed as if President Obama and Eric Holder, his nominee for the post of attorney general, were more interested in prosecuting the CIA officials who had interrogated KSM than in prosecuting KSM for the murder of three thousand Americans.

During Holder's Senate confirmation hearings, several senators sought reassurance from him that he wouldn't prosecute CIA officials for doing their duty. Holder danced. Senator Orrin Hatch asked Holder directly whether he would honor the certifications of his predecessor protecting CIA officers from any liability resulting from terror interrogations.

> **HATCH:** OK. So, if confirmed as attorney general, you will honor the certifications by Attorney General Mukasey?
>
> **HOLDER:** Yes, I believe that we would. Obviously, we have to look at if there are changed circumstances, if there is some basis to change that determination. But in the absence of that, I don't think we would.

HATCH: Well, thank you. There have been numerous calls for prosecution of various individuals, ranging from the vice president to attorneys at the Office of Legal Counsel, for their support or approval of the Terrorist Surveillance Program and the CIA's interrogation and detention program. Now, if confirmed as the attorney general, do you intend to undertake, order or support a criminal investigation of those individuals, including those individuals at the Office of Legal Counsel, who were involved in drafting legal opinions on these matters? Or are you willing to acknowledge that there can be differences of opinion, but they acted in accordance with their best good faith efforts under the circumstances at the time?

HOLDER: Well, senator, no one is above the law. And . . .

HATCH: I'll agree with that.

HOLDER: We will follow the evidence, the facts, the law, and let that take us where it should. But I think President-elect Obama has said it well. We don't want to criminalize policy differences that might exist between the outgoing administration and the administration that is about to take over. We certainly don't want to do that.

HATCH: But would you consider these policy differences, or policy decisions?

HOLDER: Well, one of the things I think I'm going to have to do is to become more familiar with what happened that led to the implementation of these policies. I've not been read into a variety of things that I will be exposed to, should I become attorney general. And that would, I think, better inform any decision that I would make in that regard.

HATCH: OK.[47]

Privately, Holder was more directly reassuring to concerned senators. In closed-door meetings in Senate offices, several senators had asked Holder about investigating CIA interrogators and prosecuting them for their use of "enhanced interrogation techniques." Holder specifically promised the senators that he would not mount investigations and pledged that there would be no prosecutions.[48]

Holder's actions belied his promises. Shortly after he was confirmed as attorney general, Holder set the wheels in motion for prosecuting CIA officials. Holder recounted to *Newsweek* how he'd spent weeks reviewing reports from the interrogations of detainees at CIA "black sites" and said it "turned my stomach." He became certain that the public would support investigating the CIA if they knew what he knew.

He pushed for President Obama to release a series of secret memos outlining Bush-era interrogation policies.[49]

Meanwhile, Holder pursued civilian trials for the detainees, including KSM. But preparing for civilian trials proved to be a bureaucratic nightmare. Amy Jeffress, Attorney General Holder's national security adviser, announced the establishment of three different task forces to review the cases of KSM and other detainees. It appeared as if the Bush administration had done nothing to prepare the cases for civilian trials, Jeffress complained. "There was no file for each detainee," she told *The New Yorker*'s Jane Mayer. "The information was scattered all over the government. You'd look at what the Department of Defense had, and it was something, but, as a prosecutor, it wasn't what you would like to see as evidence." The Bush administration "hadn't planned on prosecuting anyone. Instead, it was 'let's take a shortcut and put them in Guantánamo.'"[50]

Obama administration officials, including Jeffress, refused to consider the possibility that the Bush administration had honestly weighed the benefits and costs of civilian terror trials and concluded that they were unworkable and, in good faith, had gone with military commissions. Instead Jeffress and others presumed that their predecessors had simply made a blind ideological choice. But now that they themselves had to make an evaluation of the merits of civilian trials, the practical difficulties were slowly beginning to emerge.

Some Obama administration officials hoped to avoid the difficulty of choosing between military commissions and civilian trials by transferring the Guantánamo detainees to other countries. But this, too, proved to be far more difficult than officials initially anticipated. Few countries wanted to take the detainees without receiving something in return.

The Maldives agreed to take a handful of detainees in exchange for millions of dollars of aid from the International Monetary Fund. Yemen refused to take its own citizens, who were held at Guantánamo, without receiving millions of dollars per detainee. Other nations, like China, were ruled out as potential places to send detainees for "human-rights reasons." China had executed several Guantánamo detainees. Syria was disqualified for the same reason.

The Obama administration was quickly learning that, far from believing that a great injustice had been done to their own citizens by holding them indefinitely at Guantánamo, virtually all foreign nations considered detention to be a benefit of sorts—it spared them the cost of guarding these dangerous men.[51]

No foreign officials believed the liberal talking point that the detainees were largely innocents swept up in a dragnet by overzealous CIA officials. Obama's chief of staff, Rahm Emanuel, soon went to war with Eric Holder over his plans to prosecute CIA officers and to hold civilian trials for detainees, like KSM, in New York. Holder still wanted to prosecute CIA officials who had interrogated Khalid Shaikh Mohammed and other high-value detainees, while Emanuel feared the political ramifications of antagonizing the CIA. "Didn't he get the memo that we are not re-litigating the past?"[52]

While playing hardball with the CIA interrogators, whose work had saved hundreds of lives, Holder sought to extend every legal courtesy to KSM and other high-value detainees, who had repeatedly confessed to joyfully mass-murdering thousands of civilians. Holder was still pushing ahead on civilian trials for Guantánamo detainees, the foremost of which was KSM.

But the Obama Justice Department was already having trouble in the civilian courts. Lawyers for the detainees, some backed by the ACLU, were winning the right to habeas corpus hearings, and other liberal groups were making legal challenges on torture and detainee mistreatment. Some detainee lawyers were demanding the right to documents regarding detainee interrogation and treatment that had been drafted during the Bush years. These legal challenges, which had produced a lot of partisan glee while Bush was president, were now devouring thousands of man-hours at the Obama Justice Department. One Justice Department insider described the situation to *The New Yorker* this way: "We were buried in an avalanche of shit."[53]

At the same time, the feud between Eric Holder and Rahm Emanuel intensified. In April 2009, they were arguing about the release of four secret Bush-era memos that outlined interrogation procedures.

Holder wanted the memos released, because he was sure the public would be outraged and demand that the CIA officers responsible for interrogating KSM be prosecuted. It was his ace in the hole. Emanuel opposed releasing the memos, but was politically savvy enough to know that the memos wouldn't drive public opinion one way or the other.

Eventually President Obama agreed to release the memos and had Rahm Emanuel, of all people, appear on the ABC Sunday program *This Week With George Stephanopoulos* to declare that there would be no prosecutions of CIA officers who had acted in good faith.

In his statement announcing the release of the memos, President Obama carefully explained that it had been Holder's decision. Yet the president agreed with Rahm Emanuel substantively: "This is a time for reflection, not retribution."

While critics soon dubbed these the "torture memos," they produced little public outcry outside of liberal precincts. Interestingly, the memos outline an interrogation process that exactly matches what Al Qaeda training manuals taught captured operatives to expect, including the key fact that Americans would be afraid to harm them.

Attorney General Holder continued to barrel ahead in his quest for civilian trials for KSM and other detainees. When the Justice Department announced that it would put Ahmed Ghailani on trail for his role in bombing two U.S. embassies and killing 224 people, Holder boldly told the press: "The Justice Department has a long history of securely detaining and successfully prosecuting terror suspects through the criminal justice system, and we will bring that experience to bear in seeking justice in this case."[54]

The prosecution of Ghailani would ultimately backfire and raise new questions about the possibility of prosecuting terrorists in civilian courts. In October 2010, a New York jury would find him guilty of only a single count.

Privately, prosecutors would complain that a key witness had been excluded and, if he had not been, Ghaliani would have been found guilty on more than two hundred counts. Perhaps. But the exclusion of key testimony is always a risk in civilian trials—and one of the central reasons that they rarely work in terror cases.

In the summer of 2009, KSM continued his propaganda war against the United States. This time he cleverly used the International Red Cross. KSM spent hours posing for photos taken by a Red Cross photographer. The snapshots were supposed to reassure his family that he was in good health. After the photos were distributed to KSM's family, it took only days for them to appear on jihadi Web sites worldwide. A real propaganda coup.

Meanwhile, Holder had not given up on his plans to prosecute CIA officials for interrogating KSM or his aim of trying KSM in a civilian court, preferably in Manhattan.

Holder had been agitating for months to release the CIA's Inspector General Report. In its phonebook-size tome was a hidden bombshell: CIA interrogators had told KSM they would kill his children if another attack took place. Holder was certain that this would finally propel public outrage against the CIA. Again, he was wrong. The public shrugged. Mass murderers sometimes get threatened, the public concluded.

Holder continued to misjudge public opinion and the views of key politicians. He met with New York Mayor Michael Bloomberg and

New York Senator Chuck Schumer on November 11, 2009, to brief them on his plans to try KSM and other Al Qaeda terrorists in a Lower Manhattan federal courthouse. He believed he had their support.

Two days later, Holder held a press conference announcing plans to try KSM in New York.

At first, there was little public reaction. Yet opposition was slowly building; 9/11 family members staged demonstrations in December 2009.

At the end of January 2010, Mayor Bloomberg and Senator Schumer came out publicly against trying any Al Qaeda leaders in New York City. The mayor cited New York Police Department cost estimates showing that the city would have to pay almost $1 billion in overtime for police and the concern about blocking Lower Manhattan's narrow streets for more than a year. But everyone knows the real reason: public opinion has shifted overwhelmingly against civilian trials of terrorists in their midst.

At Rahm Emanuel's urging, President Obama publicly ordered the Justice Department to find a different venue to try KSM and other terrorists.

As the warm tropical breezes waft through the egg-crate-shaped bars of his Guantánamo prison cell, KSM is having the time of his life. For more than two years, he has humiliated U.S. military officers and other government officials, reducing every legal opportunity to a stand-up comedy routine. To those who know him well, it is reminiscent of his campus comedy skits, where he would imitate everyone from John Belushi to Hosni Mubarak. Mocking American justice certainly has its propaganda value for Al Qaeda operatives worldwide, but for KSM it is also fun. He is a performer who revels in his brief hours upon the stage, strutting and fretting for the world's attention, but, as the Bard tells us, KSM's act "is a tale told by an idiot, full of sound and fury, signifying nothing."[55]

While he claims that he has been tortured and uses this bogus claim to poke an accusing finger at the United States, he has no objections to torturing prisoners. He freely admits to torturing Daniel Pearl and, by implication, many others.

He objects to the lack of due "process of law," but has spent nearly every waking moment of his adult life plotting murder and mayhem against a world that has done him no wrong.

He dismisses the legal advisers supplied by the U.S. military on the grounds that they have indirectly been responsible for the deaths of innocent Muslims in Iraq and Afghanistan, while he has been directly and joyfully involved in the killings of hundreds of Muslims—from East Africa to the East River.

Citing the Geneva Conventions, he demanded the right to approve sketches of himself by the courtroom artist, but he thought nothing of releasing the video of Daniel Pearl's horrifying beheading without so much as a moment's warning to Pearl's family.

While denouncing the "evil laws" of the United States and its legal protections for minorities (such as homosexuals), he sought protection under those very same laws as an embattled and unpopular minority.

While the credulous may be taken in by his act and the cynical may pretend to be similarly bewitched, in the end his claims will not move any judge or juror toward leniency. They are empty and only meant to provide more time for KSM to perform.

Someday KSM may get his wish and be put to death, adding the exclamation point of martyrdom to his terrorist career.

But for now the Americans are giving him everything that he wants. Still, nearly ten years after the September 11 attacks took almost three thousand lives, no one has held the mastermind accountable.

Two years into his presidency, Obama has failed to close Guantánamo or bring KSM into a civilian court. Nor has the great orator managed to shift public opinion into believing that either one of these two goals is desirable. While KSM may be getting what he wants, President Obama decidedly is not.

Yet Obama hasn't given up hope. Eric Holder continues as his attorney general, and he continues to insist that civilian trials of terrorists will begin shortly. Holder has said he is "close to a decision" on where to try KSM as recently as a November 10, 2010, press conference.[56] Holder told *USA Today* that he "still believes his decision to try Mohammed and his alleged accomplices in a New York federal court was the correct one."[57] Holder also continues to believe that KSM and other terrorists are no worse than common criminals and deserve at least the same level of legal protection. In congressional testimony on March 17, 2010, Holder said: "These defendants, many of whom are charged with murder, would be treated just like any other murder defendants. The question is: Are they being treated the way any other murderer would be? They have the same rights Charles Manson would have."[58]

Holder succeeded in persuading the Pentagon to drop all charges against KSM and others in the hopes of clearing the decks for a civilian trial. The charges were dropped "without prejudice" in order to preserve the possibility of returning to military tribunals if Holder's crusade for civilian trials is ultimately defeated.

Still, in a nod to political reality, the Obama administration has admitted to drafting an executive order formalizing indefinite detention without trial for KSM and other Al Qaeda leaders at Guantánamo.

At the same time, Obama continues to recruit critics of his current detention policy for high-ranking posts. When the U.S. Senate objected to the nomination of James Cole as deputy attorney general, Obama put him in place anyway, on New Year's Eve 2010, using a maneuver known as a "recess appointment." Recess appointments, a creature of nineteenth-century legislative practice, allow presidents to appoint officials for up to one year while the Senate is out of session. The Senate's concerns about Cole were well-founded. On the one-year anniversary of the September 11 attacks, he'd written an op-ed contending that terrorists were no more than common criminals, and therefore entitled to the same legal protections. Now Cole will be in charge of writing the rules for the military tribunals that may try KSM and other terrorists.

President Obama continues to complain about congressional restrictions that bar the transfer of Guantánamo terrorists to the United States, such as House Resolution 1755, which was enthusiastically passed by large majorities of both parties in both houses of Congress. And, when asked, the president still worries more about the due-process rights of confessed terrorists than the aching need for closure felt by thousands of American families who lost loved ones on September 11, 2001.

KSM couldn't be happier.

13

Aftermath

Adel, Saif al-—May also be known as Mohammed Ibrahim Makkawi, a former Egyptian military officer who revealed the identity of one of KSM's accomplices in the Manila Air plot. Thought to be hiding in Iran.

Attash, Tawfiq bin (Khallad)—Now being held at Guantánamo Bay, Cuba.

bin Laden, Osama—The archterrorist is still at large.

Bybee, Jay—The co-author of the so-called torture memos is now a federal judge on the United States Court of Appeals for the Ninth Circuit.

Clarke, Richard A.—Former counterterrorism coordinator in the National Security Council. Retiring from the government in 2003, he became the bestselling author of *Against All Enemies*. He is also the founder of Good Harbor Consulting.

Clinton, Bill—The former U.S. president is currently the head of the William J. Clinton Foundation, a global nonprofit that supports various programs worldwide.

Faile, Garth—He still teaches chemistry at Chowan, which is now known as Chowan University. He was honored as teacher of the year in 2009.

Fouda, Yosri—The Al Jazeera correspondent who interviewed KSM in Pakistan now hosts a show on the Cairo-based ONTV network.

Freeh, Louis—Director of the FBI from 1993 to 2001; now founder and managing partner of Freeh Group International.

Gilani, Mubarak Ali Shah—The sixth Sultan Ul Faqr, also known as "Imam El-Sheikh Syed Mubarik Ali Shah Jilani El-Hashimi, al-Hasani wal-Husaini," Gilani is the radical cleric behind the Pakistani group called al-Fuqra, a paramilitary organization of mostly African American Muslims based in Pakistan and the United States. He is linked to "shoe bomber" Richard Reid.

Holder, Eric—The Justice Department official who wanted to move the Manila Air case to Washington, D.C., continues as attorney general of the United States.

Ijaz, Mansoor—The New York financier who introduced Daniel Pearl to the jihadis in Pakistan who ultimately kidnapped and killed the reporter. He still runs Crescent Investment. He divides his time between Monaco, Switzerland, and New York.

Janjalani, Abdurajak—The founder of the Abu Sayyaf terror group in the Philippines, he was killed in a shoot-out with Philippine troops in December 1998.[1]

John Paul II, Pope—The pontiff died a natural death on April 2, 2005.

Khalifa, Jamal—While visiting a gemstone mine in Sakamilko, Madagascar, the onetime "best friend" of Osama bin Laden and mentor to KSM was gunned down by more than a score of armed men on January 31, 2007. He died on the scene.

Khattab, Ibn al- (Samir Saleh Abdullah Al-Suwailem)—This Saudi-born militant ran an Islamist terror group in Chechnya. A veteran of wars in Afghanistan, Tajikistan, and Bosnia-Herzegovina (with the backing of Iranian intelligence), Khattab had maimed his right hand while trying to detonate a homemade bomb. He was killed during the night of March 19–20, 2002. Rumored more than once to have been killed, it appears Khattab was finally murdered by a poisoned letter from the Russian Federal Security Service, the successor organization of the KGB. Khattab's Arab mujahideen fighters earned a fearless and fearsome reputation.

Khawaja, Khalid—Mansoor Ijaz's point man, who had ties to Pakistan's military intelligence agency, Osama bin Laden, and the Taliban. He joined the Pakistani Air Force as a pilot in 1971. He was transferred to the ISI in 1985, where he was tasked to work with radical Muslim groups. He quickly developed relationships with Abdullah Azzam, Abdul Rasul Sayyaf, and Osama bin Laden. He cemented these ties by fighting alongside the jihadis against the Soviets in the battle of Jaji, in the White Mountains of Afghanistan, southeast of Tora Bora, in 1987. In an ill-fated venture in 2005, he attempted to negotiate peace with the Taliban. Like Daniel Pearl, Khawaja was kidnapped by terrorists who believed he was a spy. Seized by a Taliban remnant calling itself the Asian Tigers, he was murdered in April 2010 in Pakistan's North-West Frontier Province.

Martinez, Deuce—After being outed by *The New York Times*, the interrogator has left the CIA and currently works for the spy agency as an independent contractor.

Masri, Abu Hafs al- (Mohammed Atef)—One of bin Laden's closest advisers, he helped get the 9/11 attack plan approved by Osama bin Laden. He was killed by an American air strike in November 2001, most likely from a Predator drone plane. Shortly before his death,

Atef's daughter married bin Laden's son, Mohammed. At the time, Atef was the head of Al Qaeda's military wing. His death cleared the way for KSM's promotion.

Mohammed, Ali—The friend of el Sayyid Nosair who handed him top-secret U.S. Army training manuals while serving as an instructor for the U.S. Army at Fort Bragg, North Carolina, from 1986 to 1989; his involvement with Al Qaeda deepened in the Clinton years. After 1991, he made several trips to Sudan to train members of Osama bin Laden's entourage in small-arms tactics. He was arrested in 1998 and convicted, and is currently serving time at a U.S. federal correctional facility.

Mohammed, Khalid Shaikh—The confessed September 11 mastermind is in an American detention facility in Guantánamo Bay, Cuba, awaiting trial.

Mukasey, Michael—The former judge who presided over the Manila Air and Blind Sheikh cases went on to become the U.S. attorney general and later a partner at Debevoise & Plimpton, LLP.

Musharraf, Pervez—Coming to power by military coup in 1999, Musharraf served as Pakistan's president until his departure in 2008. During the war on terror, he walked a perilous line between working with the United States and not antagonizing religious extremists and Taliban supporters in Pakistan. Musharraf survived at least four assassination attempts.

O'Neill, John—Was America's top anti-terrorism expert. While with the FBI, he was deeply involved with the tracking and capture of Ramzi Yousef and was one of the loud early warning voices trying to focus government attention on Al Qaeda, its people, methods, and goals. He was killed trying to help rescue victims at the World Trade Center on September 11, 2001.

Padilla, José—The man who plotted to detonate a "dirty bomb" at KSM's request is now in a U.S. government supermax prison in Florence, Colorado.

Pearl, Mariane—The widow of Daniel Pearl now lives in Paris. She has not married again.

Rahman, Sheikh Omar Abdel—Known universally to the tabloid press as the "Blind Sheikh," the Egyptian cleric has juvenile diabetes that has left him blind since his first year. The spiritual guide to two noteworthy Egyptian terrorist outfits, the Jihad Group and Gamma Islamiyya (Egyptian Islamic Jihad), he is now serving a life sentence in an American prison following his conviction for plotting to blow up the Lincoln and Holland tunnels, the United Nations headquarters, and several other New York landmarks.

Revell, Oliver "Buck"—The former FBI counterterrorism chief currently serves as the president of the Revell Group International, Inc., global business and security consultants, in Texas.

Salameh, Mohammed—The driver of the Ryder truck for the 1993 World Trade Center bombing who later tried to claim back the rental deposit is now in a U.S. government supermax prison in Florence, Colorado.

Sheikh, Ahmed Omar Saeed—The British-Pakistani kidnapper of Daniel Pearl, Omar Sheikh soon found that his hope for a light sentence, given his service to Pakistan intelligence services, was a false hope. Sentenced to death in 2002, he has filed an appeal. His last chapter shows that history likes to follow tragedy with farce. Shortly after the hotel bombings in Bombay, Omar Sheikh phoned Pakistani President Zadari, pretending to be the prime minister of India. As "India's Prime Minister," he threatened war—forcing Pakistan to scramble military jets and put its ground forces on high alert. Omar Sheikh hoped to provoke war, and possibly a nuclear exchange, between India and Pakistan. When the hoax was discovered, Omar Sheikh's cell phone was taken away by his guards. Critics wondered why the kidnapper enjoyed so many unusual privileges, such as cell phones, in the first place.

Shibh, Ramzi bin al-—KSM's henchman was captured in Karachi, Pakistan, on September 11, 2002, and is now in American custody at Guantánamo Bay, Cuba.

Soufan, Ali—A former FBI interrogator who interviewed KSM, he is now CEO of The Soufan Group, in New York.

Turabi, Hassan al-—The former speaker of the Sudanese parliament who welcomed bin Laden to Sudan in 1991 was arrested in Khartoum in mid-May 2010 but released on July 1, 2010. The joke in Khartoum: "Turabi's prison cell has a revolving door."

Turki al-Faisal, Prince—Former head of Saudi intelligence. Also served as the Saudi ambassador to the United Kingdom and, later, to the United States. Now with the King Faisal Center for Research and Islamic Studies, in Riyadh.

White, Mary Jo—The no-nonsense federal prosecutor is now a partner at Debevoise & Plimpton, LLP.

Yasin, Abdul Rahman—The 1993 World Trade Center bomber who fled to Iraq. He died under mysterious circumstances in 2003.

Yoo, John—The primary author of the so-called torture memos is now a professor of law at the University of California's Berkeley School of Law.

Yousef, Ramzi—The 1993 bomber of the World Trade Center lives in a U.S. government supermax prison in Florence, Colorado. In the one hour of human contact he is permitted every day, he is often allowed within ten feet of the Unabomber—close enough to shout a conversation.[2] No one has revealed what these mass murderers say to each other, but guards confirmed that they do talk in short bursts.

Yusufzai, Rahimullah—The Pakistani journalist is a senior editor and Peshawar bureau chief with *The News.*

Zitawi, Sammy—Khalid Shaikh Mohammed's Kuwait-born classmate at North Carolina Agricultural and Technical State University now owns the Great American Food Store on Patterson Avenue in Winston-Salem, North Carolina.

Zubaydah, Abu—KSM's right-hand man in the September 11 attacks, he is now in an American detention facility in Guantánamo Bay, awaiting trial.

Acknowledgments

This book would not have been possible without the help and encouragement of many dedicated and thoughtful people.

Without the ceaseless effort of my agent, Richard Pine, of Inkwell Management, this book would not have been published. I would also like to thank Nathaniel Jacks and Jenny Witherell at Inkwell.

At Sentinel, my publisher, I would like to thank Adrian Zackheim, who saw the importance of this project immediately and was immensely supportive throughout the writing and editing process. I'd also like to thank Jillian Gray, Will Weisser, and Amanda Pritzker.

Lisa Downey Merriam, who swooped in at the last minute to save the day, spent many hours with LexisNexis.

My researcher, Martin Morse Wooster, who spent countless hours in the special-collection rooms of libraries finding documents and foreign-news accounts that are not on LexisNexis.

My interview booker, Heather L. Smith, who used her well-honed skills as a radio and television producer to track down and schedule countless interviews for me.

I am also indebted to Duke Cheston, who managed to pry old documents out of two North Carolina courthouses, and Daniel Davis, who provided valuable intelligence on the inner workings of North Carolina A&T, where KSM studied engineering.

I'd also like to thank Janet Hamlin for supplying illustrations she made of Khalid Shaikh Mohammed during his 2008 trial in

Guantánamo Bay, Cuba, and also for her recollections of those events. She can be reached at janet.hamlin@gmail.com.

I'd also like to thank Nina Rosenwald, for her constant encouragement and many lunches and dinners.

I'd also like to thank Daniel Pipes and the rest of the Middle East Forum for generous grants that enabled me to complete my reporting.

In North Carolina, I'd like to thank John Taylor and Josh Barker at Chowan University, and Mable Springfield Scott at North Carolina A&T.

In Paris, I'd like to thank Jean-Charles Brisard, who shared a treasure trove of documents. I'd also like to thank Jean-Louis Bruguière, who prosecuted most of the major terrorism cases in France over the past two decades, including cases related to KSM.

Additionally, I would like to thank Debra Burlingame, Michael Shulan, and Katie Edgerton at the September 11 Memorial Museum Foundation.

I would also like to thank Richard Perle, Daveed Gartenstein-Ross, Gawain Towler (who introduced me to a very helpful source in London), Taiseer Saleh (Yemen's military attaché in Washington, D.C.), Ahmed Charai in Casablanca, Joseph Braude (whose knowledge of the Arabic language and Islamic literature is peerless), Kate Brewster (for finding KSM's defense attorney and other helpful leads), Stephen Grey (the former head of the *Sunday Times* of London's investigative team, who shared many leads and contacts), Jeremy Slater (an indispensable help in Brussels), Rachel Ehrenfeld (who supplied an excellent source in Afghanistan), Stefan Jacobs, Keya Dashtara, Sue Saadawi, Jacki Pick (who knows her way around Capitol Hill), Joseph Szlavik (for his help with French and U.S. intelligence sources), Jim Robbins (for his encyclopedic knowledge of all things Pentagon), Philip Zelikow (the former staff director of the 9/11 Commission), Heather Higgins, and Aylana Meisel, an expert in terror financing, who knew where many of the bodies were buried.

A Note on Sources and Methods

Inevitably, when writing about a terrorist mastermind, there are two large difficulties. First, access to the subject, his comrades, and his close relatives (many of whom are themselves either wanted men or in the custody of some military or intelligence agency) is impossible, and many of those who will talk (intelligence operatives, military officers, presidential appointees) say things that cannot be independently verified. In addition, many sources insist on being anonymous, for professional or personal reasons.

Add a controversial trial and an increasingly bitter divide between our nation's two major political parties—a zigzagging fault line that runs through Washington and the minds of many of the participants in the events that I have covered here—and the reader soon sees how daunting researching and reporting a book like this one can be.

It may be decades before key documents are declassified and telling memoirs from retired government officials are written. So much of this book remains subject to revision.

Fortunately, many people agreed to sit for interviews and to supply documents—ranging from official reports to private notes—that enabled me to add tiles to this mosaic, to assemble a portrait of Khalid Shaikh Mohammed. I appreciate their time and trust.

My approach was to search out everyone who met, worked with, captured, interrogated, prosecuted, or made decisions about KSM or investigated his terrorist strikes. That produced a list of hundreds of potential sources—prisoners, police, soldiers, spies, diplomats, analysts, agents, operatives, bureaucrats, lawyers, prosecutors, judges, princes, kings, prime ministers, and presidential appointees—stretching over four continents. I talked to as many of them as I could.

I also interviewed experts who could provide perspective, analysis, and insight into events and participants. These professional observers include historians, man hunters, money trackers, intelligence analysts, and foreign correspondents. They, too, were spread across the globe—from Baghdad, Casablanca, and Paris to Brussels, London, and Washington.

"If you don't go, you don't know." It is an old saying in shoe-leather journalism. So, in the course of my interviews with police and other participants, I went to many of the places where KSM plotted. While I did go to Guantánamo Bay a few years ago, I was not able to see KSM there. I did not attempt to go back, given U.S. government restrictions. I did, however, talk to the civilian and military lawyers representing KSM and other Al Qaeda personnel, as well as some of the 9/11 family members who visited Guantánamo Bay.

While the bibliography contains an extensive list of primary source documents and books that I relied on, readers seeking more information should also consult (as I did) the CIA-run Open-Source Center (formerly the Foreign Broadcast Information Service, or FBIS) and the BBC Monitoring Service, which records and translates many radio and television reports from around the world.

I also wish to thank officials at the following embassies for assisting me in locating and contacting the appropriate persons in their countries.

Afghanistan: Adrienne Ross and Abuljalil Ghafoory, Media and Public Relations Department
Algeria: Nassima Holcine, Second Secretary
Bosnia and Herzegovina: Emin Cohodarevic, Attaché
Czech Republic: Daniel Novy, Press Secretary
France: Emmanuel Lenain, Press Counselor
Germany: Karl-Matthias Klause, Head of Press Section
India: Rahul Chhabra, Minister of Press, Information, and Culture

Indonesia: Devdy Risa, Third Secretary
Kuwait: Jasem al-Budaiwi
Pakistan: Nadeem Haider Kiani, Press Attaché and Media Spokesperson
Philippines: Gines Gallaga, Second Secretary and Consul
Qatar: Mohamed Kabir, Media Inquiries
Saudi Arabia: Nail Al-Jubeir, Director of Information
Spain: Almudena Rodriguez, Press Office
Syria: Ahmed Salkini, Press Secretary
Yemen: Taiseer Saleh, Defense Attaché

A number of current intelligence and military personnel—in the United States, Western Europe, the Middle East, central Asia, and Southeast Asia—were also interviewed but not listed here. They are not listed because they were interviewed on a not-for-attribution basis.

Any work of this kind naturally has to rely on such sources. Without anonymity, these sources would simply not talk to a reporter at all.

One major source of research material about Khalid Shaikh Mohammed is the Web site History Commons (historycommons.org). This crowd-sourced research tool is an invaluable source of citations about Khalid Shaikh Mohammed, Ramzi Yousef, and other key figures in the global war on terror—though it should be used with caution.

History Commons, however, could use an editor. Titles and authors of stories are routinely misattributed. For example, Robert I. Friedman wrote a very interesting account of the groups responsible for the 1993 World Trade Center bombing, which appeared in *New York* magazine in 1995. History Commons repeatedly says that this article appeared in *The New Yorker* (not *New York*), making it very hard to track down.

The New York Times also maintains an important online database of documents, including Department of Justice memos on interrogation practices.

LexisNexis and Factiva are the key databases to search. Factiva is generally better than Lexis, as it includes the *Wall Street Journal* and the *Financial Times*. But both need to be searched carefully. Either one, for example, will tell the reader that fewer than a dozen English-language articles mentioned Khalid Shaikh Mohammed prior to September 11, 2001, and none made the connection that KSM was the uncle of Ramzi Yousef. One must search under all variant spellings—and combinations of spellings—of Khalid Shaikh Mohammed's name. In some news accounts before 2003, he is known as simply "Khalid Shaikh."

The World News Connection is less well known than Lexis or Factiva but is nonetheless invaluable. Produced by the CIA's Foreign Broadcast Information Service, World News Connection includes many translations of articles from foreign newspapers, radio shows, and television shows. It is the primary source of translated articles from the Arab press. It's only available, in limited release, in some university libraries, such as the University of Maryland–College Park.

Most of the translations, however, are rough. Researchers need to search both under "Khalid" and "Khaled," and "Sheik," "Sheikh," "Shaykh," and "Shaikh"—and that's just for Khalid Shaikh Mohammed's first two names. The search engine for World News Connection is a strange beast. Sometimes identical search terms produce different results. Nonetheless, the World News Connection is the primary vehicle for the English-language reader to see what the Arab press is writing about terrorism.

The best source for documents about terrorists imprisoned at Guantánamo is the Torture Archive, established by the National Security Archive at George Washington University (gwu.edu/~nsarchiv). It currently comprises more than eighty thousand pages of documents about the war on terror. All of the publicly available documents about KSM's stay in Guantánamo are available from this site.

Trial transcripts are only partially available. Some of the documents from the trials related to the 1998 bombing of the embassies in Tanzania and Kenya are available on the Findlaw Web site (news.findlaw.com/cnn/docs/binladen). But the 1996 indictment of Khalid

Shaikh Mohammed, issued as part of this trial, does not appear to be publicly available.

Zacarias Moussaoui was tried in the U.S. District Court for the Eastern District of Virginia. That court has placed many nonclassified documents and trial transcripts online, including the numerous FAA bulletins and warnings issued after the collapse of Project Bojinka and testimonies of key government officials. Its Web site is vaed.uscourts.gov/notablecases/index.htm.

A larger compilation of related documents can be found on my Web site: www.richardminiter.com.

List of Aliases Used by KSM

Over the years, KSM adopted dozens of false identities.

Based on reports from the FBI, the CIA, Philippine intelligence, Afghan intelligence, Pakistan's Inter-Services Intelligence, France's Direction de la Surveillance du Territoire, Britain's MI-6, and the governments of Bosnia, the Czech Republic, Indonesia, and Malaysia, as well as published reports, here is perhaps the most complete list of his aliases:

Abdul Majid
Abdullah al-Fak'asi al-Ghamdior
Abdulrahman A. A. Alghamdi
Abu Khalid
Adam Ali
Ashraf Ahmed
Ashraf Refaat Nabith Henin
Babu Hamza
Fahd bin Abdallah bin Khalid
Hafiz
Hashim Abdulrahman
Hashim Ahmed
Khalid Abdul Wadood
Khalid al-Shaykh al-Ballushi
Khalid the Kuwaiti
Meer Akram
Mohammed Khalia al-Mana
Mohammed the Pakistani
Muk
Mukhtar al Baluchi
Mustaf Nasir
Salem Ali

Time Line

1965	▪ **April 24:** KSM born to Halema and Shaikh Mohammed Ali Dustin al-Balushi, an Islamist preacher. He grows up in Fahaheel, Kuwait.
1969	▪ KSM's father dies.
1979	▪ **February 1:** The first radical Islamic terror state, Iran, is born.
	▪ **February 14:** Jihadi extremists kidnap and kill Adolph Dubs, the U.S. ambassador to Afghanistan. There is no U.S. military response.
	▪ **November 4:** Ayatollah Khomeini declares war on the United States and seizes hostages in Tehran. There is no U.S. military response.
	▪ **November 20:** Islamist fundamentalists seize the Grand Mosque in Mecca, Saudi Arabia.
	▪ **December 25:** The Soviet Union invades Afghanistan.
1981	▪ KSM joins Muslim Brotherhood.
1982	▪ **December 6:** KSM's first passport issued, at the Pakistani embassy in Kuwait City.
1983	▪ KSM graduates from all-boys high school in Fahaheel.
1984	▪ **January 10:** KSM attends Chowan College, in Murfreesboro, North Carolina.
	▪ **Summer:** KSM transfers to North Carolina Agricultural and Technical State University, in Greensboro, North Carolina.
1986	▪ **December 18:** After attending NC A&T with Ramzi Yousef's brother, KSM graduates with a degree in mechanical engineering.
1987	▪ **Mid-1987:** KSM trains at Sada training camp, in Afghanistan.

1988

- Zahid, KSM's brother, is head of the Pakistani branch of Mercy International, which supports Muslim militants fighting in Bosnia and Afghanistan.
- **July:** Ramzi Yousef first visits Peshawar on a summer break from college.
- **August 20:** Al Qaeda ("The Base") is formed by Osama bin Laden in Afghanistan.
- **September 10:** The work of Al Qaeda commences, with a group of fifteen "brothers."

1989

- **By 1989:** KSM works at Abdul Rasul Sayyaf's University of Dawa al-Jihad and helps recruit fighters in Afghanistan for Sayyaf's faction.
- **February 15:** Soviet army retreats from Afghanistan.
- **Spring:** KSM's brother Abed is killed by a bomb.
- **November 24:** Abdullah Azzam is assassinated.
- Osama bin Laden returns to Saudi Arabia.

1991

- Yousef returns to Peshawar.
- **April:** Bin Laden flees Saudi Arabia for Sudan.
- **Summer:** Yousef makes the first of several trips to the Philippines.
- KSM goes to the Philippines, where he trains members of the militant groups Abu Sayyaf and the Moro Islamic Liberation Front in bomb making and assassination. KSM's work is discovered, and he's forced to run.

1992

- KSM helps run nonprofit that is assisting in terror operations in Peshawar and Jalalabad.
- While fighting alongside mujahideen in Bosnia, KSM works for Egypitska Pomoc, an Egyptian aid group in Zenica, Bosnia, later becoming one of its directors in 1995.
- **September 1:** Yousef arrives at JFK airport in U.S., seeking political asylum.
- **November 3:** KSM wires money to Mohammed Salameh to help fund Yousef's bombing of World Trade Center.

1993

- **January 25:** A lone gunman, Pakistani Mir Aimal Kasi, attacks CIA headquarters in Langley, Virginia.
- **February 26:** World Trade Center is bombed by Ramzi Yousef.
- **March 31:** Yousef is indicted for his participation in the World Trade Center bombing.

- **Twice in 1993:** KSM summons U.S.-trained Kuwaiti pilot Abdul Hakim Murad to Pakistan; Murad suggests that jumbo jets be used to destroy landmark buildings.
- **Spring:** U.S. investigators raid Zahid Shaikh Mohammed's house in search of Yousef, finding evidence linking Zahid, bin Laden, KSM, and government officials close to Pakistani prime minister Nawaz Sharif.
- **July:** KSM funds assassination attempt against Pakistani prime minister Benazir Bhutto; Yousef and Murad attempt to carry out the plan, but the bomb detonates too early, injuring Yousef.
- **September:** Yousef taken to emergency room in Karachi, Pakistan, due to injuries from liquid bombs.

1994

- Yousef and KSM test airport security on separate flights in the Philippines and across East Asia.
- **Spring:** Yousef moves to Thailand, where he plots to blow up Israeli embassy.
- **June:** Yousef, with his father and younger brother (Abdul Muneim), bomb the shrine of the Prophet Mohammed's grandson, Reza, in Mashad, close to the Afghan border in eastern Iran, to punish Shia Muslims.
- **August:** KSM arrives in the Philippines on a Pakistani passport issued in Abu Dhabi on July 21, under his full name, Khalid Shaikh Mohammed Ali Dustin al-Balushi; he lives at the Tiffany Mansion Condominiums with Yousef.
- **October:** KSM begins to build a cell to carry out plan to destroy key buildings; recruits Murad and Yousef; chooses to base cell in Malate district of Manila.
- **December 1:** In a test run, Yousef bombs the Greenbelt Theater, in the Philippines.
- **December 8:** KSM and Yousef move into Dona Josefa apartments in Malate, metro Manila; the planning for the Manila Air plot begins.
- **December 11:** Yousef boards Philippine Airlines flight 434, assembles bomb in bathroom, and deplanes in Cebu; bomb detonates on last leg of flight to Tokyo, killing one and injuring eleven others.
- **December 26:** Abdul Hakim Murad arrives in Manila; he's arrested at the Dona Josefa apartments two weeks later.

1995

- **January 7:** Manila Air plot, a plot to blow up eleven U.S. airplanes, is uncovered by officials when a fire breaks out in Manila's Josefa apartments.
- **January:** Yousef flees to Islamabad, possibly with KSM.
- **January 12–16:** KSM had planned to assassinate Pope John Paul II, President Bill Clinton, and Philippine president Fidel Ramos in this period; instead, he is on the run.
- **February 7:** Ramzi Yousef is arrested in Islamabad, Pakistan, at the Su-Casa Guest House; KSM boldly gives interview to the press, claiming to be an eyewitness.
- **October:** KSM is cornered in apartment building in Qatar; FBI has to wait for valid extradition order; meanwhile, KSM gets away because Qatar's minister of religious affairs tips him off.
- **October 20:** KSM possibly helps with the revenge bombing of a police station in Rijeka, Croatia. The timing device of the bomb, a modified Casio watch, closely resembled those used by KSM and Yousef in the Philippines.
- KSM visits Yemen, Malaysia, and Sudan—where he fails to meet bin Laden; in Sudan he meets Mohammed Atef, Al Qaeda's chief military official.
- **December:** KSM spends twenty days in Brazil, for mysterious reasons.

1996

- **January:** KSM indicted in the U.S. District Court for the Southern District of New York for his role in the Manila Air plot.
- **Early 1996:** FBI and Philippine authorities attempt to arrest KSM at Bandido's restaurant, in Manila, but the operation fails due to visibility of FBI and other agents; KSM again flees to Qatar.
- **May:** Sudan expels bin Laden; he returns to Afghanistan.
- **Mid-1996:** KSM outlines a plan to bin Laden that would become the 9/11 hijackings.
- **August 23:** Bin Laden declares war on U.S.
- **Late fall:** CIA receives reports that KSM is traveling in South America.
- The Taliban conquers Jalalabad and Kabul and ultimately takes control of Afghanistan.

1997

- **January:** KSM moves with his family from Iran to Karachi, Pakistan.

- KSM lives in Prague throughout much of 1997; takes identity of "Mustaf Nasir."

1998

- **January 8:** Mary Jo White, the U.S. attorney for New York's Southern District, unseals an indictment against KSM.
- **February 23:** Bin Laden and Ayman al-Zawahiri reunite and declare war on the United States again.
- **June:** KSM returns to Foz do Iguaçu, Brazil, supposedly to promote Konsojaya, a Malaysian company that funded Muslim rebels in Southeast Asia.
- Bin Laden requests that KSM move his family to Kandahar and formally join Al Qaeda.
- **August 7:** U.S. embassy bombings in Dar es Salaam and Nairobi kill 224 people, including twelve Americans.

1999

- **April:** Bin Laden summons KSM to Kandahar to tell him that Al Qaeda would support his proposal, which would henceforth be referred to as the "planes operation" within Al Qaeda.
- **Fall:** Hazmi, Mihdhar, Tawfiq bin Attash, and Abu Barra participate in elite training course at the Mes Aynak camp in Afghanistan. KSM teaches three of these men basic English words and phrases and how to read a phone book, make travel reservations, use the Internet, and encode communications.
- **November:** Bin Laden orders Nawaf al-Hazmi and Khalid al-Mihdhar to go to the U.S. and learn how to fly planes.
- **November:** Mohammed Atta, Ramzi bin al-Shibh, Marwan al-Shehhi, and Ziad al-Jarrah arrive in the Khaldan camp for a preliminary training course.
- **December:** Bin Attash tells KSM that on his reconnaissance mission, airline security checked him thoroughly.
- KSM plans another attack on the pope in Africa; this attack is thwarted only when the visit is canceled due to John Paul II's ill health.
- **December 3–31:** Millennium plot to attack U.S. and Israeli targets during millennium celebrations in Jordan.
- **Late 1999:** KSM sends Moussaoui to Malaysia for flight training.
- Ahmed Ressam captured while entering U.S. on a mission to blow up Los Angeles International Airport.

2000

- **Early 2000:** Al-Shehhi, Atta, and bin al-Shibh meet with KSM in Karachi for training.

- **January 5–8:** KSM and four key 9/11 hijackers meet in Kuala Lumpur, Malaysia.
- **January 15:** Al-Hazmi and al-Mihdhar arrive in Los Angeles and decamp to San Diego. They are the first of the 9/11 terrorists to arrive in the U.S.
- **April:** Bin Laden cancels East Asia portion of 9/11 operation.
- **Spring:** Bin Laden pressures KSM to launch the planes operation earlier than planned.
- **June:** Mihdhar abruptly returns to his family in Yemen, apparently without permission; KSM is very displeased and wants to remove him from the operation, but bin Laden intercedes and Mihdhar remains part of the plot.
- **September:** KSM meets Hani Hanjour, a future 9/11 hijacker, for the first time.
- **October 12:** USS *Cole* bombed in Aden, Yemen.
- **October:** Bin Laden appoints KSM to head all media operations for Al Qaeda.
- **December 2000–January 2001:** Abu Turab al-Urduni trains the ten "muscle" hijackers prior to their departure to the U.S.

2001

- **May 12:** Bin Laden pressures KSM to launch the planes operation on this date, exactly seven months after the *Cole* bombing in Yemen. KSM refuses.
- **Summer:** Faruq al-Tunisi, a pilot candidate for the second wave of attacks after 9/11, contacts KSM from Canada to back out of the operation.
- **June:** Mohammed Atef asks José Padilla to blow up apartment buildings in a major city using natural gas (this information would be revealed by KSM in 2003).
- **June:** KSM calls a cell phone held by a Belgian, Saber Mohammed, three times, believing he was acting as a messenger for Mosa Zi Zemmori and Driss Elatellah, two terror operatives.
- **June 12:** CIA report states that KSM is recruiting for bin Laden. The agency doesn't yet realize KSM's full role inside Al Qaeda.
- **June or July:** Bin Laden again pressures KSM to launch the attacks early, after he learns that Israeli prime minister Ariel Sharon would be visiting the White House then.
- **July:** Mohammed Atta meets Ramzi bin al-Shibh in Spain; Atta informs him of 9/11 targets, and bin al-Shibh tells KSM.

- **July 23:** KSM uses a travel agency to acquire a U.S. visa in Jeddah, Saudi Arabia, using an alias.
- **August:** KSM receives a courier from Germany, Zakariya Essabar, who gives him a letter advising him of the date of the 9/11 attacks. The information originated with Mohammed Atta.
- **August:** KSM advises bin al-Shibh to break contact with Moussaoui.
- **September 4:** Bush's National Security Council approves new presidential directive to disrupt Al Qaeda, including attacks inside Afghanistan.
- **September 10:** Deputy National Security Adviser Stephen Hadley orders CIA Director George Tenet to draft new authorities for covert action against Al Qaeda.
- **September 11:** Attacks on World Trade Center and Pentagon.
- **September 11–April 2003:** The CIA produces more than three thousand intelligence reports from detainees.
- **October 6:** American and British bombers launch their first attacks on Taliban positions.
- **October 7:** Bin Laden releases a prerecorded videotape boasting of Al Qaeda's successful operation.
- **Late 2001:** KSM becomes chief of operations for Al Qaeda; KSM hatches a plot to crash a hijacked airliner into Library Tower, in L.A.
- **December 3:** American bombers strike a cave complex at Tora Bora, and Afghan ground troops uncover more than a hundred bodies, eighteen of which are identified as top Al Qaeda lieutenants.
- **December 17:** Bin Laden writes about how he feels betrayed by the Muslims who fled in the battle of Tora Bora, a crushing loss for Al Qaeda.
- **December 22:** Richard Reid attempts to detonate a shoe bomb on Flight 63 from Paris to Miami.
- **December 28:** United Press International reports that the Singapore government, acting on intelligence gathered during U.S. special operations in Afghanistan, has arrested members of a terrorist cell with plans to attack Singapore's port.

2002

- **January 28:** Eric Holder, in an interview with CNN's Paula Zahn, says, "They [the 9/11 terrorists] are not entitled to the protection of the Geneva Convention. They are not prisoners of war," but criminals.

- **Early 2002:** KSM devises a plan to send José Padilla to set off bombs in high-rise apartment buildings in Chicago.
- **February 1:** KSM beheads Daniel Pearl in Karachi, Pakistan.
- **February:** CIA gets a lead on an Al Qaeda terrorist named Abu Zubaydah, a key KSM lieutenant.
- **March 2:** Operation Anaconda in Afghanistan begins. KSM escapes.
- **March 28:** Teams of Pakistani commandos simultaneously raid fourteen separate addresses that Zubaydah reportedly used; they find him in Faisalabad.
- **March–June:** The FBI's Ali Soufan interrogates Zubaydah.
- **April 11:** Al Qaeda bombs Djerba synagogue, in Tunisia, an attack that KSM planned.
- **May:** FBI access to high-value-detainee interrogations ends.
- **June:** KSM tells Al Jazeera that he heads Al Qaeda's military committee, a claim he later denies.
- **June:** A group of Al Qaeda operatives suspected of plotting raids on American and British ships and tankers passing through the Strait of Gibraltar is arrested by the Moroccan government.
- **September:** Pakistani police raid Karachi apartment, just missing KSM; Pakistan's Inter-Services Intelligence agency seizes KSM's two sons, Abed al-Khalid (age seven) and Yousef al-Khalid (nine).
- **September:** Al Qaeda operatives launch a KSM-planned attack on U.S. soldiers at Kuwait's Filka Island, killing one and injuring a second.
- **September 11:** Ramzi bin al-Shibh is captured in Karachi, Pakistan. At the time, he is in final stages of KSM's plot to bomb London's Heathrow Airport and Canary Wharf.
- **September 14:** Bin al-Shibh is turned over to U.S.
- KSM plans to hijack planes from mostly former communist countries to crash-dive into Heathrow.
- **Fall:** Bin al-Shibh tells interrogators that an attack on London was "planned for the same time period."
- **October 12:** Bali nightclub bombings kill 202 people.

- **December:** Bin Laden decrees in writing that KSM has been promoted to "chief of external operations."

2003

- **Early 2003:** KSM develops a plan to employ network of Pakistanis (including Iyman Faris and Majid Khan) to target gas stations, railroad tracks, and the Brooklyn Bridge, in New York.
- **March 1:** KSM captured and arrested in Rawalpindi, Pakistan, in a joint raid by Pakistani ISI and CIA Special Activities Division.
- **Before the end of March:** KSM is waterboarded. KSM gives information on the plot to fly planes into Heathrow.
- **April 29:** Ammar al-Baluchi captured (based on information from KSM), as well as others.
- **May:** Iyman Faris pleads guilty to plotting to destroy New York's Brooklyn Bridge.
- **August:** Hambali is captured.
- **September:** Rusman Gunawan (Hambali's brother) is captured in Pakistan.
- Mohammed Mansour Jabarah is captured and interrogated in Oman; he indicates that both he and Richard Reid reported to KSM.
- **November:** A second shoe bomber, Sajid Badat, is arrested.

2004

- **August 6:** Daniel Levin, a Bush administration official, writes to the CIA that waterboarding wouldn't violate the U.S. Constitution or treaty obligations.
- **October 12:** Human Rights Watch reports that eleven suspects, including KSM, have "disappeared" to a semi-secret prison in Jordan, and might have been tortured there under the direction of the CIA.

2005

- **May 2**: Abu Faraj al-Libbi—Al Qaeda's operational commander after KSM—captured and taken into CIA custody.
- **May 10:** Justice Department issues two memos declaring that the CIA's interrogation techniques complied with the federal prohibition against torture. Critics call these "the torture memos."
- **May 30:** Justice Department issues another memo finding enhanced interrogation techniques are consistent with U.S. obligations under the Convention Against Torture.
- **June 3:** CIA report "Detainee Reporting Pivotal for War Against al-Qa'ida" is created.

- **December 30:** Detainee Treatment Act is approved by the U.S. House and Senate and signed by President Bush.

2006

- **June 29:** Supreme Court issues *Hamdan* v. *Rumsfeld* decision, requiring that president seek congressional authorization for military commissions to proceed.
- **September:** KSM transferred to Guantánamo; International Committee of the Red Cross report about treatment of KSM and other terrorists is leaked.
- **September 6:** President Bush delivers a televised address confirming that the CIA held high-value detainees, including KSM, in secret interrogation centers.
- **Mid-September:** A "clean team" of senior officials from several agencies begins interviewing KSM to gather voluntary disclosures to avoid problems associated with information obtained using the CIA's interrogation approach.
- **September 27:** In a speech on the floor of the Senate, Barack Obama says: "Someone like KSM is gonna basically get a full military trial with all the bells and whistles."
- **September 29:** President Bush delivers a speech in which he reveals that high-value detainees provided information that stopped future attacks.

2007

- **March 10:** At Combatant Status Review Tribunal Hearing at Guantánamo Bay, Cuba, KSM (known as ISN 10024) confesses to 9/11 attacks, one of thirty-one terror plots he admits to attempting or executing.
- **March 19:** Ahmed Omar Saeed Sheikh's lawyers cite KSM's confession in defense of their client.
- **July:** Mariane Pearl files suit in U.S. District Court for the Eastern District of New York against terrorists, including KSM, and a bank that may have financed them for their roles in the beheading of her husband, Daniel Pearl. The suit would be dropped on October 24, 2007.
- **August 9:** Department of Defense announces that all fourteen of the high-value detainees at Guantánamo, including KSM, have been officially classified as "enemy combatants."

2008

- **February 11:** The Department of Defense charges KSM, bin al-Shibh, Hawsawi, al-Baluchi, and bin Attash for the September 11 attacks.

- **April 4:** The American Civil Liberties Union announces it has raised $8.5 million to "coordinate and defray the expenses" of lawyers working to defend terrorists.
- **June 5:** Trial at Guantánamo begins.
- **June 14:** Eric Holder addresses the American Constitution Society to say there is no tension between effectively fighting terrorists and respect for civil liberties.
- **September 23:** KSM questions Judge Ralph Kohlmann on his potential "bias" at trial.
- **October 12:** Judge Ralph Kohlmann orders that KSM and his four co-defendants be provided with laptops to prepare their defense.
- **November 4:** KSM writes a letter to military judge Colonel Stephen Henley expressing his desire to confess and plead guilty.
- **December 8:** Judge Henley reads KSM's November 4 letter aloud and announces that he will not accept guilty pleas from bin al-Shibh and Hawsawi until are afforded mental-competency hearings. KSM withdraws his guilty plea until all defendants can plead together.

2009

- **January 22:** President Obama issues Executive Order 13491, closing the CIA interrogation program and directing that all interrogations by U.S. personnel follow the techniques contained in the Army Field Manuals; he also announces plans to close Guantánamo in one year. As of 2011, Guantánamo remains open, well past the president's deadline.
- **February 2:** Eric Holder confirmed as attorney general. He immediately initiates an investigation into alleged torture of terror suspects by Bush-era officials.
- **Mid-March:** The Obama administration begins shopping Guantánamo detainees (although not KSM) to other countries in an effort to reduce the prison's population in advance of planned closure.
- **April 16:** President Obama orders release of four Justice Department memos (one dated August 1, 2002, two dated May 10, 2005, and a fourth dated May 30, 2005), which describe in detail the techniques used to interrogate KSM.
- **May:** A feud simmers between Eric Holder and Rahm Emanuel over how to handle potential CIA prosecutions,

the closure of Guantánamo, and how to deal with KSM, according to a *New Yorker* article.

- **June 9:** Suspected terrorist Ahmed Ghailani, with an alleged role in the Tanzania and Kenya embassy bombings, is sent to New York City for a civilian trial. Holder cites the history of the criminal justice system's success in handling terror cases.
- **July:** International Red Cross photographs KSM and Ammar al-Baluchi; photos are then distributed to the families of the individuals, who give them to jihadi Web sites—a propaganda boon.
- **Mid-July:** President Obama acknowledges Eric Holder's torture investigations, but rules out prosecution of CIA agents accused of conducting torture.
- **July 16:** Competency hearings for bin al-Shibh and Hawsawi take place. They are found sane enough to stand trial.
- **July 24:** Eric Holder testifies before the House Armed Services Committee, recommending changes to the Military Commissions Act of 2006 and asserting the effectiveness of civilian courts.
- **August:** CIA inspector general's report is released, revealing that CIA interrogators told KSM they would kill his children if another attack took place.
- **Late Summer through Fall:** The Eric Holder–Rahm Emanuel feud continues. Emanuel emphasizes the political ramifications and the need to bring in key opinion leaders in the Senate.
- **August 24:** Justice Department releases top-secret 2004 CIA inspector general's report on secret prisons and CIA top-secret reports for 2004 and 2005, revealing the plots thwarted due to the controversial CIA interrogation program.
- **September 2:** Photos of KSM and al-Baluchi uploaded to English-language Ansar al-Jihad Network.
- **September 3:** Photos of KSM posted to Samir Khan's English-language jihadi blog, Ignored Puzzle Pieces of Knowledge.
- **September 9:** Photo of KSM from Guantánamo posted by *The New York Times'* blog The Lede.
- **November 11:** Eric Holder briefs local New York politicians from Senator Chuck Schumer to Mayor Michael

Bloomberg about his plans for KSM and gets what he believes to be their support of the decision.

- **November 13:** U.S. Attorney General Eric Holder announces he will hold criminal trials in New York City for five detainees, including KSM.
- **November 18:** Attorney General Eric Holder testifies before the Senate Judiciary Committee in Washington, D.C.
- **November 24:** District Court Judge Gladys Kessler orders Guantánamo detainee Farhi Saeed bin Mohammed released because his prior torture in a Moroccan prison tainted later statements given to a U.S. "clean team."

2010

- **January 26:** Mayor Bloomberg and Senator Schumer come out publicly against a New York City terror trial.
- **January 28:** President Obama orders Justice Department to find a different venue to try the terrorists outside of Manhattan.
- **February 12:** *The Washington Post* reports that President Obama is "planning to insert himself into the debate" about where to try KSM and says a decision will be made "soon."
- **February 24:** Human Rights Watch executive and vocal Guantánamo opponent Jennifer Daskal is nominated for and confirmed to a high-ranking position at the Department of Justice.
- **February 24:** Fox News reports that the Pentagon is preventing lawyers of terror suspects at Guantánamo from seeing or in any way communicating with their clients.
- **February 26:** The Pentagon drops charges against KSM and his alleged coconspirators "without prejudice" to clear the way for their civilian trial.
- **March 10:** The story breaks of the "Guantánamo 9"—lawyers who until recently worked on the behalf of terror suspects and are now working for the Department of Justice.
- **March 17:** At a Justice Department budget request hearing, Eric Holder testifies that terrorists have the same rights as Charles Manson.
- **March 19:** On Al Jazeera, Osama bin Laden threatens to kill Americans if KSM is executed.
- **July 11:** On CBS's *Face the Nation*, Eric Holder says the administration will make a decision on where and how to

try KSM "as soon as we can" and decries "the politicization" of the issue.

- **October 7:** A federal judge bars critical testimony of a key witness in the Ahmed Ghailani trial because the witness had been subjected to coercive CIA interrogations.
- **November 10:** Eric Holder holds a press conference saying that he is "close to a decision" on where and how to try KSM.
- **November 17:** A New York City jury acquits Ahmed Ghailani of 284 of 285 major terrorism charges in the 1998 bombings of U.S. embassies in Kenya and Tanzania, in the first civilian trial of a former Guantánamo Bay prisoner.
- **December 6:** *USA Today* reports that Eric Holder "still believes his decision to try Mohammed and his alleged accomplices in a New York federal court was the correct one." Holder opposes Congress blocking funding for future civilian trials of terror detainees, claiming it "would set a dangerous precedent."
- **December 8:** Congress passes H.RES 1755, which contains language blocking funding of future civilian terrorist-detainee trials.
- **December 22:** *The New York Times* reports that the Obama administration is preparing a draft executive order to formalize indefinite detention of Guantánamo detainees without trial, a major reversal of Obama's stated policy.
- **December 31:** President Obama bypasses Senate opposition to the nomination of James Cole to the number-two post at the Justice Department with a recess appointment. James Cole had written a controversial op-ed on the one-year anniversary of the 9/11 attacks comparing the terrorists to common criminals. Cole will reportedly be in charge of setting up processes for military tribunals of terror suspects.

2011

- **January:** Almost a decade after the September 11 attacks, which killed nearly three thousand people, KSM is yet to be held accountable for his admitted offenses.
- **January 7:** President Obama issues a statement objecting to congressional limitations on his ability to transfer detainees. Republicans in Congress plan additional restrictions in upcoming bills.

Notes

INTRODUCTION

1. "Profile: Khalid Sheikh Mohammed," *The Times* (U.K.), March 15, 2007.
2. "Khalid Sheikh Mohammed's Isolated U.S. College Days," by Dina Temple-Raston, NPR, November 18, 2009.
3. "September 11 'Mastermind' Was Class Cutup in Carolina College," by Chad Roberts and James Gordon Meek, *Daily News* (N.Y.), August 3, 2004.
4. Author interview, May 2010.
5. "Suspected 9/11 Mastermind Graduation from U.S. University," by Susan Candiotti, Maria Ressa, Justine Redman, and Henry Schuster, CNN.com.
6. "Author Questions Trustworthiness of KSM's 'Confessions,'" by Rahimullah Yusufzai, *The* (Islamabad) *News*, March 23, 2007.
7. At a December 2008 hearing at America's naval base in Guantánamo Bay, Cuba.
8. "Capture Seen As a Windfall for Terror Fight; Suspected Sept. 11 Planner Attended 2 Colleges in N.C.," by John J. Lumpkin, Associated Press, March 2, 2003.
9. "A Brush with Evil in Murfreesboro," by Vernon Fueston, *Bertie Ledger-Advance*, December 2, 2009.
10. "The Plots and Designs of Al Qaeda's Engineer," by Terry McDermott, Josh Meyer, and Patrick J. McDonnell, *Los Angeles Times*, December 22, 2002.
11. According to a 1998 Rewards for Justice (formerly known as "Heroes") poster, KSM is 165 centimeters, or five feet four inches.
12. Author interview, January 2010.
13. Terry McDermott, "The Mastermind," *The New Yorker*, September 13, 2010, page 38.

14. Ibid.

15. "Badder than Bin Laden; Inside the Twisted Mind of the World's Most Dangerous Terrorist," by Grant Rollings, *The Sun* (U.K.), March 16, 2007.

16. Author interview, May 2010.

17. "Badder than Bin Laden," Rollings.

18. "Al Qaeda's Master Killer: The Man Who Plotted the Sept 11 Attacks, Khalid Posed the Single Biggest Threat to Global Security," by Shefali Rekhi, *The Straits Times* (Singapore), March 10, 2003.

19. Lawrence Wright, *The Looming Tower: Al Qaeda and the Road to 9/11* (New York: Alfred A. Knopf, 2006), page 308.

20. "Natural Born Killer," by Nick Fielding and Christina Lamb, *Sunday Times* (U.K.), March 9, 2003.

21. Mary Anne Weaver, "Children of the Jihad," *The New Yorker*, June 12, 1995, page 46. Interestingly, Weaver says Pakistani police had an arrest warrant for "Zahid Sheikh," Yousef's uncle.

22. Author interview with Ammar al-Baluchi's former civilian attorney, Scott Fenstermaker, June 28, 2010.

23. Ibid.

24. "Judge Allows Gang Leader to Talk with Other Infamous Prisoners," by Benjamin Weiser, *New York Times*, March 11, 1999.

25. "CIA Bio Says 9/11 Mastermind's Days in N.C. 'Helped Propel Him to Terrorism,'" by Cam Simpson, *Wall Street Journal*, August 24, 2009.

26. Ibid.

27. "Pardon him, Theodotus: he is a barbarian, and thinks that the customs of his tribe and island are the laws of nature." George Bernard Shaw, *Julius Caesar.*

28. E-mail from Mariane Pearl to author, May 12, 2010.

CHAPTER 1: THE OUTSIDER

1. "Al Qaeda's Master Killer: The Man Who Plotted the Sept 11 Attacks, Khalid Posed the Single Biggest Threat to Global Security," by Shefali Rekhi, *The Straits Times* (Singapore), March 10, 2003.

2. "Interview with Ramzi Yousef," by Raghida Dergham, *Al Hayat* (Jordan), April 12, 1995.

3. "Threats and Responses: Suspect's Hometown; A Boyhood on the Mean Streets of a Wealthy Emirate," by Marc Santora, *New York Times*, March 2, 2003.

4. "Biography of Khalid Sheikh Mohammed," Fox News, March 14, 2007.

5. Terry McDermott, "The Mastermind," *The New Yorker*, September 13, 2010, page 40.

6. While some analysts dispute the date of his birth, the author relied on the 1982 passport issued by the Pakistani Embassy (488555) that gives his birth date as April 24, 1965.

7. Terry McDermott, *Perfect Soldiers: The 9/11 Hijackers, Who They Were, Why They Did It* (New York: HarperCollins, 2005), page 108.

8. "Natural Born Killer," by Nick Fielding and Christina Lamb, *Sunday Times* (U.K.), March 9, 2003.

9. U.S. Central Intelligence Agency. *Khalid Shaykh Muhammad: Preeminent Source on Al Qa'ida*, July 13, 2004.

10. "Badder than Bin Laden; Inside the Twisted Mind of the World's Most Dangerous Terrorist," by Grant Rollings, *The Sun* (U.K.), March 16, 2007.

11. "Natural Born Killer," Fielding and Lamb.

12. Ibid.

13. Mary Anne Weaver, "Children of Jihad," *The New Yorker*, June 12, 1995, page 43.

14. U.S. Central Intelligence Agency. *Khalid Shaykh Muhammad.*

15. Author interview with an intelligence official, April 2010.

16. Yosri Fouda and Nick Fielding, *Masterminds of Terror* (New York: Arcade Publishing, 2003), page 98.

17. Thomas H. Kean and Lee H. Hamilton, *Without Precedent: The Inside Story of the 9/11 Commission* (New York: Alfred A. Knopf, 2006).

18. Weaver, "Children of Jihad," page 43.

19. "Baloch Nationalism and the Geopolitics of Energy Resources: the Changing Context of Separatism in Pakistan," by Robert G. Wirsing, published by the U.S. Army War College Strategic Studies Institute, April 2008, page 25.

20. Ibid., page 21.

21. Ibid., page 22.

22. Owen Bennet Jones, *Pakistan: Eye of the Storm* (New Haven, Conn.: Yale University Press, 2002), page 133.

23. Ibid.

24. "Pakistan: The Worsening Conflict in Balochistan," International Crisis Group, Asia Report No. 119, September 14, 2006, page 4.

25. James Wynbrandt, *A Brief History of Pakistan* (New York: Facts on File, 2008).

26. Ibid.

27. U.S. Central Intelligence Agency. *Khalid Shaykh Muhammad.*

28. Rida lived from 1865 to 1935. He was a disciple of the Egyptian scholar Mohammed Abduh (1849–1905), who also taught Hassan al-Banna's father.

29. This is drawn from a Muslim Brotherhood Web site: www.ikanweb.com. See "Hassan Al Banna and His Political Thought of Islamic Brotherhood."

30. Gilles, Kepel, translated by Jon Rothschild, *The Prophet and the Pharaoh: Muslim Extremism in Egypt* (Al Saqi Books, 1985), page 227.

31. Ibid.

32. Barry Rubin, ed., *The Muslim Brotherhood: The Organization and Policies of a Global Islamist Movement* (New York: Palgrave Macmillan, 2010), page 29.

33. Lawrence Wright, *The Looming Tower: Al Qaeda and the Road to 9/11* (New York: Alfred A. Knopf, 2006), page 25.

34. As quoted in: Rubin, ed., *The Muslim Brotherhood*, page 39. Ana Belen Solage's work, in general, as well as the work in this book, is invaluable.

35. Rubin, ed., *The Muslim Brotherhood*, page 39.

36. Ibid.

37. Ibid., page 40.

38. The judge's name was Ahmad al-Khazandar. His assassination is an important milestone in the history of the Brotherhood.

39. Rubin, ed., *The Muslim Brotherhood*, page 41.

40. Wright, *The Looming Tower*, page 25.

41. Ibid.

42. Rubin, ed., *The Muslim Brotherhood*, page 41.

43. Ibid., page 42.

44. Ibid., page 1.

45. Wright, *The Looming Tower*, page 92.

46. Weaver, "Children of Jihad," page 43.

47. Ibid.

48. McDermott, *Perfect Soldiers*, page 109.

49. Peter L. Bergen, *The Osama bin Laden I Know: An Oral History of al Qaeda's Leader* (New York: Free Press, 2006), page 148.

50. Associated Press, February 14, 1979.

51. Robert B. Cullen, Associated Press, February 1979. Nexis dates this dispatch as February 2, 1979, but that is obviously an error in that the text refers to his February 14, 1979, death as "last week."

52. "Ambassador Dubs: Eager, 'Knew Post Was Tough,' " by Stephen J. Lynton, *Washington Post*, February 15, 1979, page A21.

53. Associated Press, February 14, 1979. An eyewitness account by Mayer Stiebel, an American businessman from Highland Park, Illinois.

54. Ibid.

55. Ibid.

56. Ibid.

57. "Protecting Americans Abroad," editorial, *Washington Post*, February 15, 1979, page A18.

58. Ibid.

59. Alexander G. Higgins, Associated Press, December 4, 1979.

60. "Vote Big for Khomeini," by Alex Efty, Associated Press, December 3, 1979.

61. Wright, *The Looming Tower*, page 88.

62. Ibid.

63. Ibid., page 92.

64. Ibid., page 94.

65. National Commission on Terrorist Attacks Upon the United States, *The 9/11 Commission Report,* August 2004, page 145.

66. "The Plots and Designs of Al Qaeda's Engineer," by Terry McDermott, Josh Meyer, and Patrick J. McDonnell, *Los Angeles Times*, December 22, 2002.

67. McDermott, *Perfect Soldiers*, pages 111–12.

CHAPTER 2: CAMPUS RADICAL

1. According to U.S. Census Bureau data from the year 2000.

2. Murfreesboro now has several pizza shops.

3. It is now called Chowan University.

4. Author interview with Clayton Lewis, former dean of students, Chowan University, August 2010.

5. "Khalid Sheikh Mohammed's Isolated U.S. College Days," by Dina Temple-Raston, NPR, November 18, 2009.

6. Author interview with Clayton Lewis, August 2010.

7. "Khalid Sheikh Mohammed's Isolated U.S. College Days," Temple-Raston, November 18, 2009.

8. "Linked by Little but N.C., Islam," by Craig Jarvis and Christina Headrick, *The News & Observer* (North Carolina), March 8, 2003, page A2.

9. According to Ali, Denver, Worchester, Massachusetts, and Still Springs, Oklahoma, were the other hot spots of Muslim Brotherhood and Salafi activity at the time. Author interview, Greensboro, North Carolina, July 2010.

10. Joseph Contreras and Ed Caram, "A North Carolina Cell?," *Newsweek* (online), December 19, 2002.

11. Author interview with Clayton Lewis, Charlotte, North Carolina, August 2010.

12. The application has a number of strange anomalies. He spelled his name "Mohammed Khaled Al-Shaikh" and listed his address as "Fintass, Kuwait." He listed his date of birth as March 24, 1965. Question 16 asked, "Who or what influenced you to apply to Chowan College?" He answered:

"My friend." He said, in answer to question 17, that he planned to major in English. His signature reads: "Altini."

13. Author interview with Chowan spokesman Joshua E. Barker via e-mail, March 30, 2010.

14. "The Plots and Designs of Al Qaeda's Engineer," by Terry McDermott, Josh Meyer, and Patrick J. McDonnell, *Los Angeles Times*, December 22, 2002.

15. "September 11 'Mastermind' Was Class Cutup in Carolina College," by Chad Roberts and James Gordon Meek, *Daily News* (N.Y.), August 3, 2004.

16. Yosri Fouda and Nick Fielding, *Masterminds of Terror* (New York: Arcade Publishing, 2003), page 90.

17. "Khalid Sheikh Mohammed's Isolated U.S. College Days," Temple-Raston, November 18, 2009.

18. Author interview with Joshua E. Barker via e-mail, March 30, 2010.

19. Ibid.

20. "Khalid Sheikh Mohammed's Isolated U.S. College Days," Temple-Raston, November 18, 2009.

21. Author interview, August 2010.

22. "Khalid Sheikh Mohammed's Isolated U.S. College Days," Temple-Raston, November 18, 2009.

23. Author interview, March 2010. Also, see his book *My Year Inside Radical Islam* (New York: Jeremy P. Tarcher/Penguin Group, 2007).

24. Descriptions of KSM's life in North Carolina are based primarily on research and interviews conducted there by the author as well as an account in Terry McDermott, *Perfect Soldiers: The 9/11 Hijackers, Who They Were, Why They Did It* (New York: HarperCollins, 2005), page 113.

25. Author interview with Joshua E. Barker via e-mail, March 30, 2010.

26. Ibid.

27. Author interview with Chowan spokesman Josh Barker, July 2010.

28. Author interview, August 2010.

29. 1984–1985 Bulletin of North Carolina Agricultural and Technical State University, July 1984, page 16.

30. "Khalid Sheikh Mohammed's Isolated U.S. College Days," Temple-Raston, November 18, 2009.

31. Joseph Contreras and Ed Caram, "A North Carolina Qaeda Cell?; One of Osama Bin Laden's Most Trusted Lieutenants Was Once a Student in the Tarheel State. Now Local Muslims Fear Their Community Is Being Targeted for Special Investigation," *Newsweek*, December 19, 2002.

32. Unfortunately, Burke County purged its 1985 traffic citation records some time ago, so a copy of the physical citation is not available.

33. "Suspected Mastermind Graduated from U.S. University," by Susan Candiotti, et al., CNN, December 19, 2002.

34. "Professor Recalls Now Notorious A&T Student," by John Newsom, *News & Record* (Greensboro, N.C.), March 4, 2003.

35. "Khalid Sheikh Mohammed's Isolated U.S. College Days," Temple-Raston, November 18, 2009.

36. Bill Saporito and Tim McGirk, "Architect of Terror; Pakistani Authorities Nab Khalid Shaikh Mohammed, the al-Qaeda Bigwig Who Helped Mastermind the Sept. 11 Attacks. Can He Help the U.S. Locate Bin Laden?," *Time*, March 10, 2003.

37. McDermott, *Perfect Soldiers*, page 114.

38. "Suspected Terrorist Captured in Pakistan Was Student at North Carolina College," by Rah Bickley, *News & Observer*, March 3, 2003.

39. Ibid.

40. Waleed M. Qimlass, interview by Patrick McDonnell, Kuwait City, November 2002.

41. McDermott, *Perfect Soldiers*, page 115.

42. "Khalid Sheikh Mohammed's Isolated U.S. College Days," Temple-Raston, November 18, 2009.

43. Author interview with Gutbi al-Mahdi, former head of intelligence for the government of Sudan, in 2003 in Khartoum.

44. Sammy Zitawi, telephone interview by Terry McDermott, September 2002.

45. McDermott, *Perfect Soldiers*, page 114.

46. "Khalid Sheikh Mohammed's Isolated U.S. College Days," Temple-Raston, November 18, 2009.

47. Ibid.

48. "Fiend Mulled Pre-9/11 Kill; Wanted Rabbi Dead in '80s," by Chad Roberts and James Gordon Meek, *Daily News* (N.Y.), August 1, 2004, page 28.

49. Author interview.

50. "Taint of Terrorism Marks North Carolina University Campus," by Dahleen Glanton, *Chattanooga Times Free Press*, April 8, 2007.

51. "Is Osama's Aide a Former Aggie?" by Jim McNally, *Carolina Peacemaker*, December 26, 2002.

52. McDermott, *Perfect Soldiers*, page 115.

53. Mahmood Zubaid, interview by Patrick McDonnell, Kuwait City, November 2002.

54. UAE official, interview by Terry McDermott, United Arab Emirates, August 2003.

55. Mohammed Zubaid, interview by Terry McDermott, Kuwait City, August 2003.

56. McDermott, *Perfect Soldiers*, page 116.

57. Kuwaiti official, interview by Terry McDermott, August 2003.

58. McDermott, *Perfect Soldiers*, page 117.

59. The 9/11 Commission Report says that KSM's first trip to Pakistan was in 1987, which would seem to rule out a summer vacation trip in 1985 or 1986. However, the 9/11 Commission Report is likely to be mistaken.

60. "The Angry Rabbi," by Josh Friedman and David Firestone, *Newsday* (N.Y.), November 7, 1990, part II, page 4.

61. "Sept. 11 'Mastermind' was Class Cutup," Roberts and Meek.

62. "Jewish Defense League Leader Meir Kahane Shot," by Leslie Wines, United Press International, November 5, 1990.

63. Michael B. Mukasey, *How Obama Has Mishandled the War on Terror*, Encounter Broadside no. 9 (New York: Encounter Books, 2010), page 3.

64. Ibid.

65. "Man Accused in Terror Plot Bombed Gay Bar, U.S. Says," by James C. McKinley, Jr., *New York Times*, January 14, 1995.

66. "The CIA and the Sheikh," by Robert I. Friedman, *Village Voice*, March 30, 1993, page 22.

67. Chitra Ragaran et al., "Tracing Terror's Roots," *U.S. News & World Report*, February 24, 2003.

68. Testimony of Oliver "Buck" Revell, Committee on International Relations, U.S. House of Representatives, October 3, 2001.

69. Ragavan et al., "Tracing Terror's Roots," February 24, 2003.

70. "The CIA's Jihad," by Robert I. Friedman, *New York*, March 27, 1995, page 44.

71. Steven Emerson, *American Jihad: The Terrorists Among Us.* (New York: Free Press, 2002), page 56.

72. Lawrence Wright, *The Looming Tower: Al Qaeda and the Road to 9/11* (New York: Alfred A. Knopf, 2006), page 177.

73. Ibid.

74. "Terror Plots, Informer Links Mosque to Threats," by David Kocieniewski and Peg Tyre, *Newsday* (N.Y.), March 21, 1993.

75. Author interview with Israeli source, April 2010.

76. "The Plots and Designs," McDermott, Meyer, and McDonnell, December 22, 2002.

77. "Khalid Sheikh Mohammed's Isolated U.S. College Days," Temple-Raston, November 18, 2009.

CHAPTER 3: SEARCHING FOR WAR

1. Terry McDermott, "The Mastermind," *The New Yorker*, September 13, 2010, page 32.

2. Terry McDermott, *Perfect Soldiers: The 9/11 Hijackers, Who They Were, Why They Did It* (New York: HarperCollins, 2005), page 128.

3. Author interview with Bill Peikneg and Milton Bearden, Reston, Virginia, July 2003.

4. Author interview with Marc Sageman, May 2010.

5. National Commission on Terrorist Attacks Upon the United States, *The 9/11 Commission Report,* August 2004, page 146.

6. Jean-Charles Brisard and Damien Martinez, *Zarqawi: The New Face of Al-Qaeda* (New York: Other Press, 2005), pages 24–25.

7. Omar Nasiri, *Inside the Jihad* (New York: Basic Books, 2006), page 133.

8. McDermott, *Perfect Soldiers,* page 128.

9. Ibid.

10. Simon Reeve, *The New Jackals: Ramzi Yousef, Osama bin Laden, and the Future of Terrorism* (Boston: Northeastern University Press, 2002), page 96.

11. McDermott, "The Mastermind," page 43.

12. Ibid.

13. For a fuller discussion of bin Laden's moves, please see *Losing bin Laden*, by Richard Miniter (Washington, D.C.: Regnery, 2003).

14. John R. Schindler, *Unholy Terror: Bosnia, Al-Qa'ida, and the Rise of Global Jihad* (St. Paul, Minn.: Zenith Press, 2007), page 280.

15. Ibid.

16. Ibid.

17. Ibid., pages 8–9.

18. Ibid., page 281.

19. Jason Burke, *Al-Qaeda: The True Story of Radical Islam* (New York: Penguin Books, 2004), page 133.

20. McDermott, *Perfect Soldiers,* page 131.

CHAPTER 4: TRADEBOM

1. "A New Strain of Terrorism; Groups Are Fast, Loose, Hard to Find," by Pierre Thomas, *Washington Post,* August 3, 1993, page A1.

2. Yosri Fouda and Nick Fielding, *Masterminds of Terror* (New York: Arcade Publishing, 2003), page 95.

3. "Inspector Testifies She Urged No Asylum for Blast Suspect," by Richard Bernstein, *New York Times,* November 16, 1993.

4. "A New Strain of Terrorism," Thomas, page A1.

5. Bill Turque with Christopher Dickey et al., "The Trail to the Jihad Office," *Newsweek,* March 29, 1993, page 38.

6. "The CIA's Jihad," by Robert I. Friedman, *New York,* March 27, 1995, page 38.

7. Ibid., page 40.

8. Simon Reeve, *The New Jackals: Ramzi Yousef, Osama bin Laden, and the Future of Terrorism* (Boston: Northeastern University Press, 2002).

9. Transcript; the Yasin interview, *60 Minutes,* June 6, 2002.

10. "Trail Left by Phone Calls May Link Bomb Suspects," by Richard Bernstein, *New York Times*, January 14, 1994.

11. National Commission on Terrorist Attacks Upon the United States, *The 9/11 Commission Report,* August 2004, page 147.

12. Christopher Dickey, "America's Most Wanted," *Newsweek*, July 4, 1994, page 46.

13. "The Lesson: Incident at the Towers, 1993" by Tom Robbins, *Daily News* (N.Y.), December 9, 1998.

14. Reeve, *The New Jackals*, page 36.

15. "The Lesson," Robbins.

16. Ian O. Lesser, et al., *Countering the New Terrorism* (Santa Monica, Calif.: RAND, 1999), page 24.

17. "Suspect Is Said to Be Longtime Friend of Bombing Mastermind," by James C. McKinley, Jr., *New York Times*, August 4, 1995.

18. "The World Trade Center Bombing: A Tragic Wake-Up Call," New York State Senate report, Committee on Investigations, Taxation and Government Operations, August 3, 1993, page 9. See the testimony of Port Authority director Stanley Brezenoff.

19. Reeve, *The New Jackals*, page 21.

20. Lawrence Wright, *The Looming Tower: Al Qaeda and the Road to 9/11* (New York: Alfred A. Knopf, 2006), page 177.

21. This account is adapted from court documents and Simon Reeve's book, *The New Jackals*.

22. Lesser et al., *Countering the New Terrorism*, page 23.

23. The officer spoke with the author on the condition of anonymity in July 2010. Fox died in the mid-1990s.

24. Author interview with a senior FBI official, Washington, D.C., July 2010.

25. "Indeed, much as the 'inept' World Trade Center bombers were derided for their inability to avoid arrest, their modus operandi arguably points to a pattern of future terrorist activities elsewhere. For example, as previously noted, terrorist groups were once recognizable as distinct organizational entities. The four convicted World Trade Center bombers shattered this stereotype. Instead, they were like-minded individuals who shared a common religion, worshipped at the same religious institution, had the same friends and frustrations, and were linked by family ties as well, who simply gravitated toward one another for a specific, perhaps even one-time operation." Lesser et al., *Countering the New Terrorism*, page 22.

26. "Weaving a Wide Web of Terror," by Charles P. Wallace, *Los Angeles Times*, May 28, 1995.

27. "The Road to Ground Zero," *The Sunday Times* (of London), January 7, 2002.

28. Mark E. Rondeau, "Clinton Did Little Substantive to Fight Terror, Says Former FBI Agent," *The Advocate*, October 31, 2001.

29. Transcript, "Special Edition," *Nightline*, August 20, 1998.
30. Marc Sageman, *Leaderless Jihad: Terror Networks in the Twenty-First Century* (Philadelphia: University of Pennsylvania Press, 2008), page 30.
31. *The 9/11 Commission Report*, August 2004, page 153.
32. Ibid.
33. "Early Scheme to Turn Jets into Weapons," by Terry McDermott, *Los Angeles Times*, June 24, 2002.
34. Reeve, *The New Jackals*, page 64.
35. Ibid.
36. "Musharraf Rival Linked to bin Laden," by Maddy Sauer, ABC News, November 30, 2007.
37. "The CEO of al Qaeda," by Farhan Bokhari et al., *Financial Times*, February 15, 2003.
38. "Bhutto Says Trade Center Suspect Also Targeted Her—Pakistan: Prime Minister Says Bomb Went Off Prematurely in 1993, Injuring Plotter Instead," by John-Thor Dahlburg, *Los Angeles Times*, March 19, 1995.
39. "Womaniser, Joker, Scuba Diver: The Other Face of Al-Qaida's No 3," by Rohan Gunaratna, *Guardian*, March 3, 2003.
40. "Bhutto Says Trade Center Suspect Also Targeted Her," Dahlburg, March 19, 1995.
41. Ibid.
42. Ibid.
43. "A Former Pakistani Prime Minister Weighs In," by Benazir Bhutto, *Slate*, September 21, 2001.

CHAPTER 5: THE PLOT TO KILL THE POPE, THE PRESIDENT, AND FOUR THOUSAND AMERICANS

1. Philippines Secret Intelligence report, November 5, 2002.
2. "Bust and Boom," by Matthew Brzezinski, *Washington Post Magazine,* December 30, 2001. A truly excellent piece of reporting.
3. Ibid.
4. Ibid.
5. "Early Scheme to Turn Jets into Weapons," by Terry McDermott, *Los Angeles Times,* June 24, 2002.
6. Azmiri, whose real name is Wali Khan Amin Shah, is also known by the names Azmarai, Asmari, Asmurai, and Osmurai.
7. Jean-Charles Brisard and Damien Martinez, *Zarqawi: The New Face of Al-Qaeda* (New York: Other Press, 2005), page 20.
8. Ibid., pages 20–21.
9. "Khalifa: I Don't Know Gemma; I'm Upset," by Christine Herrera, *Philippine Daily Inquirer*, August 11, 2000, page 1.

10. "Suspect's Role in '95 Plot Detailed; Inquiry: Khalid Shaikh Mohammed, Alleged Sept. 11 Mastermind, Was a Financial Conduit in the Plan to Blow Up U.S. Jets, Philippine Official Says," by Richard C. Paddock and Josh Meyer, *Los Angeles Times*, June 7, 2002.

11. "Weaving a Wide Web of Terror," by Charles P. Wallace, *Los Angeles Times,* May 28, 1995.

12. "Revelations of Khalid Sheikh Mohammed," classified U.S. intelligence document, April 2003.

13. "Hambali Used RM2 Million Collected from Donations to Fund His Extremist Operations," by Wong Chun Wai and Lourdes Charles, *The Star* (Malaysia), January 1, 2003.

14. KSM later told interrogators that "Bojinka" was a nonsense word he had heard in Afghanistan or Bosnia.

15. "Bust and Boom," Brzezinski.

16. Maria A. Ressa, *Seeds of Terror: An Eyewitness Account of Al-Qaeda's Newest Center of Operations in Southeast Asia* (New York: Free Press, 2003), page 29.

17. Ibid.

18. Ibid.

19. Ibid., page 30.

20. Some accounts say the plane landed in Guam, but this appears to be mistaken.

21. "Weaving a Wide Web," Wallace, May 28, 1995.

22. "Bust and Boom," Brzezinski.

23. "Weaving a Wide Web," Wallace.

24. "Bust and Boom," Brzezinski.

25. Simon Reeve, *The New Jackals: Ramzi Yousef, Osama bin Laden, and the Future of Terrorism* (London: André Deutsch, 1999), page 78.

26. "Weaving a Wide Web," Wallace.

27. Yosri Fouda and Nick Fielding, *Masterminds of Terror* (New York: Arcade Publishing, 2003), page 98.

28. Ibid., page 100.

29. "Weaving a Wide Web," Wallace.

30. Ibid.

31. Melissa Boyle Mahle, *Denial and Deception: An Insider's View of the CIA* (New York: Nation Books, 2006), page 159.

CHAPTER 6: LOSING RAMZI

1. Author interview with Richard A. Clarke, July 2003.

2. This conversation is drawn from Lawrence Wright's *The Looming Tower: Al Qaeda and the Road to 9/11* (New York: Alfred A. Knopf, 2006), page 202.

3. Wright, *The Looming Tower*, page 204.
4. "Fingerprints Being Studied in Bomb Case," by Alison Mitchell, *New York Times*, May 20, 1993.
5. Wright, *The Looming Tower*, page 203.
6. Ibid.
7. Ibid., page 204.
8. "The Road to Ground Zero," *The Sunday Times* (of London), January 6, 2002. This account is also in Simon Reeve's *The New Jackals*, page 105.
9. "Report: Police Arrest Friend of Yousef," by Greg Myre, Associated Press, February 10, 1995.
10. Richard Miniter, *Losing bin Laden: How Clinton's Failures Unleashed Global Terror* (Washington, D.C.: Regnery, 2003), page 84.
11. "Interview of Ramzi Ahmed Yousef," FBI report, February 7, 1995. Taken from Peter Bergen's *The Osama bin Laden I Know* (New York: Free Press, 2006), pages 144–46.
12. "Early Scheme to Turn Jets into Weapons," by Terry McDermott, *Los Angeles Times*, June 24, 2002.
13. "Interview of Abdul Basit Mahmoud Abdul Karim," FBI report, February 7–8, 1995. Taken from Bergen's *The Osama bin Laden I Know*, pages 146–48.
14. Mary Anne Weaver, "Children of Jihad," *The New Yorker*, June 12, 1995, page 47.
15. According to an interview with a Sudanese intelligence source in Khartoum, March 2002.
16. Author interview with Janet McElligott, a former lobbyist for the government of Sudan who maintains close ties with its intelligence and political services.
17. Melissa Boyle Mahle, *Denial and Deception: An Insider's View of the CIA* (New York: Nation Books, 2006), page 247.
18. Mahle, *Denial and Deception*, pages 247–48.
19. Author interview, 2003.
20. Author interview, 2010.
21. See Robert Baer, *See No Evil: The True Story of a Good Soldier in the CIA's War on Terrorism* (New York: Crown, 2002), page 270. Baer does not specify Qatar in his book.
22. Mahle, *Denial and Deception*, page 13.

CHAPTER 7: MEETING BIN LADEN

1. National Commission on Terrorist Attacks Upon the United States, *The 9/11 Commission Report,* August 2004, page 276.
2. Author interview with Mary Jo White, June 30, 2010.
3. Ibid.

4. Rohan Gunaratna, *Inside Al Qaeda: Global Network of Terror* (New York: The Berkeley Publishing Group, 2003), page xxx.

5. Maria Ressam, CNN.com

6. Peter L. Bergen, *The Osama bin Laden I Know: An Oral History of al Qaeda's Leader* (New York: Free Press, 2006), page 300.

7. "Trail on bin Laden Grows Cold on South America's Triple Frontier," by Henry Orego, Agence France-Presse, May 4, 2003. The article is datelined: Ciuidad del Este, Paraguay.

8. Lawrence Wright, *The Looming Tower: Al-Qaeda and the Road to 9/11* (New York: Alfred A. Knopf, 2006), page 235.

9. Bergen, *The Osama bin Laden I Know*, page 300.

10. Wright, *The Looming Tower*, page 235.

11. Ibid., page 236.

12. *The 9/11 Commission Report,* August 2004, page 150.

13. Ibid., page 148.

14. Author interview with a European intelligence source.

15. *The 9/11 Commission Report,* August 2004, page 149.

16. Jason Burke, *Al-Qaeda: The True Story of Radical Islam* (New York: Penguin Books, 2004), page 175.

17. "Unheeded Warnings: A Special Report; Before Bombings, Omens and Fears," by James Risen and Benjamin Weiser, *New York Times*, January 9, 1999, page 1.

18. Ibid.

19. "1st Gunfire: Then Explosion: Toll Rises: Survivors Give Details of Attack," by Hugh Delios, *Chicago Tribune*, August 9, 1998, page 1. Note: This is from the "Chicagoland Final Edition" and is datelined Nairobi, Kenya.

20. *The 9/11 Commission Report,* August 2004, page 149.

21. Ibid., page 150.

CHAPTER 8: SEPTEMBER 11, 2001

1. "Terror Suspect Arrest Yields Names of al-Qaeda Cell Members: Official," Agence France-Presse, March 2, 2003.

2. National Commission on Terrorist Attacks Upon the United States, *The 9/11 Commission Report,* August 2004, page 150.

3. Ibid.

4. Ibid.

5. Ibid.

6. Ibid., page 154.

7. Lawrence Wright, *The Looming Tower: Al-Qaeda and the Road to 9/11* (New York: Alfred A. Knopf, 2006), page 308.

8. Yosri Fouda and Nick Fielding, *Masterminds of Terror—The Truth Behind the Most Devastating Terrorist Attack the World Has Ever Seen* (New York: Arcade Publishing, 2003), page 127.

9. "Al-Qaeda's Master Killer; The Man Who Plotted the Sept 11 Attacks, Khalid Posed the Single Biggest Threat to Global Security," by Shefali Rekhi, *The Straits Times* (Singapore), March 10, 2003.
10. *The 9/11 Commission Report,* August 2004, page 234.
11. Ibid.
12. Richard Miniter, *Losing bin Laden—How Bill Clinton's Failures Unleashed Global Terror* (Washington, D.C.: Regnery Publishing, Inc., 2003), page 95.
13. *The 9/11 Commission Report,* August 2004, page 234.
14. Ibid.
15. Ibid.
16. Ibid.
17. Ibid.
18. Ibid., page 235.
19. *The 9/11 Commission Report*, August 2004.
20. Substitution for the Testimony of Khalid Sheikh Mohammed. *U.S.* v. *Moussaoui*. Defendant's Exhibit 941.
21. Peter L. Bergen, *The Osama bin Laden I Know: An Oral History of al Qaeda's Leader* (New York: Free Press, 2006), page 304.
22. "The Nation: The 9/11 Commission Report: The Terrorist Plot," by Terry McDermott, *Los Angeles Times*, July 23, 2004, page 1.
23. *The 9/11 Commission Report*, August 2004, page 260.
24. Ibid., page 236.
25. Wright, *The Looming Tower*, pages 307–8.
26. Ibid., page 307.
27. *The 9/11 Commission Report*, August 2004, page 167.
28. Ibid.
29. Ibid., page 219.
30. John R. Schindler, *Unholy Terror: Bosnia, Al-Qa'ida, and the Rise of Global Jihad* (St. Paul, Minn.: Zenith Press, 2007), page 281.
31. *The 9/11 Commission Report,* August 2004, page 219.
32. Ibid., page 224.
33. Ibid., page 236.
34. Dominic Kennedy, *Sunday Times* (U.K.), September 9, 2002.
35. "Arrested al Qaeda Operative May Tell Secrets," CNN Saturday Morning News, September 14, 2002, http://transcripts.cnn.com/TRANSCRIPTS/0209/14/smn.09.html.
36. Bergen, *The Osama bin Laden I Know*, page 304.

CHAPTER 9: THE DANIEL PEARL MURDER

1. "Former FBI Investigator on Daniel Pearl," by Robert Windrem and Richard Greenberg, NBC News, June 22, 2007. Omar Sheikh: "Well,

he's [Osama bin Laden] out there living off the land, so he doesn't have McDonald's and he doesn't have Kentucky Fried Chicken, doesn't eat a lot of meats and gravies and starches. But there's one guy who's operating north of here and one guy who's here in Karachi who are like the left and the right hand of Osama bin Laden."

2. "Al Qaida 'Kingpin' Says Attack at 2002 World Cup Planned," Japan Economic Newswire, February 14, 2004. The article is datelined Tokyo.

3. "The News: Karachi Page," *Dawn Karachi*, February 15, 2002.

4. "Daniel Pearl Bio," retrieved from www.DanielPearlFoundation.com, June 2010.

5. Tariq Ali, *The Duel: Pakistan on the Flight Path of American Power* (New York: Scribner, 2008), page 150.

6. "NewsHour Update: Missing Reporter Masour Interview," PBS Online, January 29, 2002.

7. Author interview, July 2010.

8. "In the Line of Fire: A Memoir, Extract: How We Found Pearl Buried in Ten Pieces," by Pervez Musharraf, *The* (London) *Times*, September 26, 2006.

9. "Former FBI Investigator," Windrem and Greenberg.

10. Robert Sam Anson, "The Journalist and the Terrorist," *Vanity Fair*, August 2002.

11. "Missing Reporter Masour Interview."

12. Anson, "The Journalist and the Terrorist."

13. "Missing Reporter Masour Interview."

14. Peter L. Bergen, *The Osama bin Laden I Know: An Oral History of al Qaeda's Leader* (New York: Free Press, 2006), page xv.

15. Anson, "The Journalist and the Terrorist."

16. "Missing Reporter Masour Interview."

17. Anson, "The Journalist and the Terrorist."

18. Ibid.

19. *Washington Post*, February 23, 2002.

20. "Underworld Where Terror and Security Meet," by Rory McCarthy, *The Guardian,* July 16, 2002.

21. "Bomb Probe Eyes Pakistan Links," by Farah Stockman, *Boston Globe*, January 6, 2002.

22. Anson, "The Journalist and the Terrorist."

23. "A Murder's Aftermath: Killing of Pearl Fit Into Pakistani Web of Radical Islam," by Steve LeVine, *Wall Street Journal*, January 23, 2003.

24. "Karachi Page," February 15, 2002.

25. "Where Terror and Security Meet," McCarthy, July 16, 2002.

26. "Who Really Killed Danny Pearl?" by Asra Q. Nomani, *Salon*, October 22, 2003.

27. "Daniel Pearl—A Timeline of Events," *Gather*, June 20, 2007.

28. "Daniel Pearl Timeline," CNN.com, February 21, 2002.
29. "Karachi Page, February 15, 2002."
30. "Timeline: Daniel Pearl Kidnap," BBC News, South Asia, July 15, 2002.
31. "Daniel Pearl," *Gather*, June 20, 2007.
32. "Daniel Pearl: 1963–2002," *Time*, February 21, 2002.
33. "Karachi Page, February 15, 2002."
34. "Daniel Pearl's Killers Still on Loose," by Joel Roberts, CBS News, January 22, 2003.
35. "Former FBI Investigator," Windrem and Greenberg.
36. Ibid.
37. "Daniel Pearl 'Refused to Be Sedated Before His Throat Was Cut'; Harrowing Details of the Killing of Journalist Fuel Police Anger That 12 Suspects Have Not Been Charged," by Massoud Ansari, *The Sunday Telegraph*, May 9, 2004.
38. Ibid.
39. "A Murder's Aftermath: Killing of Pearl Fit Into Pakistani Web of Radical Islam," by Steve LeVine, *Wall Street Journal*, January 23, 2003.
40. Ibid.
41. "The Slaughter of the Spy-Journalist, the Jew Daniel Pearl, " videotape, February 21, 2002.
42. Pervez Musharraf, *In the Line of Fire: A Memoir* (New York: Free Press 2006), page 228.
43. "New Allegations Emerge in Case of Slain Wall Street Journal Reporter That Could Complicate Case," by Afzal Nadeem, Associated Press, August 18, 2002.
44. Amir Mir, *The True Face of Jehadis: Inside Pakistan's Network of Terror* (New Delhi: Roli Books, 2006), page 40.
45. "Karachi Page," February 15, 2002.
46. "Daniel Pearl Kidnap," BBC News.
47. Mir, *The True Face of Jehadis*, page 40.
48. "Who Really Killed Danny Pearl?" Nomani.
49. Musharraf, *In the Line of Fire*, page 228.
50. Verbatim transcript of combatant status review tribunal hearing for ISN 10024, conducted March 10, 2007, onboard U.S. Naval Base Guantánamo Bay, Cuba.

CHAPTER 10: EXPLOSIONS IN PARADISE

1. "Summary of Jose Padilla's Activities with Al Qaeda."
2. "Terror Suspect's Path from Streets to Brig," by Deborah Sontag, *New York Times*, April 25, 2004.

3. Ibid.
4. Ibid.
5. Ibid.
6. Ibid.
7. "Summary of Jose Padilla's Activities with Al Qaeda."
8. Ibid.
9. Mujahideen Data Form/New Applicant Form, "The Military Administration Personnel Branch, Guesthouse Management," Al Farouq Training Camp, Afghanistan, July 24, 2000.
10. "Summary of Jose Padilla's Activities with Al Qaeda."
11. "Guesthouse Management," Al Farouq Training Camp, Afghanistan, July 24, 2000.
12. Peter L. Bergen, *The Osama bin Laden I Know: An Oral History of al Qaeda's Leader (*New York: Free Press: 2006), page xi.
13. Ibid., page 346.
14. "Summary of Jose Padilla's Activities with Al Qaeda."
15. Ibid.
16. Tim McGirk, "Anatomy of a Raid," *Time*, April 8, 2002. It is datelined Faisalabad, Pakistan.
17. Ibid.
18. Ibid.
19. Ibid.
20. "Divisions Arose on Rough Tactics for Qaeda Figure," by Scott Shane, *New York Times,* April 17, 2009.
21. Ron Suskind, *The One Percent Doctrine: Deep Inside America's Pursuit of Its Enemies Since 9/11* (New York: Simon & Schuster, 2006), page 117.
22. Ibid., page 118.
23. "Al Qaeda Threatens Attack on the U.S.; Leader Takes Credit for Synagogue Bombing," by Rawya Rageh, Associated Press, May 19, 2002.
24. "Deadly Attack Keeps World on Alert," by Giles Tremiett in Djerba and Rabat, Rory McCarthy in Karachi, Luke Harding in Kabul, Julian Borger in Washington, John Aglionby in Jakarta, Michael Howard in northern Iraq and John Hooper in Berlin, *The Guardian* (U.K.), September 4, 2002.
25. "Tunisian Killed in Synagogue Blast Was Unlikely Convert to Militancy," by Chris Hedges, *New York Times*, June 9, 2002, page 22.
26. Michael Elliott, et al., "Al Qaeda Now; Is It behind the Newest Attacks Worldwide? How the Damaged Network May Be Plotting the Next Big One," *Time*, June 3, 2002.
27. "Deadly Attack Keeps World on Alert," Tremiett, et al.
28. "Terror Suspect's Path," Sontag, April 25, 2004.
29. Ibid.
30. "We'll Hit You: Pre-Bali Alert," by Marian Wilkinson, *Sydney Morning Herald* (Australia), November 16, 2002, page 1.

31. Ibid.

32. "Trial of Alleged Key Bali Bomber Begins," by Tim Palmer, ABC News (Australia), April 27, 2004.

33. Maria A. Ressa, *Seeds of Terror: An Eyewitness Account of Al-Qaeda's Newest Center of Operations in Southeast Asia* (New York: Free Press, 2003), page 184.

34. "Judge Quotes Koran as Bali Mastermind Screams Defiance; Eye for an Eye: Samudra to Die," by Wayne Miller, *Sydney Morning Herald* (Australia), September 11, 2003, page 1.

35. "In the Wrong Place at the Wrong Time," by Rob Crilly and Ian Bruce, *The Herald* (Glasgow), November 30, 2002, page 8.

CHAPTER 11: "RECOGNIZE US YET?"

1. Ron Suskind, *The One Percent Doctrine: Deep Inside America's Pursuit of Its Enemies Since 9/11* (New York: Simon & Schuster, 2006), page 102.

2. Ibid.

3. Yosri Fouda and Nick Fielding, *Masterminds of Terror: The Truth Behind the Most Devastating Attack the World Has Ever Seen* (New York: Arcade Publishing, 2003), page 37.

4. Peter L. Bergen, *The Osama bin Laden I Know: An Oral History of al Qaeda's Leader* (New York: Free Press, 2006), page 302.

5. Ibid., page 303.

6. Suskind, *The One Percent Doctrine*, page 133.

7. Ibid., page 102.

8. Fouda and Fielding, *Masterminds of Terror*, page 37.

9. Suskind, *The One Percent Doctrine*, page 138.

10. Ibid., page 139.

11. "Threats and Responses: Karachi; Karachi Radical Provides Hint of Qaeda's Rise in Pakistan," by David Rohde, *New York Times*, September 15, 2002, page 1.

12. Suskind, *The One Percent Doctrine*, page 156.

13. Suskind, *The One Percent Doctrine*, pages 204–5.

14. "The Capture: Qaeda Suspect Sound Asleep at Trail's End, Offers No Resistance," by Erik Eckholm and David Johnson, *New York Times*, March 3, 2003.

15. Mir, *The True Face of Jehadis*, page 26.

16. Suskind, *The One Percent Doctrine*, page 156.

17. "Prime 9-11 Suspect Nabbed; No. 3 Leader in al Qaida," by Martin Merzer, Jessica Guynn, and Dave Montgomery, Knight Ridder Newspapers, March 2, 2003.

CHAPTER 12: KSM AND OBAMA: THE MASTERMIND'S LAST LAUGH

1. Peter Bergen, *The Osama bin Laden I Know* (New York: Free Press, 2006), page 276.

2. Chris Mackey and Greg Miller, *The Interrogators* (New York: Back Bay Books, 2004), pages 178–81.

3. "Navy SEAL'S Mom Rejoices in His Acquittal in Iraq," Breaking Chicago News from WGN and the Chicago Tribune, April 22, 2010, 12:41 P.M.

4. "Soldier Acquitted in Afghan Prisoner Abuse," by Alicia Caldwell, AP Online, February 24, 2006.

5. Mackey and Miller, *The Interrogators*, page 181.

6. Marc A. Thiessen, *Courting Disaster* (Washington, D.C.: Regnery Publishing, Inc., 2010), page 45.

7. Ibid.

8. Ibid., page 46

9. Ibid.

10. Richard Miniter, *Shadow War: The Untold Story of How Bush Is Winning the War on Terror* (Washington, D.C.: Regnery Publishing, Inc., 2004), page 87.

11. Thiessen, *Courting Disaster*, page 46.

12. "Inside a 9/11 Mastermind's Interrogation," by Scott Shane, *New York Times*, June 22, 2008.

13. "Security Profiles; Black Hawk Down," Global Security.org, http://www.globalsecurity.org/security/profiles/black_hawk_down.htm, retrieved April 17, 2010.

14. "Security Profiles; Saudi National Guard Bombing," Global Security.org, http://www.globalsecurity.org/security/profiles/saudi_national_guard_bombing.htm, retrieved April 17, 2010.

15. "Security Profiles; East African Embassy Bombings," Global Security.org, http://www.globalsecurity.org/security/profiles/saudi_national_guard_bombing.htm, retrieved April 17, 2010.

16. "23 U.S. Troops Die in Truck Bombing in Saudi Base," by Philip Shenon, *New York Times*, June 26, 1996.

17. "Security Profiles; East African Embassy Bombings," Global Security.org, http://www.globalsecurity.org/security/profiles/east_african_embassy_bombings.htm, retrieved April 17, 2010.

18. "Security Profiles; Millenium Plot," Global Security.org, http://www.globalsecurity.org/security/ops/millenium-plot.htm, retrieved April 17, 2010.

19. "Security Profiles; USS *Cole* Bombing," Global Security.org, http://www.globalsecurity.org/security/profiles/uss_cole_bombing.htm, retrieved April 17, 2010.

20. "Official 9/11 Death Toll Climbs By One," CBN News, New York, July 10, 2008.

21. "Security Profiles; Bali Nightclub Bombing," Global Security.org, http://www.globalsecurity.org/security/profiles/bali_nightclub_bombing.htm, retrieved April 17, 2010.

22. "Security Profiles; 3-11 Madrid Train Bombings," Global Security.org, http://www.globalsecurity.org/security/profiles/3-11_madrid_train_bombings.htm, retrieved April 17, 2010.

23. "Security Profiles; London Transit Bombings," Global Security.org, http://www.globalsecurity.org/security/profiles/7-7_london_transit_bombings.htm, retrieved April 17, 2010.

24. "Raided Family of Microbiologist Denies Official Version of al-Qaida Arrests," by Rory McCarthy, *The Guardian* (U.K.), March 3, 2003.

25. "Bin Laden Threatens Americans," Al Jazeera, March 25, 2010; transcript, The Middle East Media Research Institute, March 25, 2010, http://www.memritv.org/clip_transcript/en/2432.htm.

26. Thiessen, *Courting Disaster*, page 42.

27. Ibid., page 43.

28. Ibid.

29. Ibid., page 44.

30. Ibid., page 53.

31. "A Deadly Kindness," by Richard Miniter, *New York Post*, September 15, 2006.

32. Ibid.

33. "ACLU Taps Top Legal Talent to Defend Accused 9/11 Plotters," by Carol Rosenberg, McClatchey Newspapers, April 4, 2008.

34. Ibid.

35. "I Want to Be a Martyr, Khalid Shaikh Mohammed Tells Guantánamo Tribunal," by Tim Reid, *New York Times*, June 6, 2008.

36. Ibid.

37. "Five 9/11 Suspects Defiant in Court," by Carol J. Williams, *Los Angeles Times*, June 6, 2008.

38. Ibid.

39. Ibid.

40. Ibid.

41. Ibid.

42. Jane Mayer, "The Trial: Eric Holder and the Battle of Khalid Shaikh Mohammed," *The New Yorker*, February 15, 2010.

43. "Five 9/11 Suspects Defiant in Court," Williams.

44. "9/11 Accused to Get Laptops in Cells," by Carol Rosenberg, *Miami Herald*, October 12, 2008.

45. "Goodbye Gitmo: 9/11 War Crimes Trial Adjourns for What Could Be the Last Time," Associated Press, January 20, 2009.

46. "Obama, Judge Put Brakes on Guantánamo Terror Trials," FoxNews.com, January 21, 2009.

47. "Senate Confirmation Hearings: Eric Holder, Day One," transcript reprinted in *New York Times*, January 16, 2009.

48. Jed Babbin, "Holder Tightens Grip on Intelligence Agencies," Real Clear Politics, May 18, 2010.

49. Daniel Klaidman, "Obama Doesn't Want to Look Back, But Attorney General Eric Holder May Probe Bush-Era Torture Anyway," *Newsweek*, July 11, 2009.

50. Mayer, "The Trial: Eric Holder and the Battle Over Khalid Shaikh Mohammed."

51. "Cables Depict U.S. Haggling to Clear Guantánamo," by Charles Savage and Andrew Lehren, *New York Times*, November 29, 2010.

52. Mayer, "The Trial: Eric Holder and the Battle Over Khalid Shaikh Mohammed."

53. Ibid.

54. "Ahmed Ghailani Transferred from Guantánamo Bay to New York for Prosecution on Terror Charges," Department of Justice Office of Public Affairs, press release, June 9, 2009.

55. William Shakespeare, *Macbeth* (New York: Washington Square Press, 1992), act V, scene 5.

56. "Attorney General Eric Holder: 'Close to a Decision' on 9/11 Trials," by Jason Devon and Ryan Dwyer, ABC News, November 10, 2010.

57. "Debate Snarls Process of Trying Terror Suspects," by Kevin Johnson, *USA Today*, December 10, 2010.

58. C-Span FY 2011 Budget Request for U.S. Justice Department, Testimony of Eric Holder, air date: March 17, 201

CHAPTER 13: AFTERMATH

1. Yosri Fouda and Nick Fielding, *Masterminds of Terror: The Truth Behind the Most Devastating Attack the World Has Ever Seen* (New York: Arcade Publishing, 2003), page 91.

2. "Judge Allows Gang Leader to Talk with Other Infamous Prisoners," by Benjamin Weiser, *New York Times*, March 11, 1999.

Bibliography

In any controversy, such as the case of Khalid Shaikh Mohammed, facts should be the foundation of debate. I hope this bibliography will be a good starting point for other students of international terrorism.

A. Government Reports and Trial Documents

U.S. Central Intelligence Agency. *Khalid Shaykh Muhammad: Preeminent Source on Al Qa'ida.* July 13, 2004.

———. Office of Inspector General. *Special Review: Counterterrorism Detention and Interrogation Activities (September 2001–October 2003).* May 7, 2004.

U.S. Department of Defense. Office for the Administrative Review of the Detention of Enemy Combatants at U.S. Naval Base Guantánamo Bay, Cuba. *Summary of Evidence for Combatant Status Review Tribunal—Muhammad, Khalid Shaykh.* February 8, 2007.

U.S. Department of Justice. Office of Legal Counsel. *Memorandum for John Rizzo, Acting General Counsel of the Central Intelligence Agency.* August 1, 2002.

———. *Memorandum for John Rizzo, Senior Deputy General Counsel, Central Intelligence Agency.* May 10, 2005.

———. *Memorandum for John Rizzo, Senior Deputy General Counsel, Central Intelligence Agency.* May 30, 2005.

U.S. House Permanent Select Committee on Intelligence and the Senate Select Committee on Intelligence. *Report of the Joint Inquiry into the Terrorist Attacks of September 11, 2001.* July 24, 2003.

U.S. National Commission on Terrorist Attacks Upon the United States. *The 9/11 Commission Report.* August 2004.

———. *9/11 and Terrorist Travel.* Staff report. August 21, 2004.

———. *Intelligence Policy.* Staff statements 1–17.

———. *Monograph on Terrorist Financing.* Staff report. 2004.

U.S. v. *Khalid Sheikh Mohammed et al. Defense Motion to Dismiss Military and Civilian Standby Counsel.* April 14, 2009.

U.S. v. *Khalid Sheikh Mohammed et al.* Military tribunal charges. April 15, 2008.

U.S. v. *Moussaoui. Substitution for the Testimony of Khalid Sheikh Mohammed.* Defendant's Exhibit 941.

Verbatim Transcript of Combatant Status Review. Tribunal Hearing for ISN 10018. Ammar al Baluchi. March 30, 2007.

———. Tribunal Hearing for ISN 10024. Khalid Sheikh Muhammad. March 10, 2007.

———. Tribunal Hearing for ISN 10020. Majid Khan. April 15, 2007.

Wolfowitz, Paul. Department of Defense. *Memorandum for the Secretary of the Navy, Subject: Order Establishing Combatant Status Review Tribunal.* July 7, 2004.

B. Books

Ali, Tariq. *The Duel: Pakistan on the Flight Path of American Power.* New York: Scribner, 2008.

Al-Zayyat, Montasser. *The Road to Al-Qaeda: The Story of Bin Laden's Right-Hand Man.* Sterling: Pluto Press, 2004.

Atwan, Abdel Bari. *The Secret History of al Qaeda.* Berkeley: University of California Press, 2008.

Baer, Robert. *See No Evil: The True Story of a Good Soldier in the CIA's War on Terrorism.* New York: Crown, 2002.

Bell, Stewart. *Cold Terror: How Canada Nurtures and Exports Terrorism Around the World.* Toronto: John Wiley & Sons Canada, 2004.

Bergen, Peter L. *The Osama bin Laden I Know: An Oral History of al Qaeda's Leader.* New York: Free Press, 2006.

Berkowitz, Peter, ed. *The Future of American Intelligence.* Stanford, Calif.: Hoover Institution Press, 2005.

———. *Terrorism, the Laws of War, and the Constitution: Debating the Enemy Combatant Cases.* Stanford, Calif.: Hoover Institution Press, 2005.

Brisard, Jean-Charles, and Damien Martinez. *Zarqawi: The New Face of Al-Qaeda.* New York: Other Press, 2005.

Burke, Jason. *Al-Qaeda: The True Story of Radical Islam.* New York: Penguin Books, 2004.

Byman, Daniel. *Deadly Connections: States that Sponsor Terrorism.* New York: Cambridge University Press, 2005.

Clarke, Richard A. *Against All Enemies: Inside America's War on Terror.* New York: Free Press, 2004.

Denbeaux, Mark P., and Jonathan Hafetz, eds. *The Guantánamo Lawyers: Inside a Prison Outside the Law.* New York: New York University Press, 2009.

Dwyer, Jim, et al. *Two Seconds Under the World.* New York: Crown, 1994.

Ewans, Martin. *Afghanistan: A Short History of Its People and Politics.* New York: Harper Perennial, 2002.

Fouda, Yosri, and Nick Fielding. *Masterminds of Terror: The Truth Behind the Most Devastating Attack the World Has Ever Seen.* New York: Arcade Publishing, 2003.

Friedman, George. *America's Secret War: Inside the Hidden Worldwide Struggle Between America and Its Enemies.* New York: Doubleday, 2004.

Kean, Thomas H., and Lee H. Hamilton. *Without Precedent: The Inside Story of the 9/11 Commission.* New York: Alfred A. Knopf, 2006.

Kepel, Gilles. *The Prophet and Pharaoh: Muslim Extremism in Egypt.* London: Al Saqi Books, 1985.

Kushner, Harvey. *Holy War on the Home Front: The Secret Islamic Terror Network in the United States.* New York: Sentinel, 2004.

Laqueur, Walter, ed. *Voices of Terror: Manifestos, Writings, and Manuals of al Qaeda, Hamas, and Other Terrorists from Around the World and Throughout the Ages.* New York: Reed Press, 2004.

Lesser, Ian O., et al. *Countering the New Terrorism.* Santa Monica: RAND, 1999.

McDermott, Terry. *Perfect Soldiers.* New York: HarperCollins, 2005.

Mackey, Chris, and Greg Miller. *The Interrogators: Task Force 500 and America's Secret War Against Al Qaeda.* New York: Back Bay Books, 2005.

Mahle, Melissa Boyle. *Denial and Deception: An Insider's View of the CIA.* New York: Nation Books, 2006.

Mayer, Jane. *The Dark Side: The Inside Story of How the War on Terror Turned into a War on American Ideals.* New York: Doubleday, 2008.

Miller, John, Michael Stone, and Chris Mitchell. *The Cell: Inside the 9/11 Plot, and Why the FBI and CIA Failed to Stop It.* New York: Hyperion, 2002.

Miniter, Richard. *Disinformation: 22 Media Myths That Undermine the War on Terror.* Washington, D.C.: Regnery, 2004.

———. *Losing bin Laden: How Clinton's Failures Unleashed Global Terror.* Washington, D.C.: Regnery, 2003.

———. *Shadow War: The Untold Story of How Bush Is Winning the War on Terror.* Washington, D.C.: Regnery, 2004.

Mir, Amir. *The True Face of Jehadis: Inside Pakistan's Network of Terror.* New Delhi: Roli Books, 2006.

Mukasey, Michael B. *How Obama Has Mishandled the War on Terror.* New York: Encounter Books, 2010.

Nasiri, Omar. *Inside the Jihad: My Life with al Qaeda.* New York: Basic Books, 2006.

Patterson, Robert. *War Crimes: The Left's Campaign to Destroy Our Military and Lose the War on Terror.* New York: Three Rivers Press, 2007.

Posner, Gerald. *Why America Slept: The Failure to Prevent 9/11.* New York: Random House, 2003.

Posner, Richard A. *Countering Terrorism: Blurred Focus, Halting Steps.* Lanham, Md.: Rowman & Littlefield, 2007.

———. *Preventing Surprise Attacks: Intelligence Reform in the Wake of 9/11.* Lanham, Md.: Rowman & Littlefield, 2005.

———. *Remaking Domestic Intelligence.* Stanford, Calif.: Hoover Institution Press, 2005.

———. *Uncertain Shield: The U.S. Intelligence System in the Throes of Reform.* Lanham, Md.: Rowman & Littlefield, 2006.

Qutb, Seyyid. *Milestones.* Damascus: Dar al-Ilm.

Reeve, Simon. *The New Jackals: Ramzi Yousef, Osama Bin Laden, and the Future of Terrorism.* Boston: Northeastern University Press, 1999.

Ressa, Maria A. *Seeds of Terror: An Eyewitness Account of Al-Qaeda's Newest Center of Operations in Southeast Asia.* New York: Free Press, 2003.

Risen, James. *State of War: The Secret History of the CIA and the Bush Administration.* New York: Free Press, 2006.

Robinson, Adam. *Bin Laden: Behind the Mask of the Terrorist.* London: Mainstream Publishing, 2003.

Rozenman, Eric L. *Total Jihad.* Oakton, Va.: RavensYard Publishing, 2002.

Rubin, Barry, ed. *The Muslim Brotherhood: The Organization and Policies of a Global Islamist Movement.* New York: Palgrave Macmillan, 2010.

Sageman, Marc. *Leaderless Jihad: Terror Networks in the Twenty-First Century.* Philadelphia: University of Pennsylvania Press, 2008.

Scheuer, Michael. *Imperial Hubris: Why the West Is Losing the War on Terror.* Washington, D.C.: Potomac Books, 2004.

Schindler, John R. *Unholy Terror: Bosnia, Al-Qa'ida, and the Rise of Global Jihad.* St. Paul, Minn.: Zenith Press, 2007.

Schmidle, Nicholas. *To Live or to Perish Forever: Two Tumultuous Years in Pakistan.* New York: Henry Holt, 2009.

Shenon, Philip. *The Commission: What We Didn't Know About 9/11.* New York: Twelve, 2009.

Sifaoui, Mohamed. *Inside Al Qaeda: How I Infiltrated the World's Deadliest Terrorist Organization.* New York: Thunder's Mouth Press, 2003.

Sofaer, Abraham D. *The Best Defense? Legitimacy & Preventative Force.* Stanford, Calif.: Hoover Institution Press, 2010.

Suskind, Ron. *The One Percent Doctrine: Deep Inside America's Pursuit of Its Enemies Since 9/11.* New York: Simon & Schuster, 2006.

Tal, Nachman. *Radical Islam in Egypt and Jordan.* Brighton, U.K.: Sussex Academic Press, 2005.

Tenet, George, and Bill Harlow. *At the Center of the Storm: My Years at the CIA.* New York: HarperCollins, 2007.

Thiessen, Marc. *Courting Disaster: How the CIA Kept America Safe and How Barack Obama Is Inviting the Next Attack.* Washington, D.C.: Regnery Publishing, 2010.

Vitug, Marites Danguilan, and Glenda M. Gloria. *Under the Crescent Moon: Rebellion in Mindanao.* Quezon City, Philippines, 2000.

Weaver, Mary Anne. *Pakistan: Deep Inside the World's Most Frightening State.* New York: Farrar, Straus & Giroux, 2010.

Woodward, Bob. *Plan of Attack.* New York: Simon & Schuster, 2004.

———. *State of Denial: Bush at War, Part III.* New York: Simon & Schuster, 2006.

———. *The War Within: A Secret White House History 2006–2008.* New York: Simon & Schuster, 2008.

Wright, Lawrence. *The Looming Tower: Al Qaeda and the Road to 9/11.* New York: Alfred A. Knopf, 2006.

Yoo, John. *Crisis and Command.* New York: Kaplan Publishing, 2009.

———. *War by Other Means: An Insider's Account of the War on Terror.* New York: Atlantic Monthly Press, 2006.

Index

About the Author

Richard Miniter is the author of two *New York Times* bestsellers on terrorism, *Losing bin Laden* and *Shadow War.* He has been published in *The New York Times*, *The Wall Street Journal*, *The Washington Post*, and *The Christian Science Monitor* as well as *The Atlantic Monthly*, *Reader's Digest*, *The New Republic*, and *National Review.* Previously he worked as an editorial writer for *The Wall Street Journal* in Brussels and as an investigative reporter for the *Sunday Times* of London, where he shared an award for investigative reporting on the 9/11 attacks. Later, he was editorial page editor of *The Washington Times.*

He is a regular guest on Fox News, CNN, C-SPAN, MSNBC, and Al Jazeera.

He has traveled extensively in North Africa, the Middle East (including Iraq), and Southeast Asia. He lives in Arlington, Virginia.

His Web site can be found at www.richardminiter.com.